The Power of Framing

Ivanne,
So glad you
could come.
Enjoy!

Dave Fairhurst

The Power of Framing

Creating the Language of Leadership

GAIL T. FAIRHURST

JOSSEY-BASS
A Wiley Imprint
www.josseybass.com

Published by Jossey-Bass

A Wiley Imprint

989 Market Street, San Francisco, CA 94103–1741—www.josseybass.com

Jossey-Bass books and products are available through most bookstores. To contact Jossey-Bass directly call our Customer Care Department within the U.S. at 800–956–7739, outside the U.S. at 317–572–3986, or fax 317–572–4002.

Jossey-Bass also publishes its books in a variety of electronic formats. Some content that appears in print may not be available in electronic books.

Library of Congress Cataloging-in-Publication Data

Fairhurst, Gail Theus, date.
   The power of framing : creating the language of leadership / Gail T. Fairhurst.
     p. cm. — (The Jossey-Bass Business & management series)
   Revised ed. of: The art of framing.
   Includes bibliographical references and index.
   ISBN 978-0-470-49452-3 (hardback)
   1. Leadership.   2. Communication in management.   3. Interpersonal communication.
   I. Fairhurst, Gail Theus, date. Art of framing.   II. Title.
   HD57.7.F356 2011
   658.4'092014—dc22

                                        2010032118

Printed in the United States of America

FIRST EDITION

HB Printing   10 9 8 7 6 5 4 3 2 1

CONTENTS

WEB CONTENTS

FREE
Premium Content
▼

JOSSEY-BASS™
An Imprint of
WILEY

This book includes premium content that can be accessed from our Web site when you register at **www.josseybass.com/go/gailfairhurst** using the password *professional*.

Framing Tool 1.1: Designing Leadership

Framing Tool 1.2: Critical Incident Framing

Framing Tool 1.3: Communications Style Inventory

Framing Tool 1.4: Communications Style Meshing

Framing Tool 2.1: Critical Incident Framing

Framing Tool 2.2: Identifying Your Mental Models

Framing Tool 2.3: Critical Incident Framing

Framing Tool 2.4: Your Core Framing Tasks

Framing Tool 3.1: Critical Incident Framing

Framing Tool 5.1: Critical Incident Framing

Framing Tool 6.1: Critical Incident Framing

Framing Tool 7.1: Failed Leadership

Framing Tool 7.2: Successful Leadership

Framing Tool 8.1: Framing Involving Big Projects or Campaigns

To Verne, Katie, Tom, and Kelsey

PREFACE

> *There are these two young fish swimming along, and they happen to meet an older fish swimming the other way, who nods at them and says, "Morning, boys, how's the water?" And the two young fish swim on for a bit, and then eventually one of them looks over at the other and goes, "What the hell is water?"*
>
> —David Foster Wallace, commencement address at Kenyon College, 2005[1]

SINCE *The Art of Framing* was published in 1996, I have spoken with many in the United States and abroad on the role of communications in leadership. Some really seem to grasp its importance. Too many others still do not. For them, as for Wallace's young fish, the most profound realities of life are those most difficult to see and talk about, and one of those realities is the remarkable gift of human communication. Substitute *communication* for *water*, and "What the hell is water?" wonderfully describes many leaders in organizations today. They take their communication for granted, dismissing it as something they just do automatically.

"If I am talking, I must be communicating, right?" Many leaders (and others, of course) make that assumption, because communication looks like a simple act of transmission. The "Sender → Message → Receiver" model, which describes communication in terms of a message passing over a channel subject to noise, is still commonly taught.[2] And our language is full of expressions that reinforce it—as when we say, "I got my message across," or "I can't seem to get through to this employee." The transmission model is not incorrect, but it is woefully inadequate when considering the tasks facing today's leaders.

A better way to view communication is to emphasize the way it creates a shared reality. Consider the global economic crisis that began in 2008, which according to *Newsweek* writer Daniel Gross created a whole new genre of linguistics: "financial linguistics." In a 2009 article, he recalled George Orwell's 1946 essay "Politics and the English Language," in which Orwell decried political rhetoric used "to make lies sound truthful" and "to give an appearance of solidity to pure wind."[3]

Indeed, Gross makes an excellent case that the captains of Wall Street have had a boundless energy for repackaging discredited financial products with new legit-sounding names like "legacy loans," "legacy securities," "nonprime mortgages," "high-yield debt," and the like. Framing alone didn't produce this crisis, but communications played a central role. To add insult to injury, Harry Truman's maxim—"If you can't convince them, confuse them"—appears to have become the modus operandi of leaders asked to account for their firm's performance.[4] Whether these leaders are speaking to Wall Street, Congress, or everyday citizens, they often explain their firm's actions in accounting doublespeak. If we are not left wondering just what it is they said, we are left questioning their capacity for corporate responsibility.

So the financial crisis reminds me that there is a large group of generally smart and articulate leaders out there who need to reflect on their communications and ethics a great deal more. They need to *not* take their communications for granted quite so much. They need to understand how our financial realities (and those of others) are created through their communications. They need to understand that untrustworthy leaders already understand all of this—and are betting that most others don't.

French philosopher Michel Foucault had it right when he said—and I'm paraphrasing here—that people know *what* they say, and they usually know *why* they say what they say. What they do not understand is what what they say *does*.[5] Most of us fail to understand the context-shaping features of our language and the meanings for events that we have had a hand in creating. It is easier to attribute those harsh realities to someone else's doing. However, I would be lying if I did not also acknowledge that the transmission model of communication, the "meaning-lite" model, is far easier to understand. How we create meaning with others is among the most elusive aspects of leadership communications.

With this mind-set, I am tackling the subject of framing once again as the means by which leaders and students of leadership, and not just those in the financial sector, learn to manage meaning. However, this time around my task has been made both a little easier and more difficult. What makes writing about framing easier today is that the terms *frame* and *framing* are not as foreign as they were in 1996. In part, this is because a tremendous amount of research on framing has been done in a wide range of disciplines, including communication and media studies, linguistics, economics, psychology, sociology, psychiatry, and management.

Moreover, we have seen the language of framing enter the vernacular of everyday speech with the 2006 and 2008 U.S. political campaigns. Professional pollsters like Frank Luntz have begun to use it as a campaign tool, and media outlets like the *New York Times* feature articles about the "framing wars" to analyze key campaign messages.[6]

What is a little more difficult this time around is that framing is turning out to be what the German philosopher Ludwig Wittgenstein describes as a "blurred concept."[7] Like the terms *leadership* and *communication, frame* and *framing* can be used in several different ways as people play language games. For example, does *framing* denote a cognitive process—a way of seeing—or an act of communication? Is a *frame* narrow and lens-like, or is it broad and schema-like? Do frames organize and can they expand, or are they neat little self-contained packages?

Chapters One and Two are largely devoted to answering these questions, but whichever way you slice the framing pie, it is clear that frames have consequences. After 9/11, the United States was not attacked again on its soil under the tough-talking language and action of the Bush presidency, but the "coalition of the willing" also grew perilously close to a "coalition of one" in the war in Iraq.[8] As mentioned, the consequences of irresponsible framing (among other irresponsible actions) can be seen in the near meltdown of the world's financial system. Even the financial industries themselves, according to Gross, "believed so fervently in their own rhetoric that they bet their financial houses on it."[9]

And so this book is for leaders or students of leadership who want to have a greater impact on the world through their communications. Echoing David Foster Wallace, it is for the fish who want to know about the water.

Who Should Read This Book

I have written *The Power of Framing* for three specific audiences. Carrying on the tradition of *The Art of Framing*, the first audience consists of practicing leaders and managers. If you fall into this category, you are likely battle-worn and tested in your everyday communications on the job. I am hoping that my book gives you a renewed set of ideals for communications effectiveness, a better communications vocabulary, and a means by which to analyze the many challenges that you face.

My second intended audience is MBA students. I am hoping that *The Power of Framing* supplants your usual training in public speaking and Power Point presentations as your primary introduction to communication in the workplace. This is because framing is a skill that underlies all others.

My third intended audience is communications students in upper-level undergraduate and graduate programs worldwide. You already possess a special affinity for the communications process. I am hoping that my book adds depth and understanding to your knowledge of this skill.

Given the potentially wide-ranging interests of these audiences, I have taken a different approach in this book as compared to *The Art of Framing*, which focused on routine conversations on the shop floors of the manufacturing division of a multinational consumer goods firm. The purpose there was to draw attention to framing as an everyday skill, not one reserved for special occasions in need of soaring rhetoric.

This time around I draw communication examples from a variety of sources: business, politics, sports, academia, the arts, and many more. I am hoping that the diversity of examples I supply demonstrates the widespread relevance and utility of this skill. But please do not read between the lines— I am not advancing a particular political point of view in this book, for example, as an American, whether Republican or Democrat. I try to view my role as an equal-opportunity critic!

Overview of the Contents

After an introduction to the realities of framing for leaders (Chapter One), I address the idea of framing as a skill (Chapter Two), a science (Chapter Three), an art form (Chapter Four), an emotional connection (Chapter Five), an ethical commitment (Chapter Six), a context for leadership (Chapter Seven), and a set of applications (Chapter Eight).

In addition, four other features of the book should be mentioned. First, each chapter contains a set of practice exercises designed to help you build your skills at framing. Second, each chapter ends with a chapter summary for a quick review. Third, each chapter has an extensive set of notes at the back of the book for those wishing to pursue a particular aspect of framing in greater depth (though the book can easily be read without consulting the notes). Finally, there is a glossary at the end of the book should you want to remind yourself of the definition of one or more framing terms.

More specifically, Chapter One begins with six rules for framing communications in leadership situations. Collectively, they show that when you lead, your communications help create realities to which you and others must respond. This is not to explain away the constraints that you face in your job. It does, however, underscore the importance of *how* you choose to respond to these constraints. Chapter One also shows you how to diagnose your sensitivity to the framing concept and your style of communicating, and it discusses ways to meet the challenges of your framing style while not losing any of the benefits.

Chapter Two concerns itself with framing as a skill, which is your under-lying ability to be articulate and persuasive more or less on demand. The skill sets in this chapter correspond to three concepts that are the foundation of framing:

- *Cultural Discourses*, which are where the content of your communications comes from

- *Mental models*, which are how you regulate that content

- *Core framing tasks*, which are the chief communication requirements of your job

In this chapter you will learn how to use the linguistic tool bags that accompany cultural Discourses, develop awareness of your mental models, and diagnose your core framing tasks.

Chapter Three explores the science of framing—in particular, the con-scious and unconscious learning processes that contribute to the development of frames. As Bob Sarr and I argued in *The Art of Framing*, you can exert a measure of control over your spontaneous communications when you store your memories. We called this *priming for spontaneity*, a label that I will continue to use for this deceptively simple concept. This time around, how-ever, my emphasis is on understanding what exactly priming does inside the human brain and what builds complexity into your mental models for the best framing possible. Current research supports the idea that the more you notice the better your framing.

Chapter Four concerns itself with the art form of framing. Even though many people are inclined to dismiss communication as something of an automatic process, this chapter challenges you to see framing as a craft. It deemphasizes the idea of framing as a natural ability and focuses on the work involved in honing your skills. You will discover a number of ways to create more memorable messages. For example, metaphorical frames breathe life into your communications; master frames offer great organizing potential; simplifying frames give you needle-like precision in your framing; while believability frames show you how to be a more credible communicator. The chapter concludes with a discussion of how to combine frames for maximum effect.

Chapter Five addresses the emotional connections that you can make through framing. It begins with a discussion of emotional intelligence and why you must join reason and emotion to frame effectively. Emotional contagion or "contagious emotions" in a work or team context is the second major topic with framing implications. Here the key topics include the mirror neurons in the brain, the human tendency to mirror the behavior of others, and the importance of nonverbal communications in framing emotions. The third and final topic addresses two framing techniques necessary for regulating your emotions as a leader: *priming for spontaneity* and *reframing*.

Chapter Six addresses questions of ethics and morality. It begins with a discussion of ethical codes and how to use them to morally position yourself and others in your communications. Moral positioning is a form of framing and is crucially important when you must justify certain means-end relationships or the kind of leader you claim to be. Your moral positioning may be contested by those who view you differently, so it is an important framing topic to explore. The chapter concludes with a discussion of the ways in which crucibles—events that pose great stress and require difficult choices—if properly used, can be important framing moments for leaders who mean to shape ethical organizational cultures.

Chapter Seven emphasizes the overall leadership context of your framing communications. It stresses that framing may be just one element among many in an attribution of leadership. This chapter also proposes four key questions as a way to understand how leadership, context, and framing all fit together to create an outcome. The bulk of the chapter then exposes you to a variety of leadership situations to gain practice in deciphering the ways in which framing factors into a leadership context.

Chapter Eight is about applications; it builds on the framing exercises of the first seven chapters in two ways. First, I don my hat as your executive coach and answer a number of common framing dilemmas that you might encounter as a leader. Second, I present an extended practice exercise highlighting the main points of this book in the context of framing communications involving organizational change and extended campaigns.

Gail T. Fairhurst
Cincinnati, Ohio
September 2010

ACKNOWLEDGMENTS

I **AM GRATEFUL** to all who have assisted me in writing this book. This includes those who have read all or parts of it along the way or lent support in other ways. They include Jolanta Aritz, Barbara Baranauskas, Kevin Barge, Suzanne Boys, Marthe Church, François Cooren, David Grant, Ted Dass, Katie Fairhurst, Verne Fairhurst, Evan Griffin, Danielle Hagen, Marian Lawson, Joe Levi, Marje Kiley, Olga Jacobs, Denny Moutray, Don Miller, Linda Putnam, Leland Ross, Teresa Sabourin, Pamela Shockley-Zalabak, Eugene Theus, Steve Wilson, and Edwin Young. A special thanks to Rich Kiley, marketer par excellence, who helped me visualize what this book could look like. Thanks also to Brandon Brooks, a student assistant with sage advice and a strong work ethic well beyond his years.

Since the publication of *The Art of Framing*, I have greatly benefited from opportunities to talk about framing with industry and academic audiences in the United States and abroad. A special thanks, however, to Randall Stutman of CRA, for the many summer opportunities at the Admired Leadership

Institute; Pam Shockley-Zalabak for the Aspen, Colorado conferences on engaged scholarship; Mats Alvesson at the School of Economics and Business, Lund University; and Robyn Remke, Esben Karmark, and Dan Kärreman at Copenhagen Business School for providing me with opportunities to further develop my ideas around framing.

Thanks also to Kathe Sweeney for her enthusiastic support and editorial guidance at Jossey-Bass and to Rob Brandt, editorial projects manager, for his patience in answering my many questions. I also very much appreciate the efforts of my copyeditor, Hilary Powers, and my production editors, Rachel Anderson and Nina Kreiden. Thanks also to Priscilla Ball and Corina Bizzari for all of their efforts on my behalf at the office.

Finally, I would like to thank my family, to whom I dedicate this book. I am grateful to my husband, Verne, and my children, Katie, Tom, and Kelsey, for all of their love and support. They teach me about framing every day.

1

The Reality of Framing

THE WORDS *frame* or *framing* have many meanings these days. Most often, they refer to a form or structure, as in "the house has a sturdy frame," or they refer to the act of constructing such a form, as in "framing a house." However, a "frame" can also be a structured way of thinking such as the concept of customer service (designating anything that serves or supports the purchasers of a product or service). *Framing* then is the act of communicating that concept—even something as clichéd as saying, "The customer is always right." However, the English vernacular allows for a lot of wordplay using *frame* or *framing*; we can refer to "framing someone for murder" (sometimes referred to as a *frame-up*), or to "framing an argument," or to "framing the issues."

But could you also talk about "framing reality"? If you're familiar with the old baseball yarn of the three umpires who disagreed about the task of calling balls and strikes, you might.[1] As the story goes, the first umpire said, "I calls them as they is." The second one said, "I calls them as I sees them." The third and cleverest umpire said, "They ain't nothin' till I calls them."[2] The first two might argue that the swing and a miss can be objectively determined, especially in this age of instant replays and multiple camera angles. True enough, but the third understands that one needs a society's invented game of baseball for a strike to mean something in the first place. A strike is a strike by virtue of the agreed-upon rules of baseball and pronouncement by its authorities. Without the institution of baseball, a swing and a miss could just as easily be fly or mosquito swatting. So as long as the game is under way, the third umpire understands best of all that he frames reality by gesturing and calling, "Strrriiike three. You're out!"

If leadership is like umpiring baseball, what kind of umpire are you? This book will help you answer this question. Unfortunately, the overwhelming majority of leaders are like the first and second umpires. Only a small minority come close to the third, who understands the real power of human communication. Not just a simple transmission, it is the very stuff of reality-making itself.

The Rules of Reality Construction

What is the relationship between leadership and the task of constructing reality? Well, that's what this book is all about. For starters, let's begin with a few guiding rules.

Reality Construction Rule #1: Control the Context

Leaders often cannot control events, but they can control the context under which events are seen if they recognize a framing opportunity.

Some leaders disparage communication as something they just do automatically. They may also label communication "mere rhetoric," "window dressing," or "just words" because it cannot change the hard cold facts of a situation. True as that observation may be, however, it falls far short of being complete.

Consider the situation Robert E. Murray—chairman of the Murray Energy Corporation and co-owner of the Crandall Canyon mine in Utah—faced on August 6, 2007, when the mine caved in with six miners trapped inside. It was perhaps the most important communications challenge of his career, and it serves to illustrate the effect of most of the rules in this chapter.

As soon as news of the collapse reached him, he could be sure that anxious families, the mining community, and the press would hang on his every word. But could any communication by him change the reality of a mine collapse with six entombed miners?

Of course, neither words nor symbols can alter the physical or material conditions of our world (although they may influence our perceptions of them). However, communications can play a huge role in many other issues surrounding a mine collapse—the comfort and rescue effort updates to the families and mining community; the moral and legal assignment of blame that could ultimately prove costly in a court of law; the efforts at image management for Murray Energy Corporation and its partner that could be key to future business and treatment by federal regulators; the treatment of the press as a means to an end in this regard, and many more.

Robert Murray was not in Utah at the time of the collapse, but upon hearing of it, he reportedly boarded a private jet and was at the Crandall Canyon site within hours, taking command of the rescue operation and giving frequent media updates.[3] Although not all situations so clearly mark their communication exigencies, Murray appeared to recognize an important communication opportunity with the mine collapse. This was his chance to frame reality, and he took it. But was he *competent* in his crisis communications?

Reality Construction Rule #2: Define the Situation

At its most basic level, framing reality means defining "the situation here and now" in ways that connect with others.

In the sense I use it here, *framing* involves the ability to shape the meaning of a subject—usually the situation at hand—to judge its character and significance through the meanings we include and exclude, as well as those we emphasize when communicating.[4] At his first formal news conference on August 7, 2007, how did Robert Murray define "the situation here and now"? He was adamant that an earthquake had caused the mine's collapse—not his company's practice of "retreat mining," which is exceedingly dangerous and tightly regulated. In this "situation here and now," Murray sought to portray

Murray Energy Corporation as without blame. (You can check out Murray's news conference on YouTube.[5])

But Murray went on from there, confidently proclaiming, "We know exactly where the miners are," promising, "I will not leave this mine until the men are rescued dead or alive," and then boldly predicting, "We're going to get them."[6] Curiously, at that same news conference, he spoke of subjects as wide-ranging as the essential nature of the U.S. coal industry for American consumers, new technologies, global warming, and his own rise from miner to founder, co-owner, and president of Murray Energy Corporation. On that hot August day, Robert Murray chose very specific meanings to define "the situation here and now" for those in attendance (and ruled out others that might suggest his company's culpability). That is the essence of framing.

One of the most frequently asked questions about framing is a matter of definition: Is it a structured way of thinking or an act of communicating? In reality, it is both, because a *frame* is that mental picture, and *framing* is the process of communicating that picture to others.[7] However, it can be a little confusing to talk about those "mental pictures" because they can be a single frame or snapshot of a situation, as in "I (Gail Fairhurst) am writing Chapter One right now." Or they can be rather persistent patterns of thought that I have formed, for example, about "book writing" or "first chapter book writing."

I prefer to call these more general structures *mental models* because they help organize our thoughts and serve as underlying expectations for what is likely to happen in new situations.[8] Think of them as a library of past cases from which specific frames emerge each time we communicate.[9] For example, from Robert Murray's mental models for crisis communications, his "deflect responsibility" framing emerged, coupled with the tendency to make some rather bold predictions.

What motivates us to choose one framing strategy over another? The simple and perhaps slightly cynical answer is "self-interest" or "personal goals," but the better answers are "culture" and "sensemaking." As Chapter Two discusses, *culture* supplies us with a tool bag of specific language and arguments to consider when we communicate with another. *Sensemaking* is the situational engagement of mental models (just as the mine collapse triggered Murray's mental models for crisis communications).[10] In practical terms, to have made sense is to know how to go on in a situation, that is, to know what to say or do next.[11] Chapter Two discusses how mental models make this all possible.

Language becomes a key issue not just in our own sensemaking, but in how effectively we impact the sensemaking of others. In an increasingly complex world, language that is nuanced, precise, and eloquent enables leaders to draw distinctions that others may not see or be able to describe (Chapter Four). Quite often, options for surviving a complex world lie in those distinctions.[12] However, as Freudian slips also demonstrate, more than just conscious processes are at work when we use language. We need to know how to harness our unconscious as a result (Chapter Three).

Finally, and most important, a suitable definition of "the situation here and now" requires that we connect with others in some meaningful way. We have to be able to align others' interests with our own because we are rarely free agents. We are interdependent and often so inextricably so that we cannot accomplish objectives on our own. When we operate with a sense of that interdependence, we are motivated to look for the best ways to connect to others. Robert Murray clearly aimed for such a connection, but did he succeed?

Reality Construction Rule #3: Apply Ethics

"Reality" is often contested. Framing a subject is an act of persuasion by leaders, one imbued with ethical choices.

Robert Murray might have made himself the hero of one of those uniquely American success stories were it not for the challenges to his credibility in the hours and days following the mine collapse. U.S. government seismologists from the National Earthquake Information Center in Colorado indicated that it was likely the mine collapse itself that caused the ground to shake, not an earthquake.[13] It also became clear that Murray did not know where the miners were; bore holes were drilled in several unsuccessful attempts to supply oxygen and look for signs of life. Murray's promise not to leave the mine was also broken after three rescuers died and six were injured while trying to reach the miners. By August 23, Murray was telling *National Public Radio*, "It's a deadly mountain, and I'm not going near it."[14]

What might Murray have said to draw less fire? He could have allowed that the technique of retreat mining, even within the bounds of governmental regulation, might be among several factors that could contribute to a mine collapse. Instead, he consistently forced the media to parse his words on the subject. For example, at the August 7 news conference Murray said, "The damage in the mine was totally unrelated to any retreat mining. . . . The pillars were not being removed here at the time of the accident. There are eight solid pillars around where the men are right now."[15]

When reporting on the disaster on August 16, Frank Langfitt of *National Public Radio* said, "Technically what he's saying could be true because no one knows at that very moment what they were doing underground. In fact, only the men do and at the moment certainly we can't talk to them."[16] But Langfitt's report, which was based on the opinion of experts who believed that retreat mining *was* the likely cause of the collapse, appeared more credible.

Robert Murray's lesson here is twofold. First, when we frame, we assert that our interpretations of "the situation here and now" should be taken as real over other possible interpretations. Source credibility obviously becomes a key issue when interpretations of events differ. Second, leaders may win a momentary "pass" with strategically ambiguous language, but inconvenient truths have a way of surfacing.

What else could Robert Murray have said in those early communications? He could have expressed hope, not certainty, that the miners would be found. He gambled with the forces of nature and lost, as did heartbroken families and a waiting community whose hopes were dashed. The key to understanding framing as a persuasive act is not just to focus on that which may be uncertain, unknown, or contested and then take a position. It is to do so responsibly—with an eye toward the consequences of one's communications.

As Chapter Six argues, ethical codes are communication resources that assist leaders in morally positioning themselves and others as they communicate, whether in crises or everyday matters. When reflected upon, these codes help leaders actively resist the temptation to surrender to self-interest at the expense of other stakeholders whose interests may be every bit as legitimate. There is common ground to discover when we stop thinking, "my interests or yours."

Reality Construction Rule #4: Interpret Uncertainty

It is the uncertainty, confusion, and undecidability of "the situation here and now" that opens it up for interpretation and provides an opportunity for the more verbally skilled among us to emerge as leaders.

Robert Murray could have shown real leadership during the crisis at the Crandall Canyon mine, but arguably failed. Perhaps one of the best examples of a crisis leader in recent memory is Rudolph Giuliani, who was mayor of New York City on September 11, 2001, during the World Trade Center attacks. Giuliani rose to unexpected national and international prominence with a performance on 9/11 that many felt surpassed that of President George W. Bush and New York Governor George Pataki.[17]

In the moments following the attack, Giuliani took hold of the uncertainty, confusion, and undecidability of "the crisis here and now" and gave it meaning for a stunned city and nation. He immediately took command of the city's search and rescue for victims of the Twin Towers collapse and registered the shock of a nation as he was doing so. He was a ubiquitous presence, comforting first responders and their families at some two hundred funerals of the fallen. Moreover, he helped a city and nation understand a horrific act of international terrorism through repeated references to larger resonating Discourses of God and country.

While 9/11 and the Crandall Canyon mine disaster are extreme examples, the everyday moments of uncertainty and confusion are times when leaders can have their greatest impact. Indeed, conventional wisdom tends to distinguish leaders from managers, in part, based on this notion.[18] As Chapter Two describes, each group has a different set of *core framing tasks*. Leaders are the organization's change agents. They should be able to answer followers' "why, where, what, and who" questions: *why* we are here (mission), *where* the organization is headed (vision), *what* really counts in the organization (values), and *who* we are (collective identity). By contrast, managers often answer those all-important "how" questions, typically because they are implementers, trouble-shooters, and process oriented. Their core framing tasks are to set and solve problems, envision practical futures, and motivate efforts at solution.

However, there is one caveat to all of this. Things work differently if the organization is dealing with what Rittel and Webber call *wicked problems*.[19]

Problems are wicked when they are overwhelmingly complex and broad in scope, often with no one right answer. (As examples, consider the dire state of the American automobile industry; California's intertwined budgetary crisis and drought; nation-building in a tribal Afghanistan; or the efforts to overhaul the U.S. health care system.) By nature, wicked problems are intractable, constantly morphing into new ones. Leaders aren't expected to have the answers to these problems, but they do need to foster the right collaborations to get them. They must *frame* problems and collaborate to help their organizations engage the right knowledge networks, amass the right intelligence, and collectively decide possible futures. For this reason, wicked problems can render command-and-control leadership styles obsolete.[20]

Reality Construction Rule #5: Design the Response

Ultimately, leadership is a design problem.[21] Leaders must figure out what leadership is in the context of what they do and, through their framing and actions, persuade themselves and other people that they are doing it.

Leadership always emerges in some moment—or string of moments—in which someone's performance is deemed leader-like by a situation's stakeholders. Yet, one performance, even a skilled one, does not make a leader. (Otherwise, Rudolph Giuliani would have been elected president of the United States in 2008, not Barack Obama.) The true test of leadership is not just one believable performance but a sustained believability based on evidence of reliable performance as a leader.

Inevitably, this requires us to immerse ourselves in the work or tasks at hand and to balance it with whatever idealized notions we've developed about what it would mean to excel or lead at those tasks. For example, if you lead a manufacturing company or a division of one, your action is always tempered by your definition of success at this job—whether it be through market share, sales volume, patents filed, customer satisfaction, or some other criterion. If you lead a nonprofit or captain a team, the criteria change but your focus is still on the same questions: Where are you now and where do you want your organization to be? The real and ideal are constant companions, and your job is to figure out how best to marry the two. In this sense, leadership is a design problem: *You have to figure out what leadership is in the context of what you do and persuade yourself and other people that you are doing it.*

However, it's useful to unpack this notion further by dividing it into its "design aspects" and its "persuasion aspects." Regarding the former, just how do you figure out what it means to lead at the job that you're in? This step requires critical thinking on your part, given the specifics of your job and all that your life and work life experiences have taught you about leadership. Answer the questions in Framing Tool 1.1, and take note of the picture that emerges.

FRAMING TOOL 1.1

Designing Leadership

Who are the stakeholders associated with your job? How would they define what leadership is in the context of what you do?

_____

_____

_____

_____

Whose leadership styles do you admire or emulate and why?

_____

_____

_____

_____

What have you learned, good or bad, about leadership styles from the socialization you've received into your organization's culture? (For example, does senior management "tell" middle managers to be participative with lower-level employees in your company?[22]) What cultural expectations exist regarding your leadership style?

_____

_____

_____

_____

What books have you read or are reading about leadership? How have they shaped your views of leadership?

_____

_____

_____

_____

What training, development, or coaching have you received that has helped you to match certain tasks with a particular style of leading?

_____

_____

_____

_____

What work, school, or life experiences have impacted your comfort level and attitudes toward working with and leading others?

_____

_____

_____

_____

_____

(You can download this form from www.josseybass.com/go/gailfairhurst. Feel free to adapt it to suit your needs.)

Chapter Two presents questions to help you probe the mental models that you've developed for leadership, and Chapter Three addresses ways these models can continue to develop.

Regarding the "persuasion aspects" of leadership as a design problem, imagine the following scenario. Pretend that you can travel through time and ask any of history's great monarchs, society's major industrial transformers, or even a despot or two, "Just what are you doing here?" They could well respond, "Why, I'm leading my people, of course, so that we may preserve this great nation / make a profit and keep the economy going / pursue my own agenda (which, by the way, is none of your business)." All might use the word *leadership* (or its equivalents) with very different behaviors in mind—including those that might be detrimental to society as a whole.[23]

Thus leadership is not to be found in specific concrete acts. The decision to remain a virgin queen, demand strong quarterly sales, or restrict the freedoms of the populace isn't inherently an act of leadership. All must be argued for as constituting leadership when interacting with other relevant players such as followers, customers, clients, Wall Street analysts, the press, historians, and so on. As Grint suggests, leadership performances have to be believed in the context in which they are being discussed.[24]

Richard N. Haass makes this point in a slightly different way. He is the author of *War of Necessity, War of Choice*, a chronicle of U.S. involvement in both recent wars in Iraq.[25] He writes, "All wars are fought three times. There is the political struggle over whether to go to war. There is the physical war itself. And then there is the struggle over differing interpretations of what was accomplished and the lessons of it all."

But are leaders outside politics aware of the role of persuasion as they lead? The best ones are, as demonstrated by Pamela Shockley-Zalabak, chancellor of the University of Colorado at Colorado Springs (UCCS). Her duties are to oversee a regional campus of some twelve thousand students, one of four in the sprawling University of Colorado system. Early in 2009, she received a startling telephone call. An attorney at the other end of the line said that due to her leadership, UCCS was going to receive an anonymous gift of $5.5 million dollars.[26] To her absolute astonishment, the next day the check arrived.

I had a chance to talk with Chancellor Shockley-Zalabak about why she might have won the award, and I was immediately struck by her sensitivity to the persuasion involved in the problems that she faced. For example, while the economic recession was forcing many universities to lay people off, she had declined to do this on her campus. Instead, she instituted a strategic plan that would emphasize transparency, collaboration, and a new language to help her constituents think and talk in more budgetary terms.[27]

For example, in her "2/3 of plan budget," she asked everyone to operate in the year ahead as if they had only two-thirds of their anticipated budget increases. If at the end of the year the saved money was not needed for budget cuts, the academic units would receive it back. Shockley-Zalabak's "2/3 of plan" signaled a very specific kind of budget tightening that actually calmed fears over whether needed allocations from previous years would be threatened. She also introduced the "cliff effect," which meant, from a budgetary perspective, what must units do before they cease to function effectively—before they "fall off a cliff"? Finally, the "joy of uncertainty" introduced language and arguments that prepared students afraid of the impact of the budget crisis and decision making ahead on their course of study.

Chancellor Shockley-Zalabak also thought that her outreach programs might have impressed the donor. She instituted a number of wide-ranging scholarship programs for bright but disadvantaged students from Denver public schools, area community colleges, and nontraditional women returning to school. To reach these students, the UCCS Web site links prospective students and their parents to a number of well-produced podcasts in which Chancellor Shockley-Zalabak speaks directly to its users.[28]

For example, the podcast titled "College Is Possible" is remarkable for its pithy take-away line, which also serves as a master frame organizing her persuasive arguments for those undecided about paying for a college education in today's economy. (Chapters Two and Four further explain master frames.) Along with a hard-hitting message, the strategic use of these podcasts guards against Shockley-Zalabak becoming a faceless bureaucrat in the Office of the Chancellor. On the contrary, she manages to have a real presence in these podcasts. Podcast users feel as if she is speaking to them.

It is quite likely that Chancellor Shockley-Zalabak reaped significant rewards as much through the selling aspects of her job as her design of leadership in a budgetary crisis. How about you? Later in the chapter, you will have an opportunity to evaluate yourself as a persuasive communicator.

Reality Construction Rule #6: Control Spontaneity

Effective framing requires that leaders be able to control their own spontaneous communications.

No doubt Robert Murray probably wishes he could take back some of his communication in the early hours of the Utah mine collapse. Indeed, his instinctive promise of a successful rescue of the miners proved wrong. In the end, he not only gave false hope to the miners' families, he damaged his own public image and his company's as well. However, this case raises a key question: can leaders control their spontaneous communications?

At first glance, this idea may seem both contradictory and downright impossible. Yet the truth of the matter lies with our unconscious mind and our ability to program it when we are consciously focused. Just as you might prime a pump for several seconds before water comes out, so too can you prime your unconscious mind during conscious periods to exert a measure of control over your spontaneous communications. However, it's necessary to know a little something about conscious and unconscious learning processes to do this, a topic addressed in Chapter Three.

Perhaps most important in this discussion of framing is the role that emotions and values play in our message behavior. Too often we believe that our organizational interactions are driven by logic and reason only. We either deny or fail to acknowledge the role of emotions in our framing when we ignore the way our bodies are registering pride, passion, joy, anger, and so on. Such emotions either accentuate our framing or provide a mixed message for those with whom we communicate (a point discussed in Chapter Five). The body is perhaps the most overlooked aspect of leadership behavior, but the subject of framing cannot be discussed without it.[29]

Consider also that even the most fleeting, in-the-moment responses are as value-laden as any conscious statement or affirmation of values on our part.[30] Moreover, they are especially credible to outsiders because such responses appear involuntary and thus representative of true feelings.

Despite this appearance of involuntary action, you can gain an element of control. You can go a long way toward programming your unconscious actions toward desired behavior by reflecting on what it is you would want to do. This is especially likely to be effective in close proximity to spontaneous moments of communicating. Therefore, it behooves us to explore how best to take advantage of these unconscious learning processes as we try to understand the impact of our communications on others.

To better understand the value of the six reality construction rules for leadership, select a critical incident involving your own leadership or management. The purpose of Framing Tool 1.2 is to take a first crack at analyzing this incident. As you continue to read on, you will find other analysis questions in following chapters.

FRAMING TOOL 1.2

Critical Incident Framing

Identify a key problem or critical incident involving your communications as a leader with your employees, customers, or other stakeholders. To maximize your gain from this exercise, select an incident in which you were unhappy with the outcome.

_____

_____

_____

_____

_____

How did you define "the situation here and now" for them? What specific language did you use?

_____

_____

_____

_____

How effective was this framing? What told you that your use of language was either effective or ineffective? (For example, was there a challenge to your framing? Did your framing seem to confuse people?)

_____

_____

_____

_____

If your framing was ineffective, what was your preferred outcome?

_____

_____

_____

_____

_____

(You can download this form from www.josseybass.com/go/gailfairhurst. Feel free to adapt it to suit your needs. This analysis will continue in Chapter Two.)

Test Your Framing Style

How difficult will the concept of framing be for you to understand and use? To answer this question fairly, it is important to assess the kind of communicator that you are. Since the 1996 publication of *The Art of Framing*, whenever I coach or train organizational leaders, I utilize the research of Barbara J. O'Keefe, dean of Northwestern's School of Communication.[31] In her research on what she calls "Message Design Logic," she argues that three kinds of communicator styles determine how we produce our own messages and interpret those of others, especially as the situations we face gain in complexity.[32] Complete the inventory below to determine the style that best fits your everyday communications and your sensitivity to framing.[33] Your total score should indicate whether you are an Expressive, a Conventional, or a Strategic.[34] As you will learn, each style has both strengths and weaknesses.

FRAMING TOOL 1.3

Communications Style Inventory

There are fifteen pairs of statements in this inventory. For each pair, read both statements and *quickly* decide which statement best fits your communication style. Even if both statements are partially true, select the one that is true more often than not. Circle either "a" or "b," not both. There is no right or wrong answer in this survey.

Circle "a" or "b"

1a. I pretty much say what I'm thinking most of the time.

1b. I try to be honest, but within the bounds of politeness.

2a. When communicating with another person, you have to respond to what the situation calls for.

2b. I focus on the situation, but I look for room to maneuver within it.

3a. I am sensitive to the context in which I communicate with others.

3b. When communicating with others, I try to seize the moment.

4a. I consider myself to be a straight-shooter. My communication is pretty transparent most of the time.

4b. When communicating with others, you have to really consider their thoughts and feelings.

5a. If my employees failed on an assignment that they are more than capable of handling, I would not be afraid to deliver a harsh message to them.

5b. If my employees failed on an assignment that they are more than capable of handling, I would try to couch a harsh message in a polite way.

6a. In difficult situations, I do what's right.

6b. In difficult situations, I try to redefine the context in ways that are more suitable to a beneficial resolution to the conflict at hand.

7a. People around me are shocked at times with things that I say.

7b. I try to keep most of my conversations from veering into unnecessary conflict.

8a. I am concerned about hurt feelings in a conflict.

8b. I try to seek consensus in conflict situations.

9a. I am careful in my use of language on the job.

9b. In general, I understand the power of language and the possibilities it affords, especially at work.

10a. My conflicts sometimes end with hurt feelings.

10b. Hurt feelings can usually be avoided in a conflict.

11a. I might be blunt at times, but people generally trust that I am telling them the truth.

11b. There is always a "proper" way to communicate truthfully that I try to follow.

12a. I try to persuade with the other person in mind.

12b. I've been told that I am very verbal; I could sell cars to a used-car salesman.

13a. I have one goal when I communicate, and that is to express
myself.

13b. I try to communicate with an
awareness of others' feelings
about a given subject.

14a. I don't usually play games when I
communicate.

14b. I can be subtly manipulative at
times, but not unethical.

15a. If someone is really angry and
potentially hostile, I'll back off. Otherwise, I express myself pretty freely.

15b. I try to prevent conflict as much as
possible.

How to score your results:

When your response matches the letter "b," score one point. All answers matching the letter "a" are to be scored zero.

The scale ranges from 0 to 15, with these approximate ranges:

0–8 = Expressive

9–12 = Conventional

13–15 = Strategic

Most leaders are Conventionals.

(You can download this form from www.josseybass.com/go/gailfairhurst.)

If you are an Expressive, you are likely to find it relatively difficult to develop sensitivity to the framing concept. Your primary communications goal is simply to express yourself unencumbered by most of the conventional norms of polite conversation. O'Keefe says that unless there are fairly dire negative consequences, you are a person who pretty much says what you think. Because finesse is not your strong suit, others may half-humorously suggest that you "lack an edit function." You are often blunt, surprising, or embarrassing. At times, you can also be very literal. Nevertheless, others may find you more trustworthy for these very same reasons. You are not a game-player.

Vice President Joe Biden is a classic Expressive. He is well known for his gaffes, including torpedoing his own 2008 bid for the presidency on its very first day with what many regarded as an unintentional racial slur directed toward Barack Obama, then a candidate.[35] Most recently, the swine flu epidemic in early 2009 found Biden telling the American public on the *Today Show* to stay out of airplanes due to perceived poor air circulation. With this remark, he almost single-handedly brought down the airline and travel industries, which were already struggling to survive in a tough economy.

All of us pass through an Expressive phase as children, as the youngsters who reveal embarrassing family secrets remind us. However, some of us never leave this phase even as blunt talk gets us into trouble time and again. (Incidentally, several Expressive students over the years have suggested to me that they come from Expressive families where blunt talk is the family norm, which makes a great deal of sense.) If you are an Expressive, this book can help you adapt to the people and circumstances around you, locate opportunities for influence, and avoid offending others—while not losing any of your spontaneity.

O'Keefe's second communicator style is "Conventional," and it is the style of most leaders today. Conventionals have some sensitivity to the idea of framing because they generally follow the rules for communicating with others. Conventionals do what is appropriate to the situation and readily follow social norms. If you are a Conventional, then you likely see the communication process as a cooperative venture in which others also have needs.

To take a really simple example, when a person at your dinner table says, "Are those the rolls and butter?" a Conventional understands this remark as an indirect request to pass the rolls and butter. "Yes, would you like them?" is what a Conventional is likely to say based on proper etiquette for polite company—almost certainly avoiding the somewhat more literal response of the Expressive, who might say, "Yes, they are," thus further imposing on the other diner the need to phrase the request for rolls and butter in more specific terms: "Okay, would you *please* pass the rolls and butter."

Al Gore is a good example of a Conventional. Most know him either as the forty-fifth Vice President of the United States under Bill Clinton (1993–2001) or as an environmental activist who starred in the 2006 documentary, *An Inconvenient Truth*. However, in 2000, Gore aspired to the presidency of the United States and surprised many when he lost to George W. Bush.[36] But Gore's 2000 presidential debate performances were telling. In his first debate, he was coached to be an alpha male and dominate the interaction, which he tried to do through frequent interruptions of then candidate Bush and violations of his personal space. When Gore was reviewed poorly for this, he was coached to be more affable for the next debate. Gore subsequently emphasized areas of agreement with Bush, but also adopted what many saw as an overly friendly demeanor. When this showing produced poor reviews, Gore eventually assumed a middle position by the third debate, somewhere between the two extremes. Ironically, many pundits believe that Gore's best campaign performance was his concession speech, which is the only one he wrote himself. Gore gave himself over to his handlers, switching his style each time, because that's what modern-day presidential candidates (conventionally) do.

The downside of being a Conventional is that most situations tend to seem rather fixed. That is, you minimize the opportunity to let situations work for you instead of against you by fixing the elements in the context in one particular way. It is analogous to taking a Rorschach test (a personality test based on interpreting a series of ink blots), and insisting that an ink blot could be one and only one shape. If you are a Conventional, this book can help you to understand many more possibilities when you communicate. You can realize outcomes more to your liking because "the situation here and now" becomes somewhat more pliable.

Finally, you can have a Strategic style, in which you already have a heightened sensitivity to language, and you are rather precise when choosing it. You nearly always see alternative possibilities for "the situation here and now," and you are generally confident in pursuing them. Two great examples stand out here. The first occurs in, of all places, signage at my local grocery store notifying under-age purchasers that they will not be able to buy alcohol. It reads, "If you are lucky enough to look under 27, please be ready to show your identification." The compliment is a deft touch compared to the usual straightforward announcement, "No alcohol sold to minors."

Another interesting leadership example of a Strategic comes from the world of sports and a rather unlikely source. Ohio State University (OSU) basketball player Mark Titus is a bench-warming walk-on to the team coached under Thad Matta. By their own admission, the team's starters say that Titus is taking center stage with his Club Trillion blog, "Life Views from the End of the Bench" (at clubtrillion.blogspot.com).

To say that Titus is quick with a line is an understatement. Speaking to the *New York Times*, one of his team members recounted an incident in which Coach Matta assembled the team to address a circulating e-mail about an unsanctioned party featuring OSU's football and basketball players.[37] With numerous university administrators looking on and just as Matta was about to warn players about parties of this nature, a straight-faced Titus interjected: "Coach, can you forward a copy of that e-mail to me? I never got it."

You can imagine the room cracking up. But Titus's genius here is not just to be funny. He makes the coaches and administrators momentarily share his perspective and doubt their own if, ever so briefly, they flash back to what it was like to be a student in search of the next party.

One of the coaches also recounted a time when Titus was at the scorer's table during a blowout in which his team was dominating the game. However, he did not make it into the game when a time-out was called. Titus apparently screamed "Water! Water! I need water!" to the managers as he made his way back to his seat, mockingly calling attention to his aspirations and his bench-warming plight. One of Titus's high school coaches has an interesting insight into this Strategic: "He knows the line, he'll walk it and lean over it and then pull himself back." Indeed, that's what Strategics do. They make or find opportunities when the rest of us are usually rule or role bound.

Titus's verbal skills are clearly creating buzz and, quite likely, job opportunities in the near future. However, being a Strategic also has its downside, as others may suspect you of trying to manipulate them. My students often remark that more than a few lawyers would qualify as Strategics given their ability to argue. (This may be true, but one should not overlook academics either!)

We certainly saw this demonstrated during the depositions surrounding the Monica Lewinsky scandal, when President Bill Clinton answered a question with the memorable phrase, "Well, it depends on what the meaning of the word 'is' is." Perhaps only a trained lawyer and Rhodes Scholar could have uttered such a response, which was widely mocked by the press and political pundits. Nevertheless, this book can help Strategics focus on both ethics and strategic goal formation to avoid relinquishing personal credibility to charges of manipulation.

What do you think happens when individuals with different styles get into conflict with one another? O'Keefe suggests that individuals with similar styles will likely conflict over issue-related matters, that is, specific arguments, assumptions, goals, and so on. However, individuals of different styles may conflict not only over the issues but also the other person's style—thus making resolution of the conflict all the more difficult.

For example, Strategics or Conventionals may find Expressives rude and overbearing, while Expressives or Conventionals might see Strategics as untrustworthy and manipulative. Similarly, both Expressives and Strategics may find Conventionals a bit too rule-oriented.

Consider former President George W. Bush as an example. In the early days of his presidency and after 9/11, he tended toward an Expressive style with what many Europeans saw as "Texas cowboy rhetoric" and frequent remarks like "I don't do nuance." When asked in September of 2001 if he wanted Osama bin Laden killed, he said, "I want justice. There's an old poster out West, as I recall, that said WANTED: DEAD OR ALIVE." When asked by a reporter in July 2003 about the rising attacks on U.S. troops in Iraq—two months after standing under a banner reading "Mission Accomplished" on the USS *Abraham Lincoln* flight deck—he said "My answer is, Bring them on."[38]

However, he came to regret many of those remarks when as early as January of 2005 he stated, "I watch what I say . . . . I said some things in the first term that were probably a little blunt."[39] Interestingly, Bush is the country's first MBA president and known for his aversion to lawyers, which, we can only surmise, might be a stylistic issue, as by his own admission he is not the most articulate of speakers.

One other key issue regarding Message Design Logic concerns a leader's ability to use all three styles. Interestingly, O'Keefe's work suggests that Expressives are usually Expressive most of the time.[40] Conventionals can be either Conventional or Expressive, while Strategics can be all three given their chameleon-like language skills. However, this raises a key point concerning the aim of this book, which is to move you toward a more Strategic style. It might be helpful here to recall Bill Clinton's early nickname of "Slick Willie" (from his days as governor of Arkansas) because one danger of becoming a Strategic is that others may perceive you as manipulative. It takes care with a Strategic style to realize its many benefits, and the discussion of the ethics of framing in Chapter Six is crucial to take to heart.

If you would like to further consider how the people on your team "mesh" with their different styles, especially in conflict situations, answer the questions in Framing Tool 1.4. In doing so, you may discover a conflict management strategy that you didn't know you had.

 FRAMING TOOL 1.4

Communications Style Meshing

Message Design Logic has implications for communicating with your staff, because individuals who have the same style (Expressive to Expressive, Conventional to Conventional, Strategic to Strategic) will likely conflict only over the issues when they disagree. However, individuals whose styles differ may conflict *both* over the issues and their objections to the other person's style.

If you can predict the communication styles of your staff members (or you want to give them the inventory to complete), you might gain some insight into how to better manage conflict among them.

My style is: _____

The Expressives on my staff oftentimes blurt out whatever they are thinking. It seems as though they lack an edit function most of the time. They are:

Name: _____

Name: _____

Name: _____

The Conventionals on my staff view communication as a cooperative venture. They are generally appropriate in their communications. However, they sometimes lack imagination in responding to the events of the moment.

Name: _____

Name: _____

Name: _____

Name: _____

Name: _____

The Strategics on my staff are very adept in their language use. They don't react to the context—they create it. Some, though, can be perceived as a little manipulative.

Name: _____
Name: _____
Name: _____

Conflict Dynamic #1: The Conventionals and Strategics on my staff find the Expressives rude and overbearing, regardless of the issues. Please explain.

_____

_____

_____

Conflict Dynamic #2: The Expressives and Conventionals on my staff find the Strategics to be untrustworthy or manipulative, regardless of the issues. Please explain.

_____

_____

_____

Conflict Dynamic #3: The Expressives and Strategics on my staff find the Conventionals to be overly rule-bound, regardless of the issues. Please explain.

_____

_____

_____

Key Conflict Management Strategy: Separate "communication style" from the "issues," and deal with each separately. The actual words I might use:

_____

_____

_____

_____

_____

_____

(You can download this form from www.josseybass.com/go/gailfairhurst. Feel free to adapt it to suit your needs.)

Framing Through Pictures?

Up to this point, I have focused exclusively on framing through language, which raises the question of whether there are other ways to frame—using pictures, digital images, symbolism, or even just nonverbal behavior. Most assuredly, the answer is yes! For example, consider Carly Fiorina, whose tenure as CEO of Hewlett-Packard was abruptly cut short when she was fired by its board in 2005. As business schools, executives, and the media sized up her performance, there was a lot of talk about one seemingly nonperformance issue: the placement of her portrait alongside those of the company's revered founders, William Hewlett and David Packard, in the company lobby.

No words were uttered in this simple act, but what was the possible message here? In the postmortems after her firing, it appeared to some as a lack of respect for the past and power of the company's culture.[41] To others, it was an indication of Fiorina's aspirational "rock star" status given the celebrities and politicians with whom she associated.[42] Fiorina herself said she was following company precedent, as John Young and Lew Platt had hung their portraits in the same spot when each was CEO. She also defended it in this way, "Hewlett-Packard was clearly bigger than me, but it had also become bigger than [the founders] Bill and Dave. . . . Change can only begin if its force is greater than the weight of the history and the power of the status quo."[43]

But if Fiorina had succeeded at taking Hewlett-Packard to new levels of unprecedented growth, would portrait placement have mattered quite so much? Or was this a classic case of gender discrimination when she was merely following a precedent set by her male predecessors on the job? (Interestingly, the CEO who followed Fiorina at Hewlett-Packard, Mark Hurd, chose not to have his portrait hung in the lobby.[44])

Recalling Reality Construction Rule #2, reality is often contested—and this certainly was. The controversy over her firing at the time landed her an interview on *60 Minutes*, a prominent U.S. news show.[45] The interviewer asked about the symbolism of her portrait's placement in the lobby, acknowledging that it had become a matter of considerable debate.

Consider another woman leader, Secretary of State Hillary Clinton in the Obama administration. As a U.S. senator, she ran against and lost to Senator Barack Obama for the Democratic nomination for the presidency of the

United States. One small moment in the campaign involved some interesting nonverbal behavior on her part that was deemed a framed message. It was January 31, 2006, the night of President George W. Bush's State of the Union address. Such speeches tend to draw a partisan response, although there are usually moments of bipartisanship. A smart president will try to strike a balance between partisan and bipartisan moments to avoid speaking to only half an audience of lawmakers and citizenry.

President Bush was discussing the problems associated with the U.S. Social Security system when he pointed out that the first baby boomers were turning sixty—including two of his father's favorite people (referring to President George H.W. Bush). While the audience waited to hear him name his father's two oldest sons, himself and his brother Jeb Bush, President Bush attempted a bit of humor by saying, "Me and President Bill Clinton." This was a reference to all the traveling that the elder Bush and Clinton had been doing associated with their December 2005 tsunami fundraising efforts.[46]

The cameras on the floor of the House of Representatives immediately panned to Hillary Clinton. This was to be expected, as she was the presumptive Democratic nominee at the time. Of the moment, syndicated columnist Kathleen Parker wrote, "If eyes could emasculate, Hillary's would send a man into the high octaves . . . her expression said, 'Bug off,' or sentiments to that effect. What we do know is that Bill Clinton would have loved it."[47]

Parker's take is certainly one way to interpret Hillary Clinton's putative stone face. However, it is also important to remember that Hillary Clinton had voted to go to war in Iraq, which angered many in her Democratic base. Her opponent, Barack Obama, who was not in the Senate at that time, was criticizing her heavily for doing what President George W. Bush had wanted. At every stop on the campaign trail, she was distancing herself from Bush. During the State of the Union address, it is likely that she was much more concerned with what a knowing smile or laugh might communicate to her base than with being polite at that moment. Any affiliation with the president was to be avoided if one follows this logic.

Yet, herein lies the conundrum when using nonverbal behavior, pictures, digital images, or symbolism to frame a message. They often create a visceral response, but they do not have the precision that language affords (assuming, of course, that we are choosing not to be strategically ambiguous with our word choices). For example, was Carly Fiorina's true motivation to hang her picture in the HP lobby benign, merely strategic, or blatant self-aggrandizement? What exactly was Senator Clinton thinking during George W. Bush's attempt at humor?

The answer to these questions is that we do not know. We can only speculate. Nonverbal behavior, in particular, is all about positioning ourselves or acting in relation to another. Think of the effects of a scowl, raised eyebrow, or certain tone of voice in the midst of a conversation. They clearly add meaning to verbal messages, but alone they are difficult to interpret. It is something that we must adjust to as we learn about framing without words, a subject that Chapter Five takes up directly.

A Backward Glance at Chapter One

Secretary of State Hillary Clinton, Carly Fiorina, Chancellor Pamela Shockley-Zalabak, Rudolph Giuliani, and Robert Murray are leaders thrust onto a national or international stage. They are great fodder for any book because most are so widely known. However, their status should not be misinterpreted. Differences in what they do for a living notwithstanding, they shape meaning and help construct reality by influencing "the situation here and now" just as you and I must do. The rules that apply to them also apply to you and me when we lead:

- Reality Construction Rule #1: Control the context. Leaders often cannot control events, but they can control the context under which events are seen if they recognize a framing opportunity.

- Reality Construction Rule #2: Define the situation. At its most basic level, framing reality means defining "the situation here and now" in ways that connect with others.

- Reality Construction Rule #3: Apply ethics. "Reality" is often contested; framing a subject is an act of persuasion by leaders, one imbued with ethical choices.

- Reality Construction Rule #4: Interpret uncertainty. It is the uncertainty, confusion, and undecidability of "the situation here and now" that opens it up for interpretation and provides an opportunity for the more verbally skilled among us to emerge as leaders.

- Reality Construction Rule #5: Design the response. Ultimately, leadership is a design problem. Leaders must figure out what leadership is in the context of what they do and, through their framing and actions, persuade themselves and other people that they are doing it.

- Reality Construction Rule #6: Control spontaneity. Framing reality requires that leaders be able to control their own spontaneous communication.

To help understand your own proclivities toward framing, I invoked Barbara J. O'Keefe's research on Message Design Logic as a diagnostic tool to help you categorize your communication style. The three possibilities reveal themselves in answers to the question, "Why did you say that?"

- The Expressive says, "Because that's what I was thinking!" Expressives say what they are thinking with very little editing.

- The Conventional says, "Because that is the appropriate thing to say for this situation." Conventionals follow social norms for communicating with others.

- The Strategic says, "Because that is the best course of action given my strategic goals." Strategics see situations as mutable, thus they understand that they play a major role in shaping the context.

A FINAL THOUGHT

Through framing, we create the realities to which we must then respond.

2

The Skill of Framing

I REMEMBER SITTING in church on a Sunday morning listening to a sermon given by the new president of Xavier University, Father Michael Graham. A Ph.D. from the University of Michigan and a Jesuit, he gave a sermon so spell-binding that I and others in the audience spontaneously broke into applause afterward. I remember thinking to myself, "What just happened here? We're in a *Catholic* church, and we're applauding a sermon?" Let's just say that Catholic priests are not exactly known for their oratory.[1] I had never heard a congregation spontaneously applaud a sermon, and never have since unless I attend one of Graham's masses.

After one of his rousing sermons, the communication professor in me always wants to understand how to bottle that magic. How in twenty minutes is this man routinely able to move five hundred or so half-awake people who have probably listened to more sermons in a lifetime than they can count? Well, it became a little easier when I saw him quoted in a newspaper article that featured city leaders' reflections on the meaning of Martin Luther King Day.[2] Here's what Graham said:

> Dr. King is typically remembered in a kind of soft and fuzzy way that tends to blunt his message, effectively domesticating him and, for many, making his memory less troublesome and easier to bear. What Dr. King's memory reminds me, constantly, is that the most important issues to deal with are structural, "big picture" issues, and that it's precisely at the fault lines of race, class, and I would add, gender, that America has a long way to go before it delivers on the promise of the noble words of our founding documents.

I was surprised at the prescience of his remarks. In nine other quotes from city leaders (the mayor, a city council member, two other local university presidents, another religious leader, a community action organizer, two NAACP branch presidents, and a city school superintendent), each delivered a "soft and fuzzy" take on King, however heartfelt and sincere. King was remembered for his basic values of nonviolent change and love for one's fellow man and woman; for his strength of character, which helped these leaders overcome personal adversity; and for the gratitude they felt to him for the doors that he opened.

What was a white, middle-aged male Catholic university president from America's heartland doing by suggesting that King's message had been softened, blunted, and domesticated? Was there not a touch of irony—or at least surprise—that *he* was underscoring King's more radical agenda of "structural, 'big picture' issues . . . at the fault lines of race, class . . . and gender?" Indeed, it was exactly in that side-by-side comparison of quotes that I began to understand Graham's magic—his skill at framing.

Any communication skill is an underlying ability that translates to a capacity to act.[3] Considered as a skill, framing is the capacity to be articulate and persuasive more or less on demand. This chapter zeros in on three of the most important things to know about framing as a skill:

Figure 2.1. Framing Skill Components

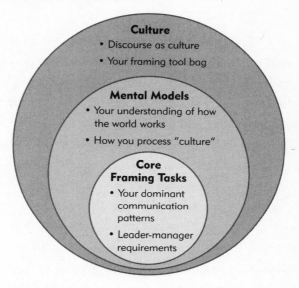

- *Cultural Discourses*, which are where the content of your communications comes from.

- *Mental models*, which are the way you regulate that content.

- *Core framing tasks*, which are the chief communication requirements of your job.

There are certainly other skill components associated with framing, but when it comes to strategizing about it, these are among the most important. Figure 2.1 reveals the terrain ahead in this chapter.

Culture and Its Discourses

Think back to the example of the sermon that opened this chapter. Imagine that Martin Luther King day has rolled around again, and your local newspaper has called upon you to reflect on the memory of King. Try writing out what you would say on the lines below:

_____

_____

———————————————————————————

———————————————————————————

While King lived in the era of racial unrest (the 1950s and 1960s) that triggered the American civil rights movement, he and his message still resonate in twenty-first-century American society. If your words in any way echo the themes or values from King's life—much as Graham and the city leaders did at the start of this chapter—then you are like millions of Americans who have been influenced by this cultural icon. Indeed, his themes of racial equality and nonviolent change, and his phrases—"I have a dream," "free at last," and others—are quite culturally familiar. You hear and see them referenced a lot, especially on and around Martin Luther King Day every year, when many honor the man by reflecting on his legacy in more modern times.[4] (If you are not an American, try a similar exercise with an admired leader from your own heritage.)

The important point here is that cultural familiarity translates into a framing resource. How so? As a historical era plays itself out, the collective experience of its defining events, people, tools, and so on gives rise to particular ways of seeing the world, including ways of talking and behaving. These systems of thought are called *Discourses* by French sociologist Michel Foucault, and they are the vehicles that transmit culture to us.[5]

A really excellent way to think about Discourse is as a system of thought with its own *linguistic tool bag,* or collection of terms and metaphors for key concepts and ideas, and its own categories for understanding, themes for stories, and familiar arguments to draw upon to describe, explain, or justify our place in the world at any given moment.[6]

For example, when you wrote your newspaper quote about Martin Luther King (MLK), you likely drew from a Civil Rights or MLK Discourse that allowed you to express what you wanted to say. Indeed, MLK Discourse has its own lingo or dialect with, as mentioned earlier, the labeling of its key ideas (such as "nonviolence"), metaphors to express them ("I have a dream"), and arguments to pose (such as basic civil rights).

Even if you only vaguely referenced that material in your quote, MLK Discourse played a role in shaping the content of your communications.

Culture left its imprint on you to the extent that you responded in a familiar or customary way. In fashion terms, it is equivalent to emulating a popular style of clothing in your own wardrobe choices. In one way or another, your use of language is influenced by what has been commonly said or done.

In later discussion on mental models, I discuss how individuals regulate what culture supplies and, therefore, how Graham's comment stands out above the others. However, for now it is important to recognize that Discourse is the common ground that all members of a culture share—be it a societal, institutional, organizational, professional, or other cultural grouping. More-over, if Discourse is the primary vehicle by which culture transmits itself, it becomes possible to evaluate specific cultural Discourses as framing resources. (Hereafter, I use the term *cultural Discourse* to signify a way of thinking and speaking that is common to all culture members.)

Cultural Discourses Used by Leaders

Most would agree that MLK Discourse presents a rich array of language and ideas to draw upon in speaking about King. However, two recent leadership books also demonstrate the power of culture and its Discourses, although nei-ther use the term. The first book is by Frank Luntz, a Republican Party and corporate pollster and author of *Words That Work: It's Not What You Say, It's What People Hear.*[7] Luntz is famous for his focus group methodology, espe-cially around election season. With focus groups, he tests out different words and phrases (inviting his audience to word-craft as well) for use in upcoming political campaigns. He is also a frequent user of the language of framing.

In his book, he offers up what amounts to a cultural Discourse of twenty-one words and phrases for the twenty-first century—as well as those words and phrases that he unabashedly claims one should never utter again for maximum persuasiveness. For example, instead of "global economy," "globalization," or "capitalism," Luntz recommends "free market economy." Instead of "inheritance or estate tax," use "death tax." Similarly, don't use words like "undocumented workers or aliens," say "illegal immigrants" or "border security" instead.

In effect, Luntz's "words that work" do so because he has vetted them with everyday Americans, whom he regards as the litmus test for American culture (and its cultural Discourses). Luntz thus sets himself up as a cultural standard bearer when he says these words *should* become part of the tool bag of any American politician or corporate spokesperson (or those wishing to do business with America). In some not-so-subtle ways then, he pressures his readers and clients to accept and use these culture-laden terms.

Culture shaping is also the subject of discussion in a book by Warren Bennis and Robert Thomas, *Geeks & Geezers: How Era, Values, and Defining Moments Shape Leaders.*[8] The book's novelty is its focus on two groups of leaders: Those under the age of thirty, or "geeks," and those over the age of seventy, or "geezers." However, it is not the generations themselves that interest these authors, it is the historical eras and those defining events in which leaders in these groups come to share history, culture, and an "arena in which to act" shaped by Discourse.[9]

For example, geezers are products of an analog era complete with tools and objects such as slide rules, record albums, and typewriters. Such tools prompt a linear and mechanical view of the world where experience is key. By contrast, geeks are products of a digital era and the profoundly transformative nature of its tools and objects such as televisions, computers, and the Internet. (Indeed, it may be difficult for them to conceive of life without such tools!) All of these encourage thinking around nonlinearity and living systems. As a result, geeks bring a fresh "beginner's mind" to their tasks that (they believe) delivers insight in ways that (geezer) experience does not.

Bennis and Thomas discerned a number of these era-based differences because geeks and geezers *each had a way of talking about their worlds.* None of them called their forms of expression a cultural Discourse, but that is exactly what they were. In interviews with both groups of leaders, the stories they told each drew upon a different set of themes. Their concepts and the terminology for them differed, and they posed different arguments. For example, influenced by the Great Depression and World War II (with their formative years being 1945–1954), geezers told stories about how they would make their living compared to the hardships of many of their immigrant parents (themes). They spoke favorably of the shaping role of the military in their organizations, as military concepts such as "chain of command" found their way into big business (metaphor for a key concept). Finally, geezers repeatedly argued that hard work was necessary to get ahead in this world, and the need to pay one's dues was crucial (familiar arguments). Theirs was an era of limits, and their language use reflected their experience of such limits.

By contrast, the historical era for geeks was an era of options (their formative years being 1991–2000). The stories they told were not about making a living but about making history and having an impact (themes). The crucial years in which geeks were molded were about technology, growth, and globalization. Theirs is not a search for a living wage as much as it is a search for meaning and identity (more themes). Gone was enduring loyalty to any organization, and in its place came the language of "entrepreneurship" and "entrepreneurial selves" in which the "self" became a project to be developed as it intertwined with one's career (terminology and metaphor for key ideas).[10] Moreover, geeks increasingly argued for work-life balance as they often experienced or saw firsthand the destructive effects of a parent's life given over to work and little else (familiar arguments).

That different story themes, metaphors, terminology, and familiar arguments mark the language of geeks and geezers is common sense. To make good use of Foucault, however, simply take the next step: recognize that geeks and geezers are each the source of a cultural Discourse—an era-based system of thought with its own linguistic tool bag. In varying degrees (depending upon how well developed a cultural Discourse is), each of these tool bags will contain its own terms and metaphors for key ideas, themes for stories, familiar arguments, and so on. Those using this Discourse can draw upon their tool bags to describe, explain, or justify their place in the world at any given moment.

For further evidence of cultural Discourses, try this experiment. Have a conversation with a geek or geezer leader and see if they draw from their respective cultural Discourses as they speak. I did this with one of my former students, Jason Delambre, who is a young environmental leader on the rise.[11] In a recent conversation with him (in which I discerned he had *not* read Bennis and Thomas's *Geeks and Geezers*), I was struck by how much he pulled terms, themes, and arguments right out of the geek tool bag!

I asked him what he wanted to do with his life, and he had no less than four "green" entrepreneurial projects in mind, framed as "wanting to make a difference." He also said that he and his wife plan to start a family while stressing a desire for work-family balance and not wanting to be an absentee father. There was no evidence of "geezer Discourse." On the contrary, only "geek Discourse" supplied him with his tool bag: his language of entrepreneurship, the theme of making a difference, and work-family arguments from which he explained his corner of the world.

But Jason's language use raises two key issues. First, his tool bag is simultaneously enabling and constraining. To borrow a cliché, imagine a real-life tool bag containing only a hammer. Owning a hammer makes it possible to pound a nail into the wall or rip one out (enablements); yet it offers little help for those tasks that require, say, twisting or turning a bolt or screw (constraints). Thus Jason's tool bag enables him to express himself at the same time it constrains him by subtly disciplining him to conform to what his "geek" cultural Discourse prescribes.

Second, we could easily imagine Jason using three or more Discourses if he talked specifically about one of his green start-up businesses (as an American, using the Discourses of capitalism and entrepreneurialism); became involved with environmental legislation of some kind (the language of the law qualifies as Discourse); joined an environmental protest movement (their frequent rhetoric qualifies as Discourse); or joined the Sierra Club (its formal statement of mission and philosophy is a Discourse).[12] In truth, leaders have many Discourses to deploy individually or in combination relevant to their work-life experiences. With such familiarity, think of how a tool bag expands with each new Discourse and the opportunity it presents to combine ideas, terms, arguments, and so on. *Anywhere we find evidence of culture, there will be one or more Discourses to capture it—and tool bags of greater or lesser size when these Discourses are combined.*[13]

Discourse Skills

Talk of combining cultural Discourses and expanding the size of your tool bag raises the issue of skills. Here, three skills stand out: discerning others' cultural Discourses, creatively combining cultural Discourses, and knowing how Discourse constrains.

Discernment It is quite useful to discern the cultural Discourses that others are using. Just think of how many intergenerational conversations between geek and geezer leaders have gone awry because each is left wondering about the values and priorities of the other. I have seen it happen often, and it is only when the parties acknowledge that they are "speaking different languages" (that is, cultural Discourses) that a first step toward understanding the other is made.

Effective, targeted framing is contingent on your ability to understand how culture and its Discourses govern others' behavior. We do this by momentarily reflecting on how culture (societal or organizational) may be impacting their talk and actions. If this proves difficult, do a side-by-side comparison of two cultural eras, just as Bennis and Thomas did in *Geeks and Geezers*.[14] The features of any given cultural era tend to stand out when compared to another.

Think back to the discussion of Message Design Logics in Chapter One (in which you scored yourself as a Strategic, Conventional, or Expressive). Conventional and Strategic communicators understand the value of discerning others' Discourses, which allows them to tailor their message by putting it into terms that others would best understand. Expressives, however, are more concerned with expressing themselves than adapting to their current target. As a result, their Expressive style may not only be shocking or irritating, it is likely to be less persuasive than the other two.

Combination You can creatively combine cultural Discourses for more framing options. Chances are, you already combine cultural Discourses automatically and unconsciously most of the time working in complex organizations today. The point here is that a conscious, creative combination of one or more Discourses may provide more room to maneuver linguistically and, sometimes, deliver fresh insight that might not otherwise have emerged. Both factors increase how articulate and persuasive you can be.

For example, in early 2010, many Toyota cars were being recalled because of accelerator problems. Toyota responded in a very public way by merging its car technology Discourse (using terms like "defective pedals" and "unwanted acceleration") with an ethics Discourse related to taking responsibility for repairs (using terms like "safety recall"). This is a very simple example, but it shows that by merging these two Discourses, Toyota names the defective product and positions itself as a responsible company. Whether or not its people did this fast and sincerely enough has been a matter of some debate, but the point remains. Combining cultural Discourses increases the size of your linguistic tool bag and gives you more maneuverability with your persuasive communications.

In the space below, write down an example of how you combined two or more Discourses in something you said recently or would like to say to someone at work. Several different types of Discourses are listed for you to select from, or you can name your own. For each Discourse you select, pay attention to the compatibility of its tool bag with the others'. You can do this by asking yourself what terms, metaphors, themes, and lines of argument are complementary enough to merge.

Type of Discourse	*What Is Culturally Shared*
Technology	Knowledge of a technology's features, uses, or applications (terms: apps, bandwidth)
Military	Issues of control, order, or hierarchy (metaphors: chain of command, top gun)
Environmental	All things ecological, sustainable, recyclable (metaphors and terms: green, sustainability)
Science	Scientific principles, research with a scientific lens (terms: controlled studies, control group)
Quality	Total quality management, six sigma (terms: continuous improvement, zero defects)
Coaching	Mentoring, support, or career advising issues (terms: mentor-protégé, coach)
Visionary Leadership	Charismatic or transformational leadership style (metaphors and terms: vision, leader versus manager)

Team	Knowledge about group influence processes (terms and metaphors: collaboration, team spirit)
Sales	Marketing information related to distribution of a product or service (terms: campaign, quota)
Change	Knowledge about complex change in organizations (metaphors and terms: vision, small wins)
Ethics	Knowledge related to moral responsibilities (terms: values, accountability)
_____	_____
_____	_____
_____	_____

How I Combined Discourses

_____

_____

_____

_____

As you might expect, Strategic communicators are always on the lookout for ways to acquire and combine Discourses. They pay attention to situations where combining Discourses worked well and even when they didn't work so well. There are lessons to be learned in each. Becoming sensitive to the prevailing Discourses in their environment allows them to grasp more of its complexity, make finer distinctions in "the situation here and now," and recognize opportunities to act in the process.

You can see this if you think of Discourse as a map to a particular territory you are trying to navigate. With two or more Discourses, you actually "see" more of that territory, for example, in the way a road map and a map of the terrain show different kinds of features. Do you always need more than one map for navigation? Certainly not, but picture driving in a new city with a GPS that isn't up-to-date on road construction. You'd learn the hard way that the quickest route is not always the shortest distance between two points! And it might be the fatally hard way: consider the people who've frozen to death the last few years as a result of letting a GPS unit lead them onto seasonally inaccessible roads in the mountains. A different kind of map (such as the trip ticket from an automobile association) might have made such construction projects known, thus providing more driving options.

Such opportunity recognition is the case with multiple Discourses, as illustrated by Graham's quote at the start of the chapter when he merged the civil rights Discourse of Martin Luther King Jr. with a more contemporary diversity Discourse inclusive of class and gender. Through this merger he created a novel framing of King's legacy.

Constraints Finally, Discourse also constrains behavior. Discourse enables communication with the tool bag it supplies, but it also limits communication in the ways it disciplines users to conform to that tool bag. Disciplined behavior can be a good thing, directing our energies to achieve a particular goal. However, discipline loses its appeal when we are no longer introspective or willing to consider change or growth. For example, perhaps a geezer leader truly wants to understand the new technologies of the modern age. Knowing how geezer Discourse has taken hold and prevented appreciation of such innovations is a crucial first step toward change. Again, conscious moments of reflection and critique of yourself should deliver the insights that you seek here.

Expressives, Conventionals, and Strategics could all benefit from these moments of reflection and self-critique. As mentioned in Chapter One, the first two would greatly benefit from reflecting on the ways in which one or more Discourses discipline them and close off language choices that they might otherwise consider. For the Strategics, those to whom words usually come easily, reflection can help them maintain a certain discipline to use verbal skills in principled ways to avoid any manipulative tendencies.

The good news for all three styles is that they can be honed through reflection, discussion with others, and exercises like the critical incident analysis presented in Framing Tool 2.1.

FRAMING TOOL 2.1

Critical Incident Framing

Recall the critical incident that you described for Chapter One, or use another one involving your leadership that you would like to analyze. Remember the focus should be on your communications as a leader with your employees, customers, or other stakeholders. Also, select an incident in which you were unhappy with the outcome.

_____

_____

_____

_____

_____

Does it seem that you and your employees (or team, customers, or other stakeholders) are "speaking a different language"? In other words, are they using terminology, metaphors, themes, or arguments so different from yours that you think you are on different wave lengths? If so, you are probably using different cultural Discourses. (Remember that Discourses are culture-based systems of thought that give us our linguistic tool bags.)

- If you know how your stakeholders have been influenced culturally through "the language they speak" (cultural Discourse), you can translate what you are saying into terms, arguments, and logics that they will understand.

Terms, metaphors, themes, or arguments (cultural Discourse) that I favor:

_____

_____

_____

_____

Terms, metaphors, themes, or arguments (cultural Discourse) that my employees favor:

_____

_____

_____

_____

Are these cultural Discourses compatible? Why or why not? Can other Discourses be introduced here to establish more common ground or open up a space to act?

_____

_____

_____

_____

_____

(You can download this form from www.josseybass.com/go/gailfairhurst. Feel free to adapt it to suit your needs. This analysis will continue in Chapter Three.)

To summarize, each Discourse contains persistent cultural features, surfacing more concretely in our linguistic tool bags. These tool bags are stylized ways of talking—terminology and metaphors for key ideas, themes for stories, familiar arguments, and so on. Frank Luntz's list of suggested twenty-first-century words is a great example of a cultural Discourse that simultaneously enables its users to communicate in certain ways and also constrains them to culturally conform. When we can combine multiple cultural Discourses to form more varied repertoires, we may discover a number of creative ways in which to frame our subject matter.[15]

Mental Models

Leaders who understand their world can usually explain their world. So when considering the resources available for framing, your own thought processes are chief among them. These thought processes are subdivided into *mental models*, which Peter Senge describes as deeply held images of how the world works.[16]

Mental models are the pictures in your head about other people, yourself, objects, events—you name it. Sometimes these pictures are rich with detail and color, other times sketchy or brand new. For example, Xavier University President Graham appears to have a richly developed mental model for Martin Luther King's message, given his ability to parse it into "soft and fuzzies" versus more radical agendas. None of the other city leaders made this distinction.[17]

Consider also what John T. Chambers, chairman and CEO of Cisco Systems, said recently when asked to describe how his leadership style has evolved over time:

> I'm a command-and-control person. I like being able to say turn right, and we truly have 67,000 people turn right. But that's the style of the past. Today's world requires . . . more collaboration and teamwork including using . . . [new] technologies.[18]

Chambers's mental model for his leadership style very clearly defines a past and present version, with a decided preference for "command-and-control" (more geezer than geek, for sure). This is also a great example of how someone can use cultural Discourses for leadership to form mental models.

As a cultural leadership Discourse, "command-and-control" has a rich pedigree, originating in the military and imported into organizations after WW II. The other, "collaboration and teamwork," defines the character of more modern-day organizational forms. These have been shaped by globalization, technological advances, and ever-changing market conditions, the net effect of which has been to push control downward into team-based systems. Chambers's mental model draws from both of these organizational Discourses to describe and justify his past and present style.

Consider another senior leader, Carol Smith, who is senior vice president and chief brand officer at the Elle Group, a large media company. On the subject of gender roles and leadership, she notes that women tend to be better at it, being less fond of hearing themselves talk. "I am so generalizing. I know I am," she says ruefully, but she adds that she's worked places where she often told people, "Call me 15 minutes after the meeting starts and then I'll come," because that would allow her to miss the football and golf stories and the jokes, and get there when the real meeting was starting.[19]

Smith has clear mental models for male and female leaders. In no uncertain terms, she tells us how she wholeheartedly endorses a cultural leadership Discourse on gender, in which male leaders are egotistical, while women are harder workers and better at management. (You can see such sentiments expressed in books like Sally Helgesen's *The Female Advantage: Women's Ways of Leadership*.)[20]

Interestingly, Smith flags her view as a mental model when she says, "I am so generalizing. I know I am." Whether or not you agree with her is beside the point. For the moment, simply note how she explains her mental model for male and female leaders using a cultural leadership Discourse on gender to do so.

Leaders' Mental Models

If you have concluded by now that people hold scores of mental models, you are quite correct. We have also known for some time now that effective leaders should have at least four mental models of their own:

- A vision for the future (Where are we headed in the next five years? The next ten years?)

- A mission (What is our purpose? Why are we here?)

- A core set of values (What really counts in this organization? What does it take to get ahead?)

- A collective identity (Who are we?)[21]

Peter Senge, John Kotter, Warren Bennis, and many others have argued since the mid-1980s that these four models are the core of a leader's governing ideas. By doing so, they have contributed to a cultural Discourse on visionary leadership. You can tell that this is a popular one because so many leadership books, lectures, editorials, and training modules echo its themes. These include the necessity of having and articulating a vision for those who wish to lead and a leader-manager distinction made on this basis. Leaders forecast change, it maintains, while managers do the implementing.

However, recall that today's leaders need not be the "I've got the answer" visionaries all the time, especially when confronting wicked problems. As it turns out, this is also true of leaders in design firms. Consider Tim Brown, chief executive and president of IDEO, a design firm based in Palo Alto,

California. In a recent interview, he argues that his people understand that it is their responsibility to bring new ideas to the table. His job is to ask the right questions, he says, adding, "And in design, that's everything, right? If you don't ask the right questions, then you're never going to get the right solution." He says he used to worry about being the one who was supposed to have the answers when he knew he didn't, but then he had the liberating insight that nobody else has all the answers either. "It's just that somehow we've got this culture of having the answers."[22]

Brown's mental models are quite clear: figure out the right questions to ask, and get over feeling insecure about not being the "answer man." As the interview continued, he argued for a more collaborative style in which questions, not solutions, get debated. He also admitted to finally realizing that no one else had all of the answers either. When he refers to "this culture of having the answers," he means the answer-giving, visionary leadership Discourse that he is trying so hard to refute.

Now it's your turn. Test out some of the mental models that you hold for yourself and your organization in Framing Tool 2.2.[23]

FRAMING TOOL 2.2

Identifying Your Mental Models

1. Circle those qualities that best describe you:

Independent	Passionate
Intelligent	Risk Taking
Generous	Loving
Assertive	Witty
Strong-willed	Articulate
Healthy	Wise

a. What other positive qualities would you attribute to yourself?

_____

_____

_____

b.   What negative qualities would you attribute to yourself?

_____

_____

_____

You have just described your mental model for yourself.

2.   What qualities epitomize your idea of an effective leader? Does someone you know or have heard about embody those qualities?

_____

_____

_____

_____

You have just described your mental model for the ideal leader.

3.   What is the purpose of your unit or organization?

_____

_____

_____

_____

You have just described your mental model for your unit's mission.

4.   How would you like your organization or unit to look in five years? Ten years?

_____

_____

_____

_____

You have just described your mental model for the vision for your unit.

5.   What really counts in your organization? What does it take to get ahead?

_____

_____

_____

_____

You have just described your mental model for your organization's values.

6. What steps or procedures do you follow in the hiring process?

_____

_____

_____

_____

You have just described your mental model for interviewing with your firm.

_____

(You can download this form from www.josseybass.com/go/gailfairhurst. Feel free to adapt it to suit your needs.)

Key Properties of Mental Models

Here are five key properties of mental models to bear in mind. First, *they can take a number of forms.* They can be an image or type of something (for example, say that your definition of a desirable leader is best represented as a "Steve Jobs type," referring to the high-octane head of Apple). Mental models can also show how something functions through a set of component parts (for example, your image of a corporate philosophy likely includes a vision, mission, and set of values). Finally, mental models can be a scriptlike sequence of actions, such as the steps you follow in the hiring process, a progressive discipline policy, or even something as simple as what to do when entering a nice restaurant (wait to be seated, wait to be handed menus, order through a waiter or waitress, and so on).[24]

Second, *mental models tell us how the world works now, and also how it is likely to work in the future.* Generally speaking, they help us to navigate the new and unfamiliar as well as the old and routine because we expect patterns to repeat themselves. For example, if someone has asked you to address them in a particular way on one occasion ("First name, please!"), it's a pretty safe bet that you should use this form of address on future occasions.

Third, *mental models organize our thoughts and assist us in understanding and remembering* key bits of information necessary to go on in the situations in which we find ourselves.[25] This is why meeting a person for the second or third time usually doesn't feel quite as uncomfortable as the first time. We have assimilated first impressions of that person into a mental model, albeit newly formed.

Fourth, it makes sense then that *mental models develop as we experience and process information about the world.*[26] For example, think about your current organization and how different your mental models of your workplace would be if you compared them at the time of the job interview to what you hold right now. As we gain experience, we usually take and assimilate new information into our mental models and build complexity into them incrementally. It stands to reason that the more complex our mental models, the better the sensemaking that feeds our framing. We can now see patterns and interrelationships or anomalies and exceptions to the rule. All of this helps us to adapt to the situation at hand, and improved frame alignment with others is usually the outcome.

Finally, according to Senge, *our mental models may be limited by certain unquestioned assumptions that we may hold,* for example, those involving stereotypes of certain categories of people in our society.[27] When we hold firmly to stereotypes, we deemphasize or ignore information that could substantially develop our mental models further. That is one reason why our mental models need to surface periodically for reexamination.

Skills for Mental Models

Two skills, in particular, pertain to mental models: keeping your mental models sharp, and priming them for spontaneity. I return to both of these skills in Chapter Three, as they are best considered in the context of new developments in brain science, including new insights about brain plasticity, and research into the mental models of experts versus novices. However, they're worth a brief look at this point.

Building complexity into mental models helps keep them sharp. As noted, the more complex our mental models, the more adaptable our framing responses. Just ask a Strategic, who is usually looking for ways to build complexity into mental models.

By priming your mental models—essentially programming your brain to respond in certain ways—you can position yourself for spontaneous communications. Priming is also a way to shift from a Conventional style to a Strategic one, because you can be more conscious of your communicative selections.

However, to underscore the role that mental models play in your framing, continue analyzing the critical incident you described earlier in the chapter. In Framing Tool 2.3, mental models and Discourse are the focal points.

 FRAMING TOOL 2.3

Critical Incident Framing

Briefly recall the critical incident that you described in Framing Tool 2.1:

_____

_____

_____

_____

_____

On the lines below, describe the key mental models for yourself and others for this critical incident. (Remember that mental models are deeply held images of how the world works and how we expect it to work in the future.)

- Generally speaking, the more you can understand others' mental models, the more you can adapt your message to suit them.

Your mental models:

_____

_____

_____

_____

The mental models of the other people involved:

_____

_____

_____

_____

Based on your answers to Framing Tool 2.1, are there particular cultural Discourses to consider that are informing, or should inform, the mental models of the others involved?

_____

_____

_____

_____

_____

Possible ways to reframe your message with their mental models and cultural Discourses in mind:

_____

_____

_____

_____

_____

_____

(You can download this form from www.josseybass.com/go/gailfairhurst. Feel free to adapt it to suit your needs. This analysis will continue in Chapter Three.)

Core Framing Tasks

If you had to describe the chief communication requirements of your job, what would they be? To answer this question, think about the patterns of communications that you regularly enact with others. Those patterns are your best clues as to the *core framing tasks* of your job.[28] For example, as a university professor, researcher, and management consultant, I would list "teaching" among my core framing tasks. Whether I am in the classroom, executive coaching, speaking to an audience, or mentoring, I would define one of my most frequent communication patterns as translating up-to-date academic research and writing on leadership communication into a usable form.

If you happened to be one of my students, someone I have coached or mentored, or an audience member, your core framing tasks would center on the relevance and use of the information I provide. You might ask or answer: Just *what* is Fairhurst saying? How relevant is it to my job? What am I learning here? What specifically can I do differently the next time a problem arises?

By contrast, during the five years I was head of my academic department, my core framing tasks were part leading, part managing. In other words, they seemed to combine aspects of the leader-manager distinction by Harvard Business School professor John Kotter, mentioned earlier.[29] In today's new-market economies, recall that *leaders* are the architects of change, while *managers* are the everyday problem solvers. My core framing tasks as an academic department head involved diagnosing and solving a lot of everyday problems (managing),[30] but they also involved answering the question, "Who are we?" for a variety of internal and external stakeholders (leading).

Given the generality of the leader-manager distinction, perhaps you feel as I do that we need more specific ways to capture our core framing tasks. Framing Tool 2.4 provides such a vehicle. It draws from leadership researchers like Jennifer George, myself, and others to suggests that leader-manager core framing tasks fall into five general categories:[31]

- Develop a collective sense of goals, objectives, and strategies.
- Instill knowledge of the organization's environment and its work.
- Generate enthusiasm, confidence, optimism, cooperation, and trust.
- Encourage flexibility in decision making and change.
- Construct and maintain a meaningful organizational identity.

In the following tool, place check marks in the boxes that best describe your core framing tasks. If the descriptions do not match what you do, then write them down in the spaces provided.

FRAMING TOOL 2.4

Your Core Framing Tasks

Develop a Collective Sense of Goals, Objectives, and Strategies

☐ Portray a compelling vision: "a promising there and then" versus "an uncertain here and now."

☐ Generate positive mood and enthusiasm for the vision.

☐ Call attention to role responsibilities that ground the mission and further it.

☐ Promote information processing by highlighting or minimizing challenges, threats, issues, and opportunities *within* ethical bounds.

☐ Stress key values, "what really counts" in the organization.

☐ To the extent possible, promote effective sensemaking and buy-in for goals and objectives.

Instill Knowledge of the Organization's Environment and Its Work

☐ Define and name problems by calling attention to issues facing your organization.

☐ Label the environment and its stressors; attribute blame when necessary.

☐ Reaffirm a commitment to ethical choices.

☐ Identify present-day opportunities in line with possible futures.

☐ Identify constraints in line with possible futures.

☐ Stress the serious yet solvable nature of the problems at hand (as in "problems are only poorly defined opportunities").

Generate Enthusiasm, Confidence, Optimism, Cooperation, and Trust

☐ To the extent possible, align the interests of the individual with your organization.

☐ Instill enthusiasm for organizational goals and objectives.

☐ Monitor, respond to, and affirm followers' moods and emotions.

☐ Instill confidence in followers' abilities to solve problems, meet challenges, and seize opportunities.

☐ Distinguish between followers' expressed emotions and possible real feelings.

☐ To the extent possible, seek win-win solutions in conflict; encourage constructive problem solving by underscoring key values.

☐ Strive to fulfill promises and point out the consistencies in doing so.

☐ Strive to resolve unfulfilled promises and commit to doing better.

Encourage Flexibility in Decision Making and Change

☐ Characterize the multiple issues facing your organization.

☐ Prioritize demands and name pressing concerns in need of immediate attention.

☐ Name and address emotions that may inhibit or bias decision making.

☐ Encourage multiple frames of a problem to brainstorm solutions, consider alternative scenarios, and avoid rigid decision making.

☐ Reflexively monitor and self-disclose your own moods and emotions that may impact problem solving and decision making.

☐ Identify connections among divergent pieces of information.

☐ Name and define followers' feelings to the extent they diverge from the emotions necessary for constructive problem solving.

☐ Engage in dialogue to overcome resistance to planned change.

Construct and Maintain a Meaningful Organizational Identity

☐ Be able to answer "Who are we?" on demand.

☐ Be able to answer "What really counts in this organization?"

☐ Be able to answer "What does it take to get ahead in this organization?"

☐ Reaffirm the "feelings of rightness" associated with the constructive norms of the organization's culture.

☐ Reward and recognize behavior consistent with the desired organizational identity.

Other Core Framing Tasks Based on the Communication Patterns in My Job

_____

_____

_____

_____

_____

_____

_____

(You can download this form from www.josseybass.com/go/gailfairhurst. Feel free to adapt it to suit your needs.)

Skills Involving Core Framing Tasks

Among the skills necessary to discharge your core framing tasks effectively, three stand out:

- Know your core framing tasks.
- Choose the right master frames.
- Select appropriate framing outcomes.

Know Your Core Framing Tasks While this may seem obvious, many leaders don't actually know all of their core framing responsibilities. For example, Harvard University's John Kotter has argued for some time now that managers undercommunicate the company mission statement by a factor of ten or more.[32] In my own research on leaders' communications during organizational change, I find that leaders are frequently guilty of assuming too much regarding employees' buy-in of their change initiatives.

In one of my studies, I taped actual work conversations of leaders and their teams during a major organizational change initiative at a large consumer goods firm. I found that employees very much wanted to talk about the change—including their problems with it, the relevance of it to their role responsibilities, how it fit with existing company initiatives, the next steps ahead, and even their leaders' enthusiasm for it. Because most leaders are Conventionals, they tend to underestimate the communications challenge of organizational change. By contrast, Strategics work the change into the very fabric of their organization by making the change relevant to the people and their job responsibilities, answering their questions, taking on their challenges, making connections, and getting them to feel a sense of enthusiasm for it.

The good news is that Framing Tool 2.4 serves as an excellent reminder of the core framing tasks of leaders in the midst of change, as well as a host of other leader-manager duties. A regular review of this list (or one like it) should serve as a reminder of your core framing tasks.

Choose the Right Master Frames Certain core framing tasks are broader in scope than others—for example, portraying a compelling vision, capturing your unit's quality standards, or emphasizing a change program's theme and shift in priorities. Your framing of these tasks thus needs to be broad in scope and have organizing potential. Unlike single-subject framing (that is, "the situation here and now"), *master frames* are umbrella-like in their power to mobilize the collective efforts of a team or organization.[33]

For example, when inducted as Xavier University president, Father Michael Graham framed a key part of his vision for his school as the "University as Citizen."[34] Far more than just a slogan, this is an example of a master frame, which represents Graham's desire for Xavier people (students first, but also faculty, staff, and alumni) to become more active participants in the city or local community by partnering with local and regional organizations for mutual benefit.

He then created the Community Building Collaborative, a coordinating body that connects Xavier to its surrounding neighborhoods and the larger community. A perusal of the Xavier Web site reveals a large and diverse number of initiatives run through the Collaborative in line with Graham's vision. Thus, the "University as Citizen" concept appears sufficiently broad in scope and inclusive of diverse enough community activities to be considered a true master frame.

However, as discussed further in Chapter Four, the language of Graham's master frame is crucial. Compare the "University as Citizen" with my own university's vision-based master frame, "UC|21," which stands for the "University of Cincinnati in the twenty-first century."[35] The latter is a catchy phrase, to be sure, and the vision itself reflects an equally strong commitment to the community as a stakeholder. But that doesn't come across immediately— at least not in the way that "University as Citizen" does. Sometimes there is word-crafting, phraseology, and perhaps even a little sloganeering involved in finding the right master frame for a diversity of stakeholders.

If you are or want to become a more Strategic communicator, these are the key master frame questions that you as a leader must ask yourself:

- Have you identified one or more master frames for your organizing efforts, or have you left them implicit, unspoken, or vulnerable to others' interpretations?

- How adequate are your master frames given the elements that you want them to include? Do they call up the meanings you desire and the actions you intend?

Finally, while the right language for your master frames is crucial, so is swift and immediate action upon introducing them. It is worth nothing that Graham created and named the Community Building Collaborative to organize and be accountable for the community activities that he and others would initiate. By taking steps like these, a university president can guard against a vision proving devoid of meaning and substance.

Select Appropriate Framing Outcomes I prefer to see framing effectiveness in terms of frame agreement or alignment with another person. *Agreement* means that you've won your targets' minds and, just maybe, their hearts. *Alignment* is a word that can have several meanings, but the one I prefer is very much like what car mechanics mean when they say, "The front wheels of your car are out of alignment."[36] In other words, I'm talking about the proper adjustment of the component parts of some entity (a car, a relationship, a work unit, or an organization) necessary for *coordinated* functioning. From a Strategic communicator's perspective, a leader's framing doesn't always have to produce agreement in others, although that is a most worthy goal. It need only produce a level of understanding necessary to coordinate action. *Thus, it behooves you to know the tasks in which only the destination matters, not the path to reach it.*[37]

Either through frame alignment or agreement, effective framing makes a difference, as communication scholar Kevin Barge neatly terms it, "a difference that connects."[38] It is an idea that Graham seems to understand intuitively. When asked to explain how he succeeds time and again as an inspirational preacher, he says, "When I tell ordinary stories from my life or others' lives, I like to think that they will help others recall [similar] episodes and reflect on them. I like to look for those sparks of humanity that are so brilliant. For when you see those sparks of humanity, they point to sparks of divinity."[39] In his search for those "sparks of humanity," Graham no doubt *prefers* to win others' hearts, minds, and agreement, but that is not always possible. When the agreement is out of reach, the Strategic leader prepares to work with frame alignment.

A Backward Glance at Chapter Two

To recap, this chapter emphasizes three key aspects of framing—culture and its Discourses, mental models, and core framing tasks—and the skills they require. More specifically:

- Culture impacts leaders through Discourse, which is a historically rooted system of thought accompanied by its own linguistic tool bag that includes terminology, metaphors, themes, and arguments for leaders to draw upon to describe, explain, or justify their place in the world at any given moment. Three cultural Discourse skills can improve your ability to become a more Strategic communicator:
  - Discern the cultural Discourses that others are using to improve your ability to adapt to and persuade them. You can do this by momentarily reflecting on how culture may be impacting others' talk and actions.

- Creatively combine cultural Discourses to maximize the size of your linguistic tool bag. A conscious, creative combination of two or more cultural Discourses creates more linguistic maneuverability. Do this by assessing the compatibility between the Discourses' respective linguistic tool bags.

- Understand how culture and its Discourses discipline your behavior in both productive and unproductive ways, the latter of which may stymie your appetite for change. Moments of critical reflection are necessary here.

- Mental models are individuals' deeply held images of how the world works and how they expect it to work in the future. They can be a type or image, a set of component parts, or a scripted sequence of actions, and they develop as we experience the world. To become a more Strategic communicator, two mental modeling skills are essential:

  - Build complexity into your mental models. Chapter Three details the ways in which this should be done.

  - Prime your mental models for use in future "spontaneous" communications, a subject also detailed in Chapter Three.

- Core framing tasks are the chief communication requirements of your job. For leaders and managers, these tasks generally fall into five categories: develop a collective sense of goals, objectives, and strategies; instill knowledge of the organization's environment and its work; generate enthusiasm, confidence, optimism, cooperation, and trust; encourage flexibility in decision making and change; and construct and maintain a meaningful organizational identity. Three skills involving core framing tasks are designed to improve your ability to be a more Strategic leader:

  - Know what these tasks are. Many leaders undercommunicate their mission statements and change efforts. Pay more attention to employees' communication needs, and use lists like Framing Tool 2.4 for a reminder of your core framing tasks.

- Choose the right master frames. Master frames are broad in scope and umbrella-like in their ability to mobilize the efforts of a collective. Word-crafting is a necessity here, a topic addressed in Chapter Four.

- Select the right framing outcome. It is important to know the tasks in which only coordination is necessary, not complete agreement.

A FINAL THOUGHT

The skill of framing requires hard work—meaning work.

3

The Science of Framing

ED HARBACH is a former CEO of BearingPoint, a management and technology consultancy firm. Several years ago, during his time as a managing partner and member of the leadership team at Accenture, I ran into him at a baseball game where we both had sons playing. I was writing *The Art of Framing* at the time, and I asked him how much he thought about his own communications. He said, "Very little, really, it's just something I do automatically." His answer had a familiar ring to it—it's often the refrain of very smart, articulate, and busy senior leaders.

On one hand, I readily understood Harbach's response; generally articulate people do know what to say in most situations. Indeed, at a minimum, they are Conventionals, right? On the other hand, the field of executive coaching is flourishing these days because senior and midlevel executives have serious communication problems related to their leadership: the tendency to fly off the handle over bad news, to make condescending and dismissive remarks to lower-status individuals, a tin ear when it comes to organizational politics, a failure to listen, an inclination toward micromanagement, inconsistencies between speech and action, and many more. Once again, this speaks directly to Foucault's notion that people know what they say, and they usually know why they say what they say. What they do not understand is what what they say does.[1]

However, in partial defense of the Ed Harbachs of the world, there may be larger forces at work here; as social psychologists like George Herbert Mead have suggested, it is part of the human condition to be "conscious always of what we have done, never of doing it."[2] In complementary fashion, management scholar, Karl Weick, neatly captures how we often make sense of the world with the question, "How do I know what I think until I see what I say?"[3] More specifically, he says that the world is "partly unknowable and unpredictable. It is a world into which people have been thrown. By *thrown*, I mean that people can't avoid acting, can't step back and reflect on their actions, can't predict the effects of their actions, have no choice but to deal with interpretations whose correctness cannot be settled once and for all and they can't remain silent. Anything they say shapes both events and themselves. These are the givens that shape sensemaking."[4]

Both Mead and Weick suggest, a bit counterintuitively, that action precedes thought, and retrospect or looking backward is fundamental to our sensemaking. The implications of these statements for framing are profound, because they suggest that we are thrust into moments of unplanned action. It is a kind of automatic pilot, if you will, in which we take to the controls afterwards to shape the meaning of what we have done. Note that Weick, in particular, is not taking aim at our ability to make and follow plans. He suggests instead that the ratio of our planned to unplanned behavior is often the opposite of what we expect it to be.

Such a view raises key questions. If we communicate spontaneously and automatically, can we exert a measure of control over our framing? How can we be effective under these conditions? I can answer the first question affirmatively, and the second with two provisos. First, we must focus on one of the tools that will enable us to go on automatic pilot, which is a process called *priming*. Here the key is to understand what is taking place in the human brain when we prime for spontaneity. Second, we must understand what builds complexity into our mental models and how we reason from them. Generally speaking, the more we notice, the better our framing. These ideas form the core of this chapter. They are the science behind framing because they concern themselves with conscious and unconscious learning processes and what brain science is suggesting about the framing process.

Priming for Spontaneity

The simple truth is that most of the time we communicate without much preparation and with little awareness of how we select and arrange our words. In all of our communications (spontaneous and planned), we communicate to make a point or convey a feeling, in other words, when we have a goal in mind. Can we be strategic and goal-oriented and, at the same time, spontaneous and automatic? Yes, because we often carry a set of overarching goals (for example, to meet a sales quota or make a sale to a customer) that shape and become shaped by the emergent goals that we formulate in the moment of communicating (for example, to answer a customer's product question).

Becoming conscious of a goal purposely but unconsciously predisposes us to manage meaning in one direction or another to communicate our frames.[5] In other words, you can be goal-conscious (without which you couldn't enter into communication), but unconscious of how you will select, structure, and exchange words with another person to achieve that goal. Your unconscious mind makes certain verbal and nonverbal options available to you for the framing that you ultimately choose. Sometimes these options are not ones you would have consciously chosen—as Freudian slips so nicely demonstrate. (Recall the classic, "A Freudian slip is like saying one thing, but meaning your mother.") That is why the best time to exert a measure of control over what you say is not when you're in the moment and about to communicate, but in moments of conscious reflection some time *before* you communicate.

For your important conversations, you can control much of what you say and how you say it by programming your unconscious toward the selection of certain options over others. A better term for *programming* is *priming*, and it has been the subject of intense study in neuropsychology, psycholinguistics (the psychology of language), and agenda setting in media studies. In all three areas, *priming* involves activating something in our short- or long-term memory, which then triggers an in-kind response in either what we say or what we do.

For example, neuropsychology seeks to understand how the brain and behavior are related. Priming in this area of study is used to demonstrate that we have an implicit memory, a not-quite-conscious body of procedural knowledge that gets triggered in routine situations, much as the cliché "like riding a bike" suggests.[6] You need not relearn how to ride a bike because the implicit knowledge of doing so never leaves you; it merely awaits activation or priming, say, when a bike is available and the opportunity to ride it presents itself on a beautiful day.

In psycholinguistics, priming is a key feature of "tip-of-the-tongue" experiments.[7] Recall the last time you talked about a restaurant whose name you could not recall. You have that maddening feeling of knowing the answer without being able to produce it. Metaphorically, it is on the "tip of your tongue." The question and your memory failure triggers or primes your unconscious to search for the name, which you later successfully recall while driving home from work or in the shower the next morning. ("Of course, that's the name of that place!") The conscious experience of wanting to remember the name primes the unconscious to search for it even after the goal of remembering leaves your conscious mind. (Think, too, of all those perfect comebacks remembered *after* an argument.) Psycholinguists want to know exactly how priming works with respect to language use—and to what extent language can be primed for apparently spontaneous use at a later time.

In media studies, priming focuses on the amount of attention that the media direct to certain stories and themes in their coverage.[8] The amount and type of media focus is thought to prime the public's reactions and interpretations. This occurs when community perceptions of heightened fear about urban crime correlate with media coverage of the sensational crime stories of the day. So a sensational murder with heavy media coverage will bias—prime—you to think that crime is actually worse than it is.

What can you take away from the scientific study of priming to improve your framing? The key lesson is that priming lays down a set of mental train tracks because, fundamentally, remembering is like reliving. Brain researchers tell us that exactly the same neurons are firing when specific content is remembered again.[9] They are also finding that the human brain is far more malleable—or "plastic," as they call it—than we have ever thought possible.[10] Psychiatrist and researcher Norman Doidge likens the human brain to a muscle: you either use it or lose it.[11] For those who choose to use it, exercising the brain develops "muscle" or brainpower through a larger number of branches among neurons. These branches drive the neurons farther apart, which then increases the volume and thickness of the brain. In short, thought develops the material structure of the brain.[12]

So think of priming as exercise that develops (brain) muscle memory. It is a conscious act that imprints your unconscious with new pathways for the brain to follow when triggered. According to brain scientist Donald O. Hebb we actually see chemical changes in neurons that fire repeatedly or in close succession, in effect, strengthening their bond. Another brain scientist, Carla Schatz, neatly summarizes Hebb's law as "neurons that fire together wire together."[13]

So the more you prime, the stronger the bond. In simple terms, the more often you think of things in connection with each other, the more likely you are to recall them together in the future. The key is to remember that if a particular thought process was a part of your recent conscious experience, then that thought process remains accessible and will be used by your unconscious mind to filter information taken in later. This occurs for some time after that thought process is no longer in your conscious awareness.

In *The Art of Framing*, Bob Sarr and I said that priming is a little like putting on sunglasses on a sunny day. You have the initial experience of less glare, but you quickly forget that you are seeing with a colored lens. It is the same with priming your unconscious mind. Your conscious experience has dissolved but has primed your unconscious with a lens that influences your view. You are quite unaware of its presence until you consciously reflect again. In such moments, you can gauge the effectiveness of priming your conscious mind for a largely unconscious, spontaneous, and yet strategic performance.

A story about Marin Alsop, the first woman to lead a major American orchestra, provides an interesting leadership example.[14] As she tells it,

> I applied to audition for Tanglewood [a Boston music festival] five times before I got an audition.[15] One day they called me in and said, "We've decided that you're going to conduct with Leonard Bernstein." I was stunned. Bernstein was more than a teacher; he coaxed the essence out of people. He talked to me about being me. There was one rather cathartic rehearsal day where he came up to me and said, "The conducting's fine but it really isn't moving me." It was so devastating. Then he said, "Let's give the orchestra a break and then you'll come back and do this again." He said forget about conducting now. Just be yourself and be the music. But then I came back in and it was the weirdest experience. I felt like I'd had a massage. I thought I had nothing to lose. I'm just going to try it. I remember in the middle of the piece—this makes me cry—he came up to me and whispered, "That's it." It was so liberating.

At Bernstein's urging—or shall I say "priming"—to be herself and the music, Alsop delivered a spontaneous performance that amazed even her. Bernstein triggered a lot of implicit knowing by Alsop of not just how to deliver the music, but how *she* delivers music, how *she* feels in her best moments of leading an orchestra. What was so liberating, what felt like a massage, was that one could actually control a spontaneous performance with a little forethought surrounding these notions ahead of time. The forethought, of course, is when we consciously store our memory as Alsop had done in reaction to her conversation with the great maestro.

Can we reduce priming to the simple recommendation to just plan ahead? No, because to understand the value of priming is to understand *exactly* what we must prime and, qualitatively, to be as mindfully deliberate as possible with this process. Doidge suggests that because so few of us engage in mental rehearsal systematically, we greatly underestimate its effectiveness.[16] To build on that insight, this chapter now turns to a way to get maximum benefit out of mental rehearsal through priming our mental models, framing opportunities, and desirable language.

But before moving on, take a moment to reflect on the times you already prime for spontaneity. This might include:

- Studying for a test before taking it
- Swinging a golf club or bat before actually hitting the ball
- Rehearsing a speech before delivering it in public
- Visualizing an acting or musical performance before actually giving it
- Saying a person's name over and over again in your head, so you will remember it the next time
- Others? _____
- Others? _____

On a scale of 1–5, how systematic are your mental rehearsals usually?

1	2	3	4	5
Not at all		Somewhat		Very

Priming Mental Models

If you take the time to consciously and periodically think through your mental models as a leader, you are priming your unconscious to select and interpret new information using the models as a reference point. Wendy Kopp, founder and chief executive of Teach for America, shows us just how she does this. Teach for America is a nonprofit aimed at getting teachers to commit to two years of service in U.S. urban and rural public schools.

In a recent interview, she talked about the need for time management in her job. Interestingly, she sets aside one hour a week to reflect on her strategic plan for herself and what she needs to do to move her priorities along. On top of that, she spends ten minutes each day saying to herself, "OK, so based on the priorities for the week, how am I going to prioritize my day tomorrow?"[17] Kopp is clearly priming her mental model of her strategic plan for a spontaneous management of her time in both weekly and daily increments. (Remember, conscious recall leaves an unconscious imprint.) Kopp claims to be obsessive about this system, but it's for all the right reasons. In a fast-moving world, it helps her to stay proactive.

Yet another proactive stance comes from leaders who turn mission statements into working philosophies by revisiting them with their employees on a regular basis. One leader of a large veterinary hospital has told me he begins his monthly staff meetings by asking a different staff member each time to read their mission statement. Then he asks the team for instances of where they have succeeded or fallen short in the past month. Another leader in a large financial firm uses Friday meetings to ask each of her direct reports what they did that week to contribute to their firm's mission.

Both leaders want to keep their organization's mission statement front and center in the minds of their staff. The leaders prime their teams' mental models regularly so that their people would be constantly thinking of the organization's purpose and direction—and disciplining themselves to adhere to its values in the process. In other words, their mental models for the organization's mission statement are consciously primed for a spontaneous and automatic interpretation of the environment around them. This is not rocket science, just allocating importance to the mission statement by taking the time to communicate about it on a regular basis.

Note, too, that you prime not just by reflecting upon your mental models but also by communicating them. Again, think in terms of the mental train tracks you are laying down. An awareness of what you say when you communicate your mental models to others primes the unconscious in the same way that reflecting on them does. Whether it is reflection or communication that brings your mental models to the surface, conscious recall leaves an unconscious imprint because of Hebb's law, "neurons that fire together wire together." The stronger or clearer the conscious imprint, the more your communications draw from the state of mental readiness that priming creates.

Before moving on, consider whether there is some advice you can use in this section. For example, can you take a page out of Wendy Kopp's book and set aside some time in which to reflect on your strategic plan (mental model) for yourself weekly and even daily? Is it time to make your firm's mission statement more of a working philosophy by discussing it more frequently with your people? On the following lines, describe the advice you can use and your plans for using it:

Advice that I can use:

_____

_____

_____

_____

_____

Priming for Opportunity

In September 2009, Crystal Lee Sutton died. You might not recognize her name, but she was the inspiration for the movie *Norma Rae*, for which Sally Field won a best actress Oscar. Set in the 1970s, the film chronicles Sutton's unlikely emergence as a leader. Crystal Lee Sutton was born in the mill town of Roanoke Raids, North Carolina. Just as generations of her family did before her, Sutton began working at J.P. Stevens & Company, a manufacturer of fine towels and brocade tablecloths for four-star hotels, before she was out of high school. But luxury was not in the cards for Sutton, especially on those days when she was forced to work near the hopper feeders. This is where men dismantled five-hundred-pound bales of Mississippi Delta cotton, spewing thick clouds of lint in the process. The lint dust found its way into her lungs and throat, not to mention her skin, hair, and even the sandwich in her lunch.[18]

By 1979, Sutton was a thirty-three-year-old mother of three, widowed and remarried, earning $2.65 an hour. She had been a spinner, a doffer, a side-hemmer, and a terry loader. Suffice it to say that the work was often grueling. Her low pay and poor working conditions inspired Sutton to take a lead role as a union organizer, much to the dismay of management who, she said later, "treated me as if I had leprosy."[19] Sutton's history could be just one more union organizing tale, especially because books like Saul Alinsky's *Rules for Radicals* had already revealed the nitty-gritty of grassroots organizing.[20] However, what was unique about Sutton was her eye for the prime framing opportunity.

It came on the day that Sutton was fired for her union organizing efforts. When the police arrived to escort her off the premises, she seized upon one last attempt to get her message out. She explained, "I took a piece of cardboard and wrote the word 'union' on it in big letters, got up on my worktable, and slowly turned it around. The workers started cutting their machines off and giving me the victory sign. All of the sudden the plant was very quiet."[21] This is the kind of scene Hollywood loves, of course, so it is no surprise that it was an iconic moment in the movie. But more than that, it points to an intuitive sense that Sutton must have had as to the power and poignancy of one last framing opportunity. That it was done with just one word, that it would be her last, and that it triggered an overwhelmingly strong and silent show of support from her coworkers only heightened its dramatic impact.

The lesson here is that leaders must develop an eye for the high-impact framing opportunity, even those that others might overlook. Recall that this was one of the key differences between Strategics and Conventionals in the discussion of Message Design Logic in Chapter One. In *The Art of Framing*, we said that those high-impact opportunities often come when there is too much information, and the leader knows it is necessary to get to the heart of the matter or risk losing others' interest; when information is suspect, and the leader knows to correct the sleight-of-hand; when information is incomplete, and the leader knows to supply the missing puzzle piece; or when collective action is thwarted, and the leader knows to find new paths forward.

Common sense all, to be sure, but there is often a large gap between knowing what one should do to be effective and actually doing it. Consider one leader who figured out a way to manage this discrepancy. Veronica is a department head at a large U.S. university and a veteran of Al-Anon due to an alcoholic first husband. As is generally known, Al-Anon is a worldwide organization of local support groups for the families and friends of alcoholics.

As Veronica's academic career progressed into administration, she was struck by the number of Al-Anon principles or "traditions" that shaped her philosophy of leadership.[22] For example, the first tradition says that, "Our common welfare should come first; personal progress for the greatest number depends upon unity." Veronica would come to see conflict as a high-impact opportunity that could be used to further "the highest good." As she describes it:

> I really had this vision of the common welfare. When conflict or doubt arises, step back and ask, "What is the highest good? *What is the highest good?*" And so when this whole thing started with Dr. Stevens [a very difficult faculty member who could be harsh with students and whose reappointment Veronica did not support], I can remember her saying in the Dean's office, "Oh, what is this going to do to my career [if I don't get reappointed]?" I had really thought about this, and I said, "How many students, though, is this going to impact?" And I argued on the grounds of the highest good for all. So, maybe somebody's mad at me; I can let go of it [using the highest good principle]. Or, maybe I don't get my own way; [I can let go of it because] it is for the common good.

When you prime for opportunity, you are always on the lookout for those framing occasions in which to make a difference. Through a great deal of reflection about Al-Anon both in and outside her job, Veronica came to view conflicts in this way and used the principle of the highest good as a reflexive device to step back and out of the situation temporarily to make that determination. In that sense, she primed herself for a spontaneous yet strategic response.

Veronica supplied yet another instance of priming for opportunity when she told me her new mantra was "pause." She explains:

> When agitated, pause. When confused, pause. When doubtful, pause. And I did it a lot last week, which was the start of school. The thing is, it made me feel better. A lot of my job is putting out fires. But I learned that I put out a lot of fires that aren't really fires. I make them fires. Having the courage to step back is really the key for me. Pausing helps me to gain a sense of perspective and consider my options—also, to ask myself the question, "How important is it?"

Veronica believes herself to be overly reactive in certain situations. In what we might term "an ounce of prevention," she essentially primes herself to adopt an observer's perspective to avoid negative framing situations. Veronica has learned that her triggers include being agitated, confused, or doubtful. Her associated mantra, "pause," cues her to acquire the observer's stance that she finds so helpful. Note that in both instances, thoughtful reflection helped prime a more effective leadership response.

Before moving on, consider whether you are on the lookout for high-impact framing opportunities. What might they be? How can you better prepare yourself to seize the moment with them in mind?

_____

_____

_____

_____

_____

Finally, are you like Veronica? Do you use guides, primers, checklists, or books to prime yourself for a spontaneous show of effective leadership (or good management)? What are they, and how do you do this?

_____

_____

_____

_____

_____

Priming for Language

In the same way that we can prime our mental models or opportunities for high-impact framing, we can prime ourselves for language use. However, priming for language use can operate in two ways. First, we can store memories around specific wording or language forms by noticing the language in use around us (and not just in work settings). Pay attention to great arguments posed in newspaper editorials or blogs. Pay attention to the turn of a phrase in great literature. Start a story file, and collect great stories to use for your upcoming speeches, presentations, or other engagements. Expand your vocabulary—learn a new word each day. Small steps, to be sure, but these steps will heighten your sensitivity to language over time.

Second, our conscious experience of the world can prime our unconscious mind for later language use. For example, consider former *60 Minutes* commentator and writer Shana Alexander, who in the 1970s was paired with James J. Kilpatrick to debate the issues of the day at the end of the broadcast. So famous was their sparring that they were often parodied on *Saturday Night Live* in its early days.[23] When Alexander died in 2005, Kilpatrick wrote in her obituary of her writing skills. He highlighted Alexander's coverage of the sensational 1976 trial of kidnapped heiress-turned-gang-member Patricia Hearst:

> Her gift was the true writer's gift, to look *intently* at the world around her, and to see similes and metaphors emerge. These she stored in her writer's attic. They would be there when she needed them . . . .
>
> At the trial of Patty Hearst she watched the defendant signal to her parents with a quick, secret wave. "Below the table, emerging from a tailored sleeve, five pink and perfectly enameled fingers flutter like the frilly fin of a Siamese fighting fish." She looked intently at Patty's lawyer, F. Lee Bailey: "He is the big fish, groupers or a sheepshead bass, all massive head and strong shoulders." Presiding over the courtroom, "dead center and motionless, sitting so still he might be barnacled to the back wall of the tank, hangs the black-robed judge."
>
> At the trial, the court stenotypists became "human ear trumpets who funnel every word through trained fingers into the little, terrier-sized tripod that sits between their legs." Tension "hangs across the court like a trapeze net." After several days of trial, reporters and spectators came to recognize one another, but kept their thoughts to themselves: "We behave as if we are meeting at a bus stop."

Shana watched Patty Hearst come into the courtroom: "She was tiny and jailhouse sallow, with a copper coin's profile. Roman nose, red-gold hair gone dark at the roots, no makeup, dressed in a matronly brown suit . . . . " As the trial neared its end, Hearst became "a Madonna dolorosa, a classic image of female suffering. She sits motionlessly, and tears fall from her eyes as from a Sicilian painting."

How did my old antagonist bring it off? She looked *intently* at Siamese fighting fish, groupers, sheepshead bass, trapeze nets, bus stops, copper coins, billboards, Sicilian paintings, and hair gone dark at the roots. She stored the images like fresh-cut lumber. Years later, when it came time to build a descriptive paragraph, they awaited her command."[24]

"Fresh-cut lumber" is an apt metaphor for the potential supplied by a keen eye. Shana Alexander's intense scrutiny of the world primed her unconscious for a spontaneous use of language that greatly enabled her writing ability. While few of us can claim this level of authorship, the principle nonetheless stands. To the extent you are conscious of your experience of the world (rather than acting mindlessly), you prime your unconscious mind for spontaneous use down the road. It stands to reason, then, that heightening your powers of observation (including others' use of language) will develop your ability to see and describe when framing. More about this later in the chapter.

Another example of priming for language (and in this case opportunity) comes from entrepreneurship expert and syndicated columnist Rhonda Abrams. Given the centrality of networking in today's business climate, she urges entrepreneurs not to underestimate elevator rides and chance meetings at trade association conferences, conventions, large sales meetings, and the like. Similar to the comedy routine of a stand-up comic, a consciously primed "elevator pitch" can create a great first impression in a short time—about as long as it takes to ride the average elevator a few floors. However, she urges you to keep it short and, *using the right language*, be as memorable as possible to secure that positive first impression.[25] (But don't forget direct eye contact, a smile, and a strong handshake to reinforce your message.) Those chance encounters could pay dividends.

Finally, it is important to note that we can use priming to *avoid* a specific use of language. Perhaps this language is insensitive to one or more social categories of people—such as referring to women in the workplace as "the girls in the office." In another instance, I knew a leader who viewed himself as having a democratic style, but he was also fond of authority-based expressions like "you have my permission to . . . " with his key people. Leaders can and should strike such expressions from their repertoire by consciously reflecting on them one or more times to set up a mental signal to use alternative language in work discussions.

To recap, priming mental models and opportunities or language use is exercise for the brain. Such exercise develops "brain muscle" that can, in turn, be used to exert a measure of control over your spontaneous communications at a later time.

Priming After Mistakes and Gaffes

Most leaders are verbally skilled. Nevertheless, you can be generally articulate and not be aware of the context-shaping features of your language. For this reason, all leaders misspeak, say things they regret, and wish for do-overs. Some leaders are chronically gaffe-prone—such as CNN founder Ted Turner (nicknamed "The Mouth from the South"), President George W. Bush (his mispronunciations were parodied on *Saturday Night Live* with attributed words like "strategery"), and Vice President Joe Biden (who, as mentioned in Chapter One, derailed his own bid to become president on the first day of his campaign with an unintended racial slur toward Barack Obama).

Alpha males all, these leaders have strong egos and can be fairly dismissive of the need to focus on their communications (often, executive coaching's raison d'être).[26] However, even rhetorically gifted leaders occasionally misspeak, as Barack Obama did during his 2008 campaign for the U.S. presidency, when he stated that he had campaigned in all fifty-seven states with one to go.[27] (At last count, there were only fifty states.) To avoid repeating the mistake, priming for a spontaneous error-free performance the next time around is crucial.

For example, one fairly new manufacturing leader that I studied, let's call her Jean, was in her office one day when one of her people, Beth, came in to complain about another member of the team, George. Beth had heard folks in another department complain about George's sometimes over-the-top alpha male dominance, and she thought that Jean needed to coach George to tone it down. Both Jean and Beth agreed that George's antics could damage the reputation of the entire team. However, Beth did not want to be revealed as the source of the information, which Jean promised not to reveal. When I interviewed Jean after the incident, here's what she said:

> I got caught in the middle and wanted to make everybody happy and couldn't. My deep gut instinct told me don't get involved here, but I wanted to pounce on this [issue with George] but I also wanted to please Beth. So even though the first rule of interpersonal communication is to give specific feedback, I brought it up with George and said something like, "Somebody said they heard grumblings in processing. . . . " Well, he went pretty psycho. [He said,] "Well, who? Well, this isn't fair. Well, you just can't tell me this and not tell me who." He was really mad, and . . . after a couple of days he came to my office and said, "You know, you really bummed me out the other day." So the situation became about me, that I had handled it wrong. Then Beth got mad at me because I was pressuring her to let me tell George everything. So there was no solution, and that really made it worse . . . .
>
> What I realized is that I wasn't true to myself to begin with, and I got in the middle. And so I came up with a rule that, from now on if you are complaining about somebody and you want me to do something about it, then you have go on record. [This is] because this situation really backfired. It was not effective, and it was me taking too much responsibility to make everything better. So the Beth-George situation never got a good resolve, but I didn't do that again and, in that way, it was really a good lesson for me. In a recent leadership training class, I brought this situation of people not going on record up to the group. What we pretty much decided was to focus on making my own observations.

What is interesting about this example is that Jean was not able to repair the Beth-George conflict. Yet the formation of a clear rule reveals a lesson learned *through conscious reflection*. She created new mental train tracks for her brain to follow the next time someone complains. What is especially interesting about this example is that Jean goes to school on this incident in a leadership training seminar and primes yet another possible behavior path to follow (stick to personal observations). This effort marks Jean as a continuous learner, someone who tries to keep her mental models sharp. This is an apt theme as I turn next to helping develop your own mental models.

But before doing so, can you describe a situation in which you might prime for a spontaneous use of specific language? Or, alternatively, the avoidance of specific language?

_____

_____

_____

_____

Also, have you misspoken recently or said something you should not have? How can you avoid such mistakes in the future?

_____

_____

_____

_____

_____

Building Complex Mental Models

Thus far, I have been emphasizing the value of priming for spontaneity. However, I cannot leave this subject without also addressing how good your mental models need to be when you prime. It stands to reason that priming incorrect or weakly developed mental models can be as much of a problem as not priming at all. But what do well-developed mental models look like? From the earlier discussion, it's clear that you want large numbers of branches among your neurons, but what produces such growth? In other words, how do you go about *developing* mental models?

Reasoning from Mental Models

To answer this question, consider first the two kinds of mental models from which people can reason—rules and cases. When we reason from a set of rules, we have looked across a set of similar situations and derived a general rule. For example, after the events of September 11, 2001, Bush's policy to fight terrorism seemingly hinged on a simple rule: spread democracy to troubled nation-states (because free societies generally do not breed terrorism). U.S. involvement in the wars in Iraq and Afghanistan soon factored into this logic.

However, by Bush's second term of office, U.S. colonels and captains on the ground in these countries found that "spreading democracy" was far too simplistic a rule to serve as policy. As *New York Times* columnist David Brooks wrote in 2008: "They . . . could clear a town of the bad guys, but they had little capacity to establish rules of law or quality of life for the people they were trying to help." Their biggest challenge was not taking out the enemy but "repairing the zones of chaos where enemies grow and breed."[28]

Because security, democratization, and development efforts had proven to be impossibly intertwined in these conflicts, Secretary of State Condoleezza Rice and Defense Secretary Robert Gates called for a transformational diplomacy. Such diplomacy would individualize broad planning efforts with military personnel, the creation and support of local governments, and the initiation one or more development projects by locale or region. So what worked in one locale might be very different than what worked in another. As Brooks points out, the Bush administration's simple rule-based policy was not terribly helpful to those on the ground, who needed to grasp the possibilities inherent in more localized solutions—they needed more case-by-case knowledge.

There is nothing inherently wrong with reasoning from a set of rules, but it is interesting that cognitive scientists who study the knowledge of experts compared to that of novices believe that experts are more likely to reason from cases than from rules.[29] In problem-solving episodes, novices often do little more than apply one or more rules they believe fit the situation, which might be both efficient and appropriate for simple problems. However, for complex problems, the novices continue to try to apply rules, while the experts spend a great deal of time qualitatively analyzing a problem, gaining perspective, considering the principles that might apply, weighing constraints, and the like.[30] In short, they reason from the case, the qualities of which they have taken time to assess.

Psychologists Christopher Riesbeck and Roger Schank use baseball to distinguish case-based from rules-based reasoning.[31] For example, which second baseman should the manager of the Mets play regularly in the upcoming World Series—the rookie sensation, the steady hustler who helped with the World Series the preceding year, or the guy who did the best this year? Certainly, it's possible to name a rule, such as "Experience is the most important factor in a pennant race," but the answer is not readily apparent. As Riesbeck and Schank suggest, "even though we can cite rules like these, actual decision making in such cases is usually more seat-of-the-pants in nature. We have a gut feeling about the situation as a whole."[32]

For the experienced baseball manager, a pressure-packed game case presents all sorts of contingencies, for example, not being able to play at home for half of the games; a rookie player who has never been to the playoffs; heightened media coverage on the players; the win-loss record of the two teams and the series to date; the health and endurance of the experienced player; cold-weather playing ability (the Series is held in October); clubhouse leadership; and so on. As such, the "wholes" of these types of situations are best preserved in our memories as cases rather than rules.

Thus a partial answer to how we go about developing our mental models is to aim for case-based knowledge for complex problems, while remaining aware that rules-based knowledge may suffice for simple problems. However, such an acknowledgment still raises the question, How do we go about *developing* case-based knowledge?

Developing Your Mental Models

The simple answer to the question of how you develop case-based knowledge is age and experience. The more years and experience you accrue, the more developed your mental models become for a given subject. The more complex answer involves incremental training and "massed practice." Again, from the frontiers of brain science, we are learning from stroke patients that the brain can and will reorganize itself when training is done in increments that increase in difficulty over time. Also, the training must be intensive, or what Norman Doidge quotes brain scientist Edward Taub as labeling "massed practice."[33]

Doidge likens massed practice to learning a foreign language, which can be far more hit-and-miss in your average language course instruction compared to in-country immersion.[34] Simply trying to meet life's daily necessities like food and lodging in a foreign country prompts "massed practice" because survival depends on communication. Moreover, he adds, "our accent suggests to others that they may have to use simpler language with us; hence we are incrementally challenged, or shaped."[35]

Interestingly, these same two brain development principles of incremental training and massed practice apply to organizations of a type known as *high-reliability organizations*, or HROs for short. These organizations are concerned with failure and reliability rather than success and efficiency. As one group of management researchers explain these organizations: "They all operate in an unforgiving social and political environment, an environment rich with the potential for error, where the scale of consequences precludes learning through experimentation, and where to avoid failures in the face of shifting sources of vulnerability, complex processes are used to manage complex technology."[36]

Can you guess some of these organizations? Think of aircraft carriers, firefighting organizations, police units, nuclear power plants, mining operations, oil tankers, NASA, and the airlines, to name a few. All have teams that must operate with a strong sense of mission and highly developed collective mental processes to bring off the safe rescue, the safe take-off and landing, or the safe environment. Interestingly, Weick and Roberts suggest that the best HROs have a *collective mind*—not one where everybody thinks and does the same thing, but one with overlapping knowledge, a hierarchy that envisions the right configuration of overlapping knowledge, and continuous training on real-life cases.[37]

Weick and Sutcliffe thus call HROs "smart systems" because they are continuously developing their mental models.[38] Consider such an example from a police organization that a colleague and I studied several years ago.[39] One cold February evening in 1998, a police unit from a Midwestern city got an emergency distress call from one of its rookie officers: she had been shot and needed help.

Unfortunately, the shooter was in control of her car, and she made the call in the midst of a violent struggle. GPS units were not yet standard issue in police cars, so police supervisors could not decipher this rookie's location until she managed to fatally shoot her assailant and radio back to the dispatcher. In about four minutes from that time, her supervisors found her and subsequently got her the medical assistance that she needed. She had been shot four times with a .357 magnum, but she survived. While most of us would conclude that this was a successful rescue, in fact, an effective HRO frames it as a near-failure.

Why? To treat this incident as a success breeds complacency, according to Weick and Sutcliffe. By contrast, to treat this incident as a near-failure is to trigger massed practice for the police unit, practice that stringently assesses what went wrong and what went right; what the officer, supervisors, and dispatcher could have done better; how various protocols performed; and what must they recall (read: prime) for the next emergency.

Such training *incrementally* builds on the training of previous critical incidents. Over time, it creates fine-grained mental models derived from case-by-case knowledge of past emergencies and the many contingencies they present. Indeed, police supervisors stressed to me how their training around real-life incidents is exactly what they prime on their way to their next emergency. The priming allows them a measure of strategic yet automatic behavior when the crisis is upon them.

As "smart systems," HROs differentiate themselves from other organizations by the breadth of what members monitor, expect, and fear. Obviously, less breadth means more opportunity for surprise and potentially less reliability. Effective HROs, according to Weick and Sutcliffe, become *preoccupied with failure*. This is not a matter of subconsciously desiring failure, as in a self-fulfilling prophecy, but of remaining in a mindful state by surfacing mental models regularly and consciously reflecting upon them.[40] Such reflection greatly facilitates members' effectiveness as they prime for spontaneous crisis management. For this reason, effective HROs tend to see more—and to see it *earlier*, when they can act to correct a situation. The implications for framing are clear. How effectively we frame depends upon how much we notice.

Weick and Sutcliffe thus recommend that all organizations take a page out of the HROs' playbook to deal with the unexpected in the work environment. To take just one example, note how Vince, a manager of a small manufacturing firm, uses the concept of preoccupation with failure:

> I live in a world of uncertainty, I'm not naive any longer. . . . I come in in the morning now and I'm a skeptic. I say, "Okay, first tell me about all of the casualties, I want to set priorities. What are the things that might take us out of business today?" I'm not being wise, I'm being a realist. . . . Right now we're wrestling with keeping two boilers up and running. . . . Yeah, we gotta game plan and we try to set a course of direction, but then I live with the reality of the situation. I can go back Monday and the boiler is gone—so how do we address this problem? You really have to be nimble of foot here, you've got to be able to react, you don't know what's going to be thrown at you. You try to prepare yourself for the unexpected, and with a number of eyes looking ahead with me, maybe we'll see a few of the potholes that are approaching us. . . . If you look at the plant, the plant itself is like a rickety old car with band aids and rubber bands.[41]

Concepts such as a preoccupation with failure build complexity into Vince's mental model for his plant operations, nicely summed up as a "rickety old car." Through such a metaphor, he periodically surfaces his mental models (triggering incremental learning), intensively assesses "the situation here and now" for potential pitfalls (triggering massed practice), and trains on events of the past (primes for spontaneity).

However, what if you are short on experience in which to train? Fortunately, there are other ways to build complexity and rich case material into your mental models. One important way involves *fantasy*, a technique that psychotherapists consistently use. For example, in the school of therapy known as *brief therapy*, therapists pose "miracle questions" to help clients clarify their goals and discover potential solutions to their problems.[42] A therapist might ask a client, "If your problem were suddenly solved, what would that look like? Who would be a part of this solution? What kinds of conversations would you be having? How would you be feeling about yourself?"

By asking questions such as these, two kinds of apparent miracles can occur. First, the more often clients discuss the future, the more of a possibility it becomes. As therapists Berg and de Shazer observe, "As client and therapist talk more and more about the solution they want to construct together, they come to believe in the truth or reality of what they are talking about. This is the way that language works, naturally."[43] Second, clients connect with their own expertise for solving problems.[44] Thus, miracle questions can develop mental models through the words and thoughts involved in fantasizing possible futures.[45] As discussed in the first two chapters, leaders who ask the right questions can generate productive solutions to vexing problems—even from a tool box that is limited to fantasy techniques.

For some time now, miracle questions have been a staple of organizational consultants, who use visioning exercises to foster widespread organizational change. According to management consultant Jean Duck, their goal is to get leaders to ask themselves, "If we were managing the way we say we want to manage, how would we act? How would we attack our problems? What kind of meetings and conversations would we have? Who would be involved? How would we define, recognize, compensate, and reward appropriate behavior?"[46] Again, fantasizing answers to questions like these triggers mental model development.

If organizational consultants use psychoanalytic fantasy techniques, why not everyday leaders? Using fantasy exercises like miracle questions offers some great ways to build case-based knowledge into your own mental models, so long as these techniques spur further learning or discovery by you. You can also be assured that brain science supports the effectiveness of these techniques given new understandings about how learning enhances the structures and synaptic connections among neurons.[47]

Before moving on, use the framing tool below to analyze a critical incident with this chapter's key learnings.

FRAMING TOOL 3.1

Critical Incident Framing

Recall the critical incident that you identified in earlier chapters or use another one involving your leadership that you would like to analyze. Remember the focus should be on your communications as a leader, with your employees, your customers, or other stakeholders. Also, select an incident in which you were unhappy with the outcome.

_____

_____

_____

_____

Briefly, name all of your mental models involved in this incident. Allow for the possibility that there could be several when you factor in all of the people and organizations involved, the situation, and so on.

1. _____

2. _____

3. _____

4. _____

5. _____

6. _____

7. _____

Which of these mental models were insufficiently primed? Remember that the key to priming is conscious, systematic rehearsal. This can mean going over things in your head or practicing what you want to say out loud. Either lays down the mental train tracks necessary for your neurons to fire appropriately.

_____

_____

_____

_____

_____

_____

How can you better prime for spontaneity the next time around?

_____

_____

_____

_____

_____

Which of the mental models you have listed are still in their early stages of development and could benefit from more case-based knowledge?

_____

_____

_____

_____

_____

In what ways could you further develop these mental models? What specifically could build case-based knowledge, including miracle questions? Think expansively at this stage, and complete the sentence "In the best of all possible worlds, I could get this knowledge by . . . ."

_____

_____

_____

_____

_____

Whether it is through acquiring a coach or a mentor, attending an off-site training event, spending time with another person, asking for projects that will build specific skill sets, reading and reflecting, scheduling time for fantasy exercises, or other course of action, write down your plan to aggressively pursue development of these mental models. It includes . . .

_____

_____

_____

_____

_____

(You can download this form from www.josseybass.com/go/gailfairhurst. Feel free to adapt it to suit your needs. This analysis will continue in Chapter Four.)

A Backward Glance at Chapter Three

Much of the science behind framing involves understanding conscious and unconscious learning processes and what brain science is beginning to tell us. Such an understanding helps with a basic dilemma that human beings face in our desire to communicate spontaneously and automatically, yet strategically. The aim of this chapter is to show how this might be done. More specifically,

- We can control much of what we say and how we say it through priming for spontaneity. Priming is a conscious act that imprints the unconscious with a path for the brain to follow. Much like the tip-of-the-tongue phenomenon, if a particular thought process was a part of one's recent conscious experience, then that thought process remains accessible and used by the unconscious mind to filter information that arrives later.

- Leaders can prime their mental models either by reflecting on them or by communicating them to others.

- Leaders can prime for opportunity and look for instances in which to seize the moment or, alternatively, avoid troublesome situations.

- Leaders can prime for language use and adopt specific arguments, labels, or stories or, alternatively, avoid poor language choices.

- Our ability to frame effectively and prime for spontaneity is deeply impacted by the quality or complexity of our mental models. Research has shown that experts' mental models look like cases rather than rules.

- Case-based reasoning appears necessary for complex problems, while reasoning from rules may be appropriate for simple problems.

- The simple answers to the question of how we build complexity into our mental models are age and experience. The more complex answers involve incremental training and "massed practice." Brain science shows us that the brain will reorganize itself with incremental training that increases in complexity over time and immersion in the subject at hand.

- HROs or high-reliability organizations encourage members to train themselves to be preoccupied with failure, periodically surfacing their mental models and intensively scanning the environment for potential problems.

- Fantasy also builds complexity into our mental models, especially those that may be underdeveloped.

A FINAL THOUGHT

Because so few of us engage in mental rehearsal systematically, we underestimate its effectiveness.

4

The Art of Framing

ART CAN BE a difficult word to define because the experience of it is so personal and subjective. The aesthetics that delight my senses, arrest my thoughts, or capture my emotions may not be the same as the ones you respond to. It is the same with framing aesthetics, with one or two possible exceptions. For instance, many regard Martin Luther King's "I Have a Dream" as one of the greatest speeches of the twentieth century. You have likely seen bits and pieces of it over the years, especially if you're an American. But take a moment to go on YouTube, and watch the entire the speech start to finish.[1] Given on August 28, 1963, in Washington, D.C., it is considered one of the defining moments of the U.S. civil rights movement.

King's speech was delivered on the steps of the Lincoln Memorial and begins with a powerful allusion to this sixteenth president of the United States "in whose symbolic shadow we stand today." King's use of metaphor was masterful, as when he spoke of slaves "seared in the flames of withering injustice," their lives "crippled by the manacle of segregation and chains of discrimination." He deftly used an extended metaphor when referring to coming to the nation's capital to "cash a check" for equal rights. He spoke of the Bible and founding fathers' texts like the U.S. Constitution and Declaration of Independence. Phrases like the desire to be judged by the "content of [one's] character" would find their way into the speeches of countless others to follow. Finally, King repeated key phrases for dramatic appeal, thus delivering among the most remembered lines of the speech.[2] "I have a dream . . . " and "Free at last" became signature lines, delivered in a voice that was exquisitely mournful yet hopeful at the same time.

Now read leadership scholar Keith Grint's "executive summary" of King's speech:

It's been a hundred years since we were promised freedom and we still haven't got it. This state of affairs cannot continue. We must not sink to violent tactics but we want freedom now. This isn't just a black problem, it's an American problem. I have a dream that one day we will achieve our rights. Everyone go home and keep up the good work.[3]

The point that Grint so brilliantly makes here is that a seventeen-minute speech or a fifteen-second one can deliver the same basic message, but the irony of the latter is that it is about as stimulating as an afternoon nap. Indeed, one cannot see a video of King deliver his speech and not be moved by his eloquence, passion, and crystallization of a key moment of the civil rights movement.[4]

Unfortunately, the case for eloquence is a tough sell to many managers, who prefer a no-frills, straight-talk approach to their communications. They are functional in their language choices, and often happily so, because their attention is directed elsewhere. And for many everyday business communications, no-frills works perfectly well.

But there are other times when you need to inspire, especially as you move up in the organization and your voice projects louder and further. Rote behavior or compliance with authority just won't do when you need to win hearts and minds. Other times "the situation here and now" is complex, and you've got to help your people understand this complexity. To do all this, management scholar Karl Weick suggests cultivating "nuanced vocabularies" and "stockpiles of metaphors."[5] In short, you need eloquence, which you can learn by focusing on the *art* involved in framing.

In this chapter's discussion of the aesthetics or art form of your framing communications, the key message is simple. Whether you are verbally skilled or not, the art of framing should be practiced like a craft.

Framing as a Craft

Harvard English professor Marjorie Garber says that most Americans have an overly romantic view of the artistic process. We think of it as being driven by some transcendent moment of genius or inspiration, captured in metaphors like the lightning bolt or the lightbulb going on over someone's head. What we minimize is the labor that a true craft requires—all the practice, mistakes, rehearsals, experiments, and course-corrections.[6]

Immediately, I saw in Garber's observation a powerful analogy to how most people view articulate and charismatic leaders. That is, they must have been born that way, "naturally gifted" or "divinely inspired" in a way that others cannot be. But the truth of the matter is that those who are viewed as the most gifted orators, for example, a Martin Luther King, Ronald Reagan, or Abraham Lincoln, spent considerable time in the craft of framing by paying attention to how they used language. All are known to have labored over their most important framing communications—and, significantly, maintained an interest in "word crafting" as a lifelong pursuit. As with actors who never stop learning their craft, so too with framing and the verbally skilled.

American writer, comedian, and actor Steve Martin gives us a glimpse of this when writing about his time on the road as a stand-up comedian.[7] To the naive, Martin seems like a naturally gifted comic in these early days. (You can catch his routines on YouTube.) But his words tell a story of perspiration more than inspiration:

> I did stand-up comedy for eighteen years. Ten of those years were spent learning, four years were spent refining, and four were spent in wild success. My most persistent memory of stand-up is of my mouth being in the present and my mind being in the future: the

mouth speaking the line, the body delivering the gesture, while the mind looks back, observing, analyzing, judging, worrying, and then deciding when and what to say next. Enjoyment while performing was rare—enjoyment would have been an indulgent loss of focus that comedy cannot afford. After the shows, however, I experienced long hours of elation or misery depending upon how the show went, because doing comedy is the ego's last stand.

As Martin so beautifully demonstrates, cultivating a funny bone night after night is hard work. He accumulated jokes, developed routines, and honed his timing. He paid attention to the ways that others before him told jokes, funny or not so funny, and gauged their responses. He experimented with word choice, vocal emphasis and stress (Martin was famous for, "Well, excuuuse me!"), and props to help deliver a line (famously, his banjo, arrow through his head, and white suit). Fortunately, few of us face the same pressures as Martin, but depending upon your job, there may be no less work involved.

To stay on target day after day, you need to focus on language, because it is at the heart of all great framing. There are also two key lessons to keep in mind. First, heightening your sensitivity to language will make you a better framer. Recall from Chapter One's discussion of Message Design Logics, that Strategics are defined by their sensitivity to language beyond that of Conventionals and Expressives. Also, remember Chapter Three's lesson, which is that heightening your sensitivity to language primes your unconscious with a wider selection of language choices from which to communicate.

Second, there are no simple linguistic recipes or formulas for framing success. No one can say, "Add two parts metaphor, one part story, a master frame, and voilà, you will have constructed an artful message!" On the contrary, what is simultaneously fascinating and maddening about language use is the way in which the same word or turn of phrase can resonate or be off-sounding as we change sentences, topic, situation, or person with whom we are communicating. Just ask former New York City Mayor Rudy Giuliani—for whom "9/11" was once a master frame and term of regard—that is, until he turned it into a tired expression through overuse in his bid to become a U.S. presidential candidate.

To understand more about language issues, begin with some basic language forms such as the ones listed in Table 4.1. Think of these language forms as

Table 4.1. Commonly Used Language Forms in Framing

Form	Description
Metaphorical	It portrays a subject's resemblance to something else that is not literally applicable to the topic, as in "This project is a *breeze*."
Story	It frames a subject through narrative, as in *"Remember the time we worked until midnight on that project, and we had to call security to get us out of the building."*
Contrast	It describes a subject in terms of a comparison or what it is not, as in "This project is *not as complex as the last one*, thankfully."
Spin	It places a subject in a positive or negative light, as in "This project has a *huge negative—time!*"
Jargon or Catchphrase	It frames a subject in familiar terms as in, *"Think outside the box* on this project, and it will pay dividends."
Analogy	It frames a subject's parallels to another subject, as in "The personnel issues that you experienced with your project are similar to what I'm experiencing with mine."
Argument	It frames a subject in reasoned, rational terms, as in "It's an important project *given the changing market here and an economy in recession, as the numbers show.*"
Feeling statement	It frames a subject in terms of felt emotions, as in "I *absolutely love* what I get to do with this project."
Category	It frames a subject in terms of membership (or lack of membership) in a class or group, as in "This project is *need-to-know* only."
Three-part list	It organizes a subject in easily remembered "threes," as in "This project is *safe*. It's *cost effective*, and most of all, it is *environmentally friendly*."
Repetition	It dramatizes a subject through parallel form, as in *"This project is safe. This project is cost-effective. This project is environmentally friendly."*

your artist's palette. Instead of paint colors, your palette is a linguistic one. Note that Table 4.1 is not an exhaustive list of all the language forms available to you, but they are all fairly common in the English language. (If you speak another language, you may have to modify the list.)

Just how do these language forms differ from the cultural Discourse tool bags in Chapter Two? Tool bags are mostly content-related: *what* we communicate about. The language forms in Table 4.1 are the means by which we communicate that content. For example, Chapter Two discussed the geek and geezer Discourses and their respective tool bags of terminology and arguments for two different generations of leaders. However, note that the words *geeks* and *geezers* are actually examples of jargon—for computer experts (as in computer geeks) and older people, respectively. Jargon is one of the language forms listed in the table.

While I tried to define the language forms in Table 4.1 as simply as possible and demonstrate them with a set of messages all involving a nondescript project for easy comparison, they are certainly capable of a great deal more. To demonstrate their capabilities in specific leadership examples, the rest of this chapter addresses five types of frames commonly used by articulate leaders: the metaphorical, master, simplifying, gain and loss, and believability frames. Each of these frames and its examples uses one or more of the language forms in Table 4.1. I italicize them throughout the chapter so that you can note just how they are used in the framing process.

Metaphorical Frames

Metaphorical frames may involve *simple metaphors*, such as when we say, "It was a monster of a storm" to indicate a storm's magnitude. But more often than not, they involve *complex metaphors*, where we find "an intricate organization of parallel elements" according to Genie Laborde, author of *Fine Tune Your Brain*.[8] For example, Albert Einstein famously described relativity through *analogy* and *contrast*: "Put your hand on a hot stove for a minute, and it seems like an hour. Sit with a pretty girl for an hour, and it seems like a minute. That's relativity."[9]

Complex metaphors are often the foundation for *stories* and other narrative forms like parables, fables, and folktales. As a result, Laborde argues that our conscious mind responds to simple metaphors, but our unconscious mind delights in the complex metaphor.[10] Our unconscious searches for the deeper meanings and purposes behind the intricate series of comparisons drawn by the metaphor. For example, consider one senior executive's complex metaphor for corporate mergers:

> Well, it's almost like dating somebody . . . you talk about culture and what you like and don't and how you work and don't, [but] you don't know until you live together, right? You're on your best behavior in merger meetings . . . the ugly isn't coming out. You're not arguing with someone about whether you should have a policy over something or not. You're not doing more high level kind of due diligence. Whether you have 14 people approving something or one doesn't come out in due diligence. Nobody says in due diligence, "Now how many approvals does it take to give somebody a $500 bonus?" That's not the level of detail you're working at. But when you live together, that's the kind of thing that drives you crazy. Now [their] company says five people have to sign this to give somebody a $1,000 bonus; [ours] says their manager can approve that. So trying to bring that kind of stuff together you would never know that in due-diligence. You don't get to that level.[11]

Complex metaphors work best when listeners derive pleasure from novel or surprising comparisons, as with dating for due diligence and living together for after a merger. By allowing a subject to take on new meanings, metaphors boost our sensemaking abilities.[12] Add to this the leader's dash of humor—when he suggests "the ugly isn't coming out" in merger talks—and the complex metaphor embedded in this executive's merger *story* becomes even more effective. When faced with explaining complex subject matter, there's nothing better than metaphorical framing of this nature.

Interestingly, Laborde's major point on complex metaphors—and it is one consistent with the message of this book—is to actually aim your communications at the conscious *and* unconscious minds of others (and yourself, for that matter). Advertisers, she reminds us, do it all the time.[13]

One really great example of this comes from Candace Matthews, chief marketing officer for Amway Global. In a difficult economy, her innovations helped boost Amway's revenues to $8.2 billion, up 15 percent from 2008.[14] One of those innovations involved recognizing culture's impact on brand acceptance and regional sales models. In an interview, Matthews recounts a discussion with her chief marketing officers on global-regional operations. She introduced the complex metaphor of an octopus and used a stuffed toy to demonstrate her point:

> I said, "We need to think globally here," she explains, touching the head of her colorful sea creature, "and then we implement through each of our areas," in which she points to the octopus' tentacles. "So I gave everyone a stuffed octopus and when we get into one of our meetings and people get too far down into their details, I say, 'Whoa, whoa, whoa; get back to the head of the octopus.'"[15]

No doubt, distributing stuffed animals must have elicited a chuckle or two from senior staff members who likely take their on-the-job toys a bit more seriously. But with both conscious and unconscious underpinnings, this complex metaphor and prop beautifully illustrate the kind of organizational form she seeks. Also, by introducing the complex metaphor in one discussion, it allows Matthews to extend the metaphor and communicate in a more efficient, shorthand fashion in subsequent ones. (Note also her use of *repetition*—"Whoa, whoa, whoa"—for emphasis.) Complex metaphors will pay these kinds of dividends as long as all aspects of the metaphor match the situation.

But do you think that you needed to be an English major in college or possess a literary bent to become adept at metaphorical framing? Consider Edwin Young, an African American manager from a large U.S. insurance firm, who had only been out of college for a few years. Edwin was personable, well-spoken, even charismatic save for one problem: his occasional use of nonstandard English.[16] Edwin's manager, Denny Moutray, wanted him to talk with me to see if the public speaking training Edwin was receiving was also meeting his needs regarding nonstandard English. Here is a portion of my conversation with Edwin after we introduced ourselves:

Edwin: I started out working for a financial services firm and ended up being
       recruited by a representative from this company. I took the job and

two years later was recruited for management. Two years after that, I got another promotion to regional multicultural director, which is where I am today. I have been here for six months. I can hardly believe my luck.

Gail: No doubt, luck had only a small part to do with things, Edwin. You must be impressing somebody at your firm to have had such a quick rise through the ranks. Now, I know how Denny has sized up the situation. Tell me the situation from your perspective. What are your needs?

Edwin: Do you remember the days of taking the Polaroid picture? Click the camera, and instantly a picture spits out. The way I see it, people can take a quick Polaroid of me when they see me make a presentation at our sales meetings, but if they work with me on a daily basis, they can see the movie. I *know* I can impress folks when they can see the movie. What I've got to work on is my Polaroid image by getting my grammar and presentation skills up to par, so that I can impress the largest number of folks right off the bat.

Gail: But how do you feel about that, Edwin? I mean, what we are talking about is the use of nonstandard English, sometimes found in African American communities and others. You're working for a company that wants you to be able to speak two different languages, one language for the corporate community and, ironically, another language for black communities you might also be doing business with in the future. In the literature, it's called "code switching"— switching from one language code to another.

Edwin: *I know!* I go home, and my family says to me, "Why are you talking so funny?" I seem like an outsider to them, but I'm an outsider at work, as well, without this ability to "code switch" as you call it. Here's the way I see it, though. A few years ago, Tiger Woods all of a sudden doesn't like his golf swing. *Imagine,* Tiger Woods! Perhaps the most successful golfer of all time says his swing is not working for him anymore. So he relearns a new swing by breaking the process down, getting down to the basic mechanics, and learning to swing anew. I figure, that's what I'm doing. For example, I have a bad habit of switching "were/where" or "are/our" in sentences. It's not as apparent when I'm presenting information to a group of people versus them reading (e-mail) communication from me. So let me "aks" you, what would you do in a situation like this?[17]

Gail: Well, I think I would do exactly what you are doing—checking out all of the resources available to you. Before we're done, I think you'll see quite a range of resources that you can use. Now, I understand that you've met once or twice with a public speaking coach who also helped you with grammar issues. Tell me about that. Was it useful?

Needless to say, Edwin made a terrific first impression, in part, because he used complex *metaphors* like "Polaroids" and changing golf swings to good effect. As it turns out, Edwin went to college on a basketball scholarship, which meant listening to countless motivational speeches by coaches trying to rouse their teams to victory. Those speeches had more than just a motivational effect on Edwin. He developed an unconscious appetite for metaphorical frames—and his understanding of the power of language came through the world of sports, not literature.

Before leaving Edwin, note also the variety of language forms he used in addition to *metaphor*. He told a *story* of his career trajectory. He posed *arguments* regarding the need to switch to a more standard use of English. He used *spin* to mark this as a good thing. He uses a *feeling statement* when he expresses confidence in his ability to impress others, and he used the *category* of "outsider" to describe himself both with his family and at work. These language forms seamlessly fold into Edwin's metaphorical framing in this situation.

Now it's your turn. Develop a complex metaphor for a subject you have explained recently or one that you want to explain in a future conversation. You can do this by following these four steps:

1. Identify your subject matter and the specific points you want to emphasize (for example, Candace Matthews wanted to communicate what "thinking globally" meant to her marketing team).

   _____

   _____

   _____

_____

_____

2. Brainstorm similarities with various other subjects that might serve as the metaphor (for example, Matthews used the anatomy of an octopus to represent global-local operations, but your subject may compare better to a journey, war, theater, sports competition, brain, anatomy, prison, or machine, or to cooking, giving birth, or some other activity).

_____

_____

_____

_____

3. Select the metaphors whose parallel elements are the most consistent with your subject matter's points of emphasis.

_____

_____

_____

_____

4. Select the metaphor your listeners would relate to best.

_____

Master Frames

In Chapter Two, I pointed out that *master frames* operate in a wider context than single-subject framing, illustrating this with the master frame of "Xavier University as citizen." Master frames are a pithy way of expressing an organizational vision. Indeed, they can represent a corporate philosophy or ideology of most any kind. Because master frames can be potent organizing tools, it is appropriate to discuss their aesthetics. If worded correctly, they have great power to inspire and mobilize people to act.

First a little history is necessary. The concept of "master frame" comes from the study of social movements where social scientists are interested to know, what inspires a group of people to organize themselves to collectively protest some existing condition in society? Examples abound in today's world: the fledgling democracy movement in Iran, the "Tea Party" movement in the United States, and global social movements of various kinds like the G8 protestors who lobby world leaders for more responsible positions on climate change, nuclear proliferation, and poverty.

Sociologists David Snow and Robert Benford tell us that there is a relationship between master frames and cycles of protest (in other words, framing and action).[18] This is because social movements, even fledgling ones, are meaning-making machines where ideology comes to life in the communications of members.

From the many interactions inside the movement, *master frames* take shape. They are much more specific than ideologies, perhaps dealing only with one specific theme with broad appeal. But they have the potential to stir people to act. They are an ideology's best advertisement—and they can do as much for a corporate philosophy. There is often sloganeering involved, but it is not only a matter of wordsmithing. It is the encapsulation of a key idea and turn of phrase all at once.

For example, the frequently used expression, "Women helping women" is a master frame with great resonance and scope. Unspoken but implicit is a more elaborate ideology rooted in women's rights, social welfare, and often philanthropy. A Google search on this phrase produces well over 300,000,000 hits for women's causes both large and small. Several of these are nonprofit and community-based organizations whose actual name is "Women Helping Women" and whose mission is simultaneously and powerfully encapsulated in the master frame of the same name. More than simple sloganeering, it is a succinct call to action for a host of women's causes.

Consider a second master frame from another organization serving women's causes, the NoVo Foundation. In 2006, Warren Buffett pledged the tidy sum of $1 billion to each of his three children for philanthropic causes. His son Peter and Peter's wife, Jennifer, founded NoVo, which is dedicated to helping women and adolescent girls in developing countries who suffer from violence, poverty, and discrimination.[19] Jennifer is president of this nonprofit.

When Jennifer and Peter Buffett were interviewed on the efforts of NoVo, the master frame they presented was the simple but unlikely word *no*. It fit because saying no had been necessary to manage the huge number of would-be suitors trying to get a piece of the action from this nonprofit. It fit because Jennifer had become the self-described "'no' person" as her husband was proving to be a soft touch to the artful persuader. Most important, it fit because *no* is the word that too many adolescent girls in developing countries *don't* feel empowered to use—"no to early marriage and unsafe sex (thereby lessening HIV exposure) and yes to education."[20] The very simplicity of this master frame is noteworthy because it has evolved into this organization's mission statement.

Can you think of master frames that you already use? Write a few of them in the spaces below.

_____

_____

_____

_____

What is the mission and vision of your organization currently?

_____

_____

_____

_____

Create a master frame for one or both of them.

_____

_____

_____

_____

_____

Simplifying Frames

As the name suggests, *simplifying frames* reduce the chaos or complexity of the moment. The best simplifying frames are elegant in their clarity. For example, many felt that the late Tim Russert, Washington bureau chief of NBC news and moderator of the long-running television show *Meet the Press*, used this framing to good effect. Russert was renowned for holding U.S. politicians accountable by creating visuals of their previous quotes and asking them to reconcile those words with their current perceived flip-flopping.

In the 2000 U.S. election cliffhanger between Al Gore and George W. Bush, Russert famously chose to avoid computer graphics for updating electoral results, using instead a small whiteboard. One of his incisive renderings of election night chaos were the words, "Florida, Florida, Florida" scrawled across it. This framing proved prophetic of the outcome as Florida's twenty-five electoral votes went to Bush, thus helping him win one of the country's closest elections ever. Russert's whiteboard is now located in the Smithsonian Institution.[21]

As Tim Russert's "Florida" message shows us, the "art" involved in simplifying is needle-like precision that reduces the complexity, confusion, or chaos of the moment. Simplifying leaders wade through chaos by reflecting, detecting patterns, and using verbal signposts or linkages to the familiar. The great financier Warren Buffett of Berkshire Hathaway does it through homespun *metaphor* or *stories*—drafting annual reports as if writing to his sister, who reportedly knows nothing about investments. Ronald Reagan was famous for reducing complex economic issues to simple, clear themes that voters could grasp, such as "Get the government off our backs," and "Are you better off than you were four years ago?" In just a few well-chosen *catchphrases*, he was able to depict his vision of economic growth through less government interference.[22]

Communicating numbers is a special case of simplifying frames. The usual advice here is to follow "law of large numbers," which is to translate them into terms that will be meaningful to recipients. For example, writing in *Fast Company*, Dan Heath and Chip Heath argue that the $800 billion stimulus package, created in 2009 to boost a faltering U.S. economy, is too difficult a number for most people to grasp. Better to characterize it as "the rough equivalent of seven weeks' income for an American household."[23] Then *argument* can proceed as to whether individuals would be willing to sacrifice this amount to stave off a possible depression. Or, is this amount outrageous and further evidence of the irresponsibility of the financial sector (an acknowledged scapegoat in this crisis)?

However, we live in complex times, and communicating about the meaning of some numbers can be difficult. PepsiCo, owner of the Tropicana brand, found this out in trying to document the carbon footprint of its orange juice production. It determined that the equivalent of 3.75 pounds of carbon dioxide is emitted into the atmosphere for each half-gallon carton of orange juice.[24] But outside the company, communicating about this number (for example, using it as a marketing tool) proved difficult because companies may interpret the standards for calculating the carbon footprint in different ways. What should you do if you find yourself in a similar situation? Here are a few guiding rules:

- First and foremost, don't go beyond your data and exaggerate your claims. You lose credibility immediately when others find out.

- Communicate the sources of uncertainty and acknowledge the assumptions being made. You *build* your credibility through honest disclosures of this kind.

- Consciously reaffirm the set of ethics you are upholding here and those that may be tested. Should you be challenged, your rebuttal is already formulated.

Chapter Six takes up the issue of ethical framing in more specific terms. For now, understand that your framing is also a window into your ethics as a leader.

Can you identify a simplifying frame that you have used recently? Write it on the lines below.

_____

_____

_____

_____

_____

Identify one or more numbers that you must communicate and translate them into terms that might be easier for your targeted listeners to understand.

_____

_____

_____

_____

Gain and Loss Frames

Did you know that the subject of framing is a mainstay not just for social scientists who study social movements, but those who study decision making, conflict, and negotiation as well? The main reason for this is the popularity of the gain or loss frame. A gain frame *spins* or emphasizes the potential rewards of choosing one particular course of action, while a loss frame spins the disadvantages and the potential losses.

If you're in the business of risk management, no doubt you've heard about "prospect theory," developed by psychologists Amos Tversky and Daniel Kahneman. It explains how the same problem can be framed as either gains or losses to produce markedly different decision choices.[25] A number of studies have gone on to suggest that people tend to be more concerned about losing something than they are about gaining something.[26]

However, as communication scholar Laurie Lewis argues, most of this research involves controlled experiments.[27] Little or no relationship exists between the person framing a message and the audience, nor is one anticipated in the future. As a result, we know little about framing that actually combines gains and losses, which should be a common everyday occurrence in *arguments* about pros and cons. For example, when framing a message about the need for organizational change, senior leaders might speak of potential gains in market share *and* the avoidance of job loss or plant closure. Moreover, the effectiveness of this combined framing depends upon any number of factors related to the organization, the competitive environment in which they operate, the workforce or other stakeholders, and so on—all conditions that are difficult to replicate in a lab.

Interestingly, research also tells us very little about the art involved when leaders or other communicators creatively use the gain or loss frame. For example, consider Daniel P. Amos, chief executive of Aflac Insurance. In a recent interview, he was asked to identify the lessons he learned as a young manager. One of those lessons involved never explicitly giving his salespeople quotas, which all of them do indeed have. Instead he would tell them how much income he wanted them to accrue, such as "I want you to make $60,000." He said it worked best to give it to them in the form of a compensation number, "[because] they don't know how to argue when you say, 'I want you to make more money.'"[28] Of course, they're wise to his strategy, but it's an artful gain frame of "win-win" nonetheless.

Likewise, video game designer Will Wright leads a team of creative professionals who are much more likely to respond positively to "presenting things to them in such a way that, a year later, they are definitely going to be a better artist or a better programmer . . . . Even if you give them tough critical feedback, they see the benefit and value of it, as opposed to just a typical performance review."[29] Wright found that the gain frame was an "amazing amplifier" if he could find the things that they really like to do. Of course, the fear generated from a "loss frame" can be equally motivational, especially if a performance review makes clear that someone's job is on the line. However, the consequences of a consistent pattern of fear-based framing are rarely helpful to an organization's culture.

Can you identify a particular powerful gain frame that you've been exposed to in the past? How was it presented, and what made it so powerful?

_____

_____

_____

_____

_____

Now identify a particularly powerful loss frame that you've experienced. How was it presented, and what made it so powerful?

_____

_____

_____

_____

How do you use gain and loss frames? Do you favor one or the other? When do you use them in combination?

_____

_____

_____

_____

Believability Frames

The final category of frames that leaders consistently use is the believability frame.[30] With this type of frame, we position ourselves as truthful, objective, or legitimate. Unlike the earlier metaphorical, master, simplifying, and gain and loss frames, believability frames can hide in plain sight. We're often unaware of when we use them, and others tend to pay less attention to them unless our credibility is suspect.

Truth and Reality Frames A legendary newscaster in the early days of television, Walter Cronkite used to end every broadcast with the simple expression, "And *that's* the way it is." Such an expression is the quintessential example of a *truth and reality frame* where speakers explicitly claim that their framing of events represents the truth of "the situation here and now."[31] If you are thinking that truth and reality frames occur every time a declarative sentence is spoken, you are correct.

However, many of the most noticeable truth and reality frames explicitly emphasize their "fact-like" nature, or as the comedian Stephen Colbert likes to say, their "truthiness."[32] For example, consider today's brand of broadcasters and bloggers, who proffer a distinct political or religious philosophy. They often proclaim their version of the truth with an artful, evangelical zeal that spells "charisma" to some and "charlatan" to others. Histrionics notwithstanding, they do four things effectively:

- They conjugate the verb *to be*, using *is, are*, and *be* in key statements such as "If you don't support this proposal, management *is* in serious trouble."

- As mentioned, they frame their pronouncements in terms of facts, truth, or reality. Phrases such as, "The simple truth is . . . ," "The facts are . . . ," and "The situation here and now is . . . ." are typical.

- They avoid hedges ("This is kind of the way it is—I think,"), hesitation ("I, I'm, I am sure,"), and questioning intonations ("This is right?")

- They sound authoritative by using nonverbal emphasis and stress in key places for dramatic effect; for example, "I *know* why you came today," or "*Without question*, she's the best manager we have *ever* had."

Verbally and nonverbally then, they reinforce a "this is truth" message. However, as Chapter One indicated, framing any subject, including "the situation here and now," is an act of persuasion that can always be contested, power dynamics permitting.

Should your version of the facts strain credulity, your credibility is at risk as a leader. For example, one manager I know seriously risks his credibility by emphasizing the negative in every situation. Routinely claiming that the sky is falling teaches your team to read you that way and not recognize those instances when the sky really is about to fall.[33]

Objectivity Frames Recall Mark Twain's line, "There are three kinds of lies: lies, damned lies, and statistics!" Twain was given to such a sentiment because the use of numbers, statistics, charts, and graphs often communicate the appearance of objectivity, much as the cliché "the numbers don't lie" expresses.

In the *objectivity frame*, speakers make claims about themselves or their positions so as to appear neutral or unbiased.[34] If you think about it, such expressions are quite common, "In all fairness," "Objectively speaking," or "Look, I don't have a horse in this race, but . . . . " Whenever you assert your fairness, neutrality, independent judgment, or freedom from bias, you are using an objectivity frame.

Moreover, the same observation about truth and reality applies to objectivity: asserting your objectivity is a persuasive act. Such a claim can be contested. If you are found not to be objective, but biased or self-interested instead, your credibility as a leader takes a hit. By any measure, Walter Cronkite was a leader in his time—and it is interesting how his signature sign-off, "And *that's* the way it is" can also be read as an objectivity claim. Cronkite rarely shared his opinions publicly and was reportedly uncomfortable doing so. He once said, "I am a news presenter, a news broadcaster, an anchorman, a managing editor—not a commentator or analyst. . . . I feel no compulsion to be a pundit."[35] His objectivity claims were hugely successful. At one time, "Uncle Walter" was labeled "the most trusted man in America."

Legitimacy Frames Legitimacy frames attach importance to your arguments through appeals to principle or values, established practices, legitimate authority, or strong evidence.[36] Put simply, they rationalize a course of action by invoking another credible source. For example, in the Republican primaries leading up to the 2008 U.S. election, John McCain often told the *story* of a mother who requested that he wear a bracelet bearing the name of her son, who had been killed in the war in Iraq. McCain would explain,

> She said to me, "Senator McCain, I want you to make me one promise . . . and that is that you will do everything in your power to make sure my son's death was not in vain." I think you understand very clearly, as I do, that puts everybody's priorities and ambitions in the right perspective.[37]

This story not only has powerful emotional appeal (*feeling statement* and *argument*), but along with his POW background, McCain felt it legitimated him as the candidate best suited to deal with wars in two countries. He could also claim to speak for those American families whose members have made the ultimate sacrifice.

In the business world, leaders often rationalize a course of action by appealing to a corporate philosophy, established standards and practices, a collective identity, a management philosophy, or a personal code of honor. Of course, trouble often surfaces when there are competing legitimating sources, and it becomes difficult to assign a priority to one or another. When multiple claims to legitimacy must be negotiated, false claims are often revealed—which should be a word to the wise for those leaders likely to make them.

To recap, truth and reality, objectivity, and legitimacy framing can be more subtle approaches to framing than others reviewed in this chapter because they frame what we say as real, truthful, objective, or legitimate. For this reason, it is crucial that they be used responsibly, because they greatly impact your credibility as a leader should they be misused.

In the space below, write an example of a truth and reality frame that you have used recently.

_____

_____

_____

Write an example of an objectivity frame that you have used recently.

_____

_____

_____

Write an example of a legitimacy frame that you have used recently.

_____

_____

_____

The $1,000,000 Question: Combining Framing Devices

Leaders are generally articulate people, but they are often specifically igno-
rant of the context-shaping features of their language. Dominating alpha
leaders are testimony to this because they generally distrust words, considering themselves to be men or women of action instead. It is worth recalling
here how George W. Bush, perhaps the poster child for this category, came
to regret key remarks in his first term as president that may have actually
fueled the Iraq war. (Recall his being asked by a reporter in 2003 about the
rising attacks on U.S. troops in Iraq—two months after standing under a
banner reading "Mission Accomplished" on the USS *Abraham Lincoln* flight
deck—he said "My answer is, Bring them on.")[38] As Karl Weick has argued,
though, approximate and imprecise words will not do when nuance, understatement, and precision are required.[39]

Weick's key idea leads us to "the $1,000,000 question" (the ultimate chal-
lenge on the television game show, *Who Wants to Be a Millionaire?*). It seems
a fitting metaphor to address how leaders must learn to combine language
forms to master the art of framing to achieve eloquence.

As it turns out, the answer to the $1,000,000 question is both easy
and hard. The easy part is that it involves a simple threefold refrain: *trial,
error*, and *critical reflection*. Certainly, the hard part is that in trying and
failing, we risk looking foolish, unprepared, or inarticulate. Yet, in most
situations, that is a calculated risk worth taking because second chances
and do-overs are possible. You will do better with practice. But *critical
reflection* is also a key step on the path to eloquence. It involves conscious
attention to what language forms or frames *felt* right or wrong at a particular
moment based on the outcomes. Whether the reflection is immediate or
delayed, such conscious attention helps prime you for a better spontaneous
performance the next time around.

Critical reflection can be accomplished in a myriad of ways—asking
colleagues for some quick feedback on how well you did in a meeting or
interview; spending moments in a car, train, or airplane reflecting on lessons learned, for example, about specific words to use or avoid; stockpiling

metaphors and creating a file of great stories to use in future communications; networking with people who can be communication resources for you; or working directly with an executive coach, to name just a few.

If you are among the large group of leaders out there who do not believe that they have time to reflect, this is certainly understandable given today's fast pace of change and ever-mounting workloads. However, as demonstrated in the Strategic style, to the extent that attention to framing aesthetics produces more persuasive framing and room to maneuver, not even the most overworked leader can afford to ignore these lessons.

A Backward Glance at Chapter Four

This chapter began by considering framing as an art and a craft that, like any other, requires time, effort, and a healthy dose of critical reflection. Such reflection is necessary to understand how language functions to produce framing eloquence.

- A variety of language forms make framing interesting:
  - *Metaphorical language* portrays a subject's resemblance to something else that is not literally applicable.
  - *Story* frames a subject through narrative.
  - *Contrast* describes a subject in terms of what it is not.
  - *Spin* places a subject in a positive or negative light.
  - *Jargon or catchphrases* frame a subject in familiar terms.
  - *Analogy* frames a subject's parallels to another subject.
  - *Argument* frames a subject in reasoned, rational terms.
  - *Feeling statements* frame a subject in terms of felt emotions.
  - *Categories* frame a subject in terms of its membership (or not) in a category and of category limits.
  - *Three-part lists* organize a subject in easily remembered "threes."
  - *Repetition* dramatizes a subject through parallel form.

- These language forms surface in the frames leaders commonly use, five of which were reviewed in this chapter:

    - *Metaphorical frames* use metaphorical language and stories. They can involve a simple comparison or a more complex arrangement of parallel elements often captured in narrative or story form. Metaphorical frames involving a surprising comparison work best.

    - A *master frame* is an organizing frame that is broad in scope and from which other, more specific frames emerge. It synthesizes ideological elements into more simplified ideas and calls to action.

    - *Simplifying frames* reduce the chaos or complexity of the moment. For example, when communicating numbers, translate them into terms more understandable to an audience.

    - *Gain and loss frames* emphasize the potential advantages and disadvantages of a particular course of action, respectively. However, they can also be used in combination to create strategic value.

    - *Believability frames* often hide in plain sight, but they are crucial to leader credibility. Leaders use them to frame themselves (or their message) as truthful, objective, or legitimate.

- Combining these frames is the real challenge in any framing encounter, but through trial, error, and critical reflection, we can develop greater sensitivity to language use.

A FINAL THOUGHT
Eloquence creates impact.

5

The Emotion of Framing

I **HAVE A GUILTY PLEASURE** I must confess to. I am a huge fan of the television show *The Office*, an American spin-off of Ricky Gervais's British version. The latter has become such a runaway success that there are several international versions of *The Office*, and I think I know why.[1] Before I get to that, though, a little background is necessary for the uninitiated. The show is set in Scranton, Pennsylvania, at a regional office of "Dunder-Mifflin," a declining paper company struggling to compete with the big paper suppliers of our day.

This fictional office is occupied by "Michael," a cringe-worthy boss; "Dwight," an authority-obsessed salesman; "Jim," a likable everyman; and "Pam," the erstwhile receptionist turned salesperson who, along with Jim, copes with Dwight through humor and pranking. There are also a host of richly drawn supporting characters, but the uniqueness of this situation comedy is that it appears to be shot documentary style. The actors interact not only with one another but with the camera, allowing us to peer directly into the emotional worlds of their characters' lives.

For many years, emotions were a veiled aspect of organizational life. The people who ran organizations and the people who studied and wrote about them liked to pretend that emotions didn't exist.[2] But they were always present—and I think that's the real reason why *The Office* has been such an international success. Audiences powerfully identify with the emotions wrought by organizational life in this show. We identify with characters who are, at times, *bored* with the office routine, *ambivalent* about career choices, forced to tolerate *annoying* coworkers, *conflicted* when they compete and cooperate with each other simultaneously, *happy* in stolen moments of office hijinks, *raging mad* at perceived injustices, witnesses to jokes both *cruel* and *amusing*, and swept away by *love*.

Emotions are the subject of this chapter, for good reason. They are an important and overlooked aspect of leadership communications because, all too often, leadership is cast in overly rational terms. To wit, a good leader supposedly sets feelings aside to "objectively" choose the right course of action. Today, we know that this is a distorted view of human decision making. As the mounting evidence on emotional intelligence shows, feelings play a central role in memory recall, reasoning processes, creativity, and decision making.[3] They help us to weigh our options, make choices, and act wisely in the moment. While it is true that intense emotions can interfere with our ability to make decisions, the work on emotional intelligence tells us that the dearth of emotion may be equally harmful.[4]

Emotional Intelligence and Framing

Generally speaking, *emotional intelligence* involves the ability to join emotion and reason effectively. Psychologists Mayer and Salovey describe it as "the ability to perceive emotions, to access and generate emotions so as to assist thought, to understand emotions and emotional knowledge, and to reflectively regulate emotions so as to promote emotional and intellectual growth."[5] If both reason *and* emotion are among the defining qualities of the human experience, then any discussion of framing must proceed accordingly. But how does one capture such a complex relationship in relation to framing?

Perhaps an example will help. Consider a midlevel workforce restructuring manager I'll call "Tom," who came to his position after witnessing a very harsh initial downsizing of a one-time cold war manufacturing site, which was moving into multiyear environmental remediation in preparation for eventual site closure.[6] Tom had to deal with a large number of "legacy workers," people who had expected to spend their careers at the site (as generations had done before them), but were now being required to leave it. Tom was credited by the U.S. Department of Energy (hereafter, DOE) with arriving at a more humane downsizing program (a "velvet boot") that productively managed the tension between company and employee interests.

However, Tom's velvet boot was actually the site's third downsizing. It was a second downsizing at the site that had been a turning point for him. In advance of it, Tom scheduled information sessions for fifty or so legacy workers at a time so they could learn about their separation options. Here is what he said about those trying times when I interviewed him:

Gail: Were you charged with workforce transition at that time?

Tom: Not officially. It was still one of those quasi-portfolio assignments at that time, but I stepped up to the plate, I guess, is the best way to put it. And my manager at that time later acknowledged the fact. Finally, somebody had to stand up. And one of the things they complimented me on was the fact that when there's people actually targeted to be part of that reduction process, none of the [invited] senior leadership people ever showed up to [employee] meetings. And my manager was just irate about the fact that they sent me to the slaughter, and none of them bothered to show up to offer any support.

Gail: And were you "slaughtered"?

Tom: No . . . . Was I nervous? Absolutely, because these were people who worked at this facility, some of them for twenty-eight years, who were literally within hundreds of days of retirement—full retirement—who had just been told either voluntarily leave the facility or we're going to fire you or lay you off. We had people who had sick children in the hospital, who had wives who were sick, who had husbands who had lost their jobs. It was a very threatening time. And I wouldn't be lying to you if I told you that probably was the most gut-wrenching time of my entire life . . . . I got the stories. I got the heartache from the employees, and it was tough to look at those people . . . . Somebody had to look at them and talk to them openly and honestly and say, "This is not your fault. It's not something you did; it's not something you said." And I went home . . . with my guts in knots with the dry heaves and the whole works . . . . But that was a life-changing moment for me. Those four or five days we met with people I decided we have got to approach this [downsizing] from a better, faster, cheaper, smarter, kinder, gentler, more moral way of doing things.[7]

In this day and age, downsizings are routine; however, they are no less painful for workers unaccustomed to the uncertainty. It is not an exaggeration to say that in each employee meeting, Tom faced angry, even hostile workers. However, Tom had the verbal skills of a Strategic in the Message Design Logic terms of Chapter One. Interestingly, he was a hog farmer in his off-hours and often told humorous stories of farm life to get his message across at work. More than once, he had been told that he was "the world's greatest schmoozer." Tom would say that he just loved people—meaning talking to them. (At one time, an administrative assistant answered the calls of some twenty faculty members in my department. I could always tell when Tom was calling because our assistant was cheerful and laughing within seconds of answering his call.) He was also known for a disarming use of "I'm just an ol' country boy" disclaimers, followed by incisive analyses. Tom fit the bill for a Strategic for sure. Using Tom as an example of an emotionally intelligent Strategic leader, several framing lessons emerge:

- Recognize a framing opportunity when emotions run strong.

- Prioritize listening amid the framing.

- Handle toxic emotions as an exercise in framing.

- Take the time to reflect, heed your emotions and reason, and do— say—the right thing.

Framing Opportunity in Strong Emotions

Recognize a framing opportunity when emotions run strong. Chapter One began with the notion that leaders often cannot control events, but they can control the context under which events are seen if they recognize a framing opportunity (Reality Construction Rule #1). Tom recognized a framing opportunity created by the downsizing and scheduled face-to-face meetings with fifty employees at a time. He recognized their need for information during a period of great uncertainty and the company's need to actively manage the message of the downsizing.

As mentioned, he asked for a vice president to accompany him to each meeting; regrettably, none ever showed. Several of his counterparts at other DOE facilities were actually shocked that he would go into those meetings alone; they saw a potential for escalating conflict, if not real threat. Tom knew that he would be challenged in these meetings. If anything, he under-estimated the emotional response that he would have to them.

Prioritize Listening

Prioritize listening amid the framing. An important factor in Tom's success is that his mental model for this meeting wasn't that of a monologue but a dialogue. Tom had information to share, to be sure, but it was best communicated in a format that would meet the specific needs of the legacy workers, which meant questions and answers and the opportunity for give-and-take. Listening through dialogue was thus crucial to employees' feeling they had been heard. The listening could not be perfunctory; it had to be a full-on commitment to hear their stories. On this subject, dialogue expert Bill Isaacs reveals the keen insight of a manager in a program that he was leading. "You know," said the manager, "I have always prepared myself to speak. But I have never prepared myself to listen."[8] Truer words were never spoken by the vast majority of the managers that I have studied and with whom I've worked. But Tom bucked this trend, and he did listen. As he said, "I got the stories. I got the heartache from the employees, and it was tough to look at those people."

Face Up to Toxic Emotions

Handle toxic emotions as an exercise in framing. When Tom spoke of "stepping up to the plate," he became what the late management scholar Peter Frost called a "toxin handler": one of the leaders who, "more than others, assume the pain in their organizations for the benefit of everyone—essentially handling all the company's emotional 'toxicity.' . . . "[9] Such a description perfectly captures Tom, who didn't back away from the toxicity of employees' anger, hostility, and fear. Instead, he listened to the employees, absorbed what they were saying, and affirmed the feelings of fear and anxiety behind the anger they showed.

Unlike the vice presidents, Tom felt a moral responsibility to communicate directly with the legacy workers. As he said, "Somebody had to look at them and talk to them openly and honestly and say this is not your fault. It's not something you did; it's not something you said." This is a great example of the ways we can use framing to morally justify our actions. Chapter Six discusses this in terms of "moral positioning," but suffice it to say here that Tom wasn't afraid of "morality talk." It was the right thing to do. It came from an authentic place within him, and it gave him the credibility he needed to manage those meetings effectively.

Reflect and Heed Both Emotions and Reason

Take the time to reflect, heed your emotions and reason, and do—say—the right thing. There is no question that Tom's meetings with employees were personally painful to him. As he said, he went home with his "guts in knots with the dry heaves and the whole works." However, for emotionally intelligent leaders like Tom, personal feelings become data that can improve decision making. As suggested at the start of this chapter, the work on emotional intelligence shows that feelings inform our decision making, helping us weigh options and make the right choices.

The impact of emotions is magnified when an intense emotional experience becomes a crucible, another Chapter Six concept that involves transformative experience. Tom describes his crucible when he says: "But that was a life-changing moment for me. Those four or five days we met with people I decided we have got to approach this [downsizing] from a better, faster, cheaper, smarter, kinder, gentler, more moral way of doing things."

Although it is difficult to convey in writing, Tom's framing of his crucible was utterly persuasive, spoken with the moral authority of one who was on a mission to correct unnecessary suffering due to job loss. It is important to note here that he was neither attempting to prevent reductions in the workforce nor favor employees over management. He was looking for a more humane way to downsize and hold the bottom line steady at the same time. That's the mark of an emotionally intelligent leader forced to downsize. It also shows the presence of a clear, focused mental model in which the framing to follow would be "both-and," not "either-or."

And Tom did just that with a "velvet boot" plan called "managed attrition," in which those in decreasing job classifications only (not just anyone wishing to leave), as determined through official manpower planning estimates, were given up to two years' notice of their separation. For this group, separation benefits for education or retraining did not commence upon departure; they could be used any time during that two-year window.[10] In other interviews, I learned that Tom's velvet boot and the framing of his crucible (much like the one Tom gave in my interview with him) galvanized Tom's staff, his boss, and his company's president. It also galvanized the DOE, which sent Tom on a tour of its other sites to speak to local officials, and, in an unusual move, to his counterparts from other contracting firms.

In summary, Tom's case demonstrates a strong relationship between emotional intelligence and framing, which is reflected in the following four rules:

- Emotionally intelligent leaders recognize a framing opportunity when emotions run strong. They often discover framing opportunities that others seek to avoid.

- Emotionally intelligent leaders prioritize listening amid the framing, especially when dialogue is key. Quality framing that is more adaptive to the target pays dividends.

- Emotionally intelligent leaders treat toxic emotions as an exercise in framing and an opportunity to productively manage them.

- Emotionally intelligent leaders reflect and treat their own emotions as data, joining reason and emotion to facilitate the right kind of decision making and framing for the benefit of those involved.

Answer the following questions, reflecting on your level of emotional intelligence. Circle the answer that best reflects what you do.

When emotions run strong in my organization, I generally try to address them.

Always   Usually   Rarely

I try very hard to listen to my people, especially when I can see they are emotional.

Always   Usually   Rarely

I try to productively manage negative emotions when they surface in my unit.

Always   Usually   Rarely

I make decisions based on both reason and my emotions.

Always   Usually   Rarely

When it comes to dealing with the emotions of people in your unit or organization, what is the most difficult problem that you face?

_____

_____

_____

_____

_____

What resources are available to you that might help you address this problem?

☐ Books on emotional intelligence

☐ Talks with a mentor or more senior leader

☐ Time by myself for critical reflection

☐ Training or executive coaching

☐ Other?

_____

☐ Other?

_____

Emotional Contagion and Framing

Despite Tom's best efforts, the accumulating force of one painful story after another stoked the fire of toxic emotions at the employee meetings. Organizational scientists would label this a case of "emotional contagion," an academic-sounding term better thought of as _contagious emotions_. We actually have certain English language expressions to suggest this, such as "that enthusiasm is infectious," and "the bad apple poisons the barrel."

Yale University's Sigal Barsade says that when we enter a group we are inevitably exposed to the emotions on display, and these emotions can be characterized in terms of _valence_ (positive or negative) and the _energy level_ of the emotions expressed.[11] In the current example, Tom became a toxin handler of negative emotions with high energy levels, given employees' manifest anger and hostility. We could compare this with low-intensity emotions like depression.

As it turns out, the energy levels of emotions help drive emotional contagion (also sometimes known as mood contagion) in which a person's or group's emotions and energy levels influence others, consciously or unconsciously, to adopt such a mood.[12] This is a common human experience—beyond downsizings, when you think about it. We all know what it's like to be in the presence of positive and upbeat people; they make us feel good. Likewise, others who are "real downers," as the slang suggests, have the opposite effect; they tend to bring us down with them.

Again from the frontiers of brain science, we are learning a lot about emotional contagion and its implications for the ways we communicate. There are some rather obvious things like the fact that emotional contagion is influenced by how much attention we pay to the situation at hand (and thus our receptivity to emotional cues) and that certain emotional expressions are more arresting than others. (Scream "Fire!" and you've got my attention.)[13]

However, what is not so obvious is the work that is being done on *mimicry*, or the automatic, subconscious ways in which we mirror the behavior of those around us.[14] We routinely mimic others' facial expressions, body language, speech patterns, and vocal tones in social interaction, and *only sometimes are we aware of it*.[15] The fact that mimicry effects have been found in newborns suggests that humans have an innate tendency to mimic.[16] This certainly explains our inclination to yawn after someone else in our presence does. And it explains why the pop star Madonna, from Detroit, Michigan, suddenly adopted an English accent when she married a Brit and moved to England.

Remarkably, mimicry of another's vocal, facial, and postural cues helps us feel the emotions the mimicked person is experiencing. As neuroscientist Marc Iacoboni explains in *The New Science of How We Connect with Others: Mirroring People*, "Mimicking others is not just a form of communicating nonverbally; it helps us to perceive others' expressions (and therefore their emotions) in the first place."[17] Counterintuitive as it may seem, mimicry *precedes* and aids in the recognition of emotion.

How so? As it turns out, there are "mirror neurons" in the human brain that copy the expression and emotion of others. They can recreate in us a screen actor's *panic* in a horror movie, the *sadness* of a breakup in a romantic tear-jerker, or the *delight* of a surprise twist in a comedy. As Iacoboni says, "We have empathy for the fictional characters—we know how they're feeling—because we literally experience the same feelings ourselves."[18] It makes sense then that our ability to imitate is also related to our ability to empathize.[19]

But what does mimicry have to do with framing? Well, *first, it puts our verbal and nonverbal communications into perspective*. In a frequently cited 1972 study of emotional communications, Mehrabian reported that only 7 percent of participants' emotional understanding of others came from the words spoken.[20] By contrast, 38 percent and 55 percent were attributed to verbal tone and facial expression, respectively. If true (and I am aware of no study that contradicts this one), we should not overestimate the power of language. The impact of framing comes just as much from both conscious and unconscious nonverbal cues that we convey. Consider also that when a verbally framed message contradicts a nonverbal message, listeners routinely believe the latter because it is assumed that people have less control over the nonverbals, political candidates and actors notwithstanding.

Second, because mimicry often operates unconsciously and automatically, people may not be aware of the emotional contagion to which they have been subject or how it works.[21] Certainly, there's a message here for leaders: realize that emotional contagion exists; that it can energize or poison team dynamics and decision making; and that framing opportunities become apparent with such awareness.[22] However, this is not always so easy. The late Andy Pearson, CEO of PepsiCo, had a self-described style of "unmitigated toughness," what others saw as "brutally abrasive . . . relentless . . . interrogation in meetings."[23] Pearson relays such an incident:

> I remember bringing one of our market-research women to tears because I told her that the information she was gathering wasn't producing anything. I could just see the breath come out of her. I realized that in today's world . . . that kind of treatment demoralizes people. I don't think that woman was ever the same.[24]

Even though Pearson "could just see the breath come out" of this woman, the emotional milieu wasn't important enough to him at the time (an enduring characteristic of many alpha leaders) to do anything about it. Nor was he attuned to the dispiriting contagion he likely triggered when the market researcher returned to her team.[25] What was it like to work with this woman? What did her people or coworkers unconsciously mirror?

Clearly, you need to be an emotionally intelligent leader to be wise to the possible emotional contagion of this moment. You must take a deep breath and steady yourself, separate the learnings from the dysfunction of the confrontation, and self-consciously regulate your emotions to prevent passing the toxicity of this encounter on to your people. In short, you must become the target of your own framing.

While the focus of this book has been on our framing communications with other people, common sense tells us that much of what we "talk ourselves into" involves a lot of framing—and never more than in the case of emotional intelligence. Often the emotions that we communicate are not those we initially experience, because we frame them to ourselves as "too reactionary" or "unhelpful" for the situation at hand. The emotionally intelligent leader has a lot of inner conversations that begin, "On second thought . . . ."

Third, *because attention is a prerequisite to mimicry, high-energy framing (that attracts attention) is instrumental to emotional contagion.* As noted, receptivity to the emotional cues of others requires attention—and certain emotional expressions can direct that attention. Those expressions are usually *high-energy*—as defined by voice volume, voice variation, vocal pitch level and range, facial and hand gestures, and posture.[26] Apple's Steve Jobs and management guru Tom Peters are two great examples of high-energy leaders; Peters has an almost evangelical delivery style.

Communicators with a real presence rely as much on strong nonverbals as on words in framing their message, if not more. You can see this even more clearly if you have ever communicated with someone with what is clinically called "flat affect." These individuals communicate primarily through verbal means. We can read little in their nonverbal behavior to support what they are saying and are often confused as to their true feelings. Beginning public speakers often fall prey to this criticism. They speak in a monotone, read their speeches, and "white-knuckle" the podium, thus minimizing gestures or movement.

The research on emotional contagion shows that, generally speaking, people who express their emotions more forcefully or expressively attract more attention and hold it for longer periods.[27] The more one's attention is held, the sharper the clarity and accuracy of the emotional message received, thus paving the way for a contagious transfer of such emotion. Barsade's research shows this to be true for both positive and negatively valenced emotions, although he originally thought that negative emotions would demonstrate this effect most profoundly.[28]

What is the message here? Throw your body *and* heart into framing. Avoid speaking in monotones and vary your voice. Direct your eye contact, gesture for emphasis and stress, and use facial expressions appropriate to the emotions you wish to communicate. When high-energy framing is combined with rich metaphors, stories, and other aesthetically appealing language, the conditions are right for emotionally resonant framing.

Fourth, *framing in the service of authentically positive emotions increases positive emotional contagion through mimicry.* While the benefits of the power of positive thinking related to self-esteem have been known for some time, research by Jennifer George and her colleagues has demonstrated that feeling positive affect motivates people to go beyond their job description, increases the helpfulness and cooperativeness they show, and promotes positive thoughts about the organization.[29]

The veterinary hospital owner profiled in Chapter Three (for priming the hospital's mission statement with his staff) took over a management role from a previous owner whose style was not unlike the one Andy Pearson used at PepsiCo. He regularly berated employees, and he didn't care who was present. Turnover was a chronic problem for the hospital; employees stayed only until they could find something better.

The new owner took a different tack and directed his energy first toward simple, small, and subtle changes, such as greeting each employee with "Good morning" and saying "Thank you" at the end of the day. He asked and listened to their opinions on matters about which they were knowledgeable. He also didn't hover over them, instead treating them like adults who could make responsible decisions in line with the mission and values of the organization.

The second major change he undertook was to get his employees health insurance and profit sharing for the first time, actions that reinforced the everyday signs of respect. As a result of *both* sets of actions, the culture of the animal hospital changed radically. Note that mirror neurons get triggered far more frequently in everyday signs of respect than in the big things like insurance and profit sharing that, while crucial to "walking the talk," likely have a more fleeting effect. Yet "walking the talk" is crucial to employees' feelings about the everyday signs of respect as *authentic* or *genuine*, not an attempt to manipulate. Unless both are in place, positive mood contagion is likely stymied.

Today, turnover at the animal hospital is no longer a problem because the individuals who work there have begun to see themselves as career employees. This veterinarian understood that his rise to owner and manager was like throwing a rock into a pond. Though other factors also have an impact, he is a prime source of the everyday emotions and moods that ripple out to his charges, both human and animal.

To recap, there is a strong relationship between framing and emotional contagion, a relationship scripted by the human tendency toward mimicry and the mirror neurons in the brain. As a result of this relationship, the following points are clear:

- The presence of mirror neurons in the brain puts verbal and nonverbal communications into perspective; framing is not achieved by verbal means alone, especially in more emotionally charged messages.

- Because mimicry often operates unconsciously and automatically, people may not be aware of the emotional contagion to which they have been subject or how it works. Emotionally intelligent leaders will likely be more sensitive to these dynamics than others less emotionally attuned.

- Because attention is a prerequisite to mimicry, high-energy framing is instrumental to emotional contagion. High energy takes shape in vocal emphasis and stress, voice volume and pitch, facial expressions, gestures, and posture.

- Framing in the service of authentically positive emotions increases positive emotional contagion through mimicry. The combined effect of "talking the walk" and "walking the talk" has never been more important.

Can you remember the last time you observed emotional contagion in your work unit or organization? What were the circumstances?

_____

_____

_____

_____

Do you try to promote positive emotional contagion in any way? Explain how you "walk the talk" and "talk the walk."

_____

_____

_____

Emotional Regulation and Framing

Hillary Clinton, the U.S. Secretary of State, toured Africa in 2009. She reportedly had a grueling schedule of official meetings and private events in seven countries over eleven days. At one gathering in Kinshasa, Congo, in which the press was invited, a male Congolese university student posed a question to her about a multibillion-dollar Chinese loan offer to Congo.[30] The exchange went as follows:

> Student: (Through the voice of an interpreter.) Thank you. Mrs. Clinton. We've all heard about the Chinese contracts in this country. The interference is from the World Bank against this contract. What does Mr. Clinton think, through the mouth of Mrs. Clinton, and what does Mr. Mutombo think on this situation? Thank you very much.

> Sec. Clinton: (She looks displeased and pauses for a moment, removing the translation device from her ears.) Wait, you want me to tell you what my husband thinks? My husband is not Secretary of State, I am. (She fixes her gaze on the student and gestures as if to emphasize this distinction.) So you ask my opinion, I will tell you my opinion. I am not going to be channeling my husband!

This is an interesting display of emotion by a political leader used to tightly regulating her emotion on an international stage. Most secretaries of state conform to the strict protocol of the diplomatic corps. They choose their language carefully and try not to offend because they mediate international conflicts and the strong, culturally rooted emotions attached to them. Unguarded moments for these leaders are rare, so this is an interesting case of emotional regulation to consider.

You may recall that *emotional regulation* is part of the definition of emotional intelligence because it involves the management of one's own emotions. It includes being open to a wide range of feelings and emotions, both positive and negative, and being able to reflexively monitor them, step back or engage them, and manage the emotions of others.[31] As the two prior discussions in this chapter focused on the management of others' emotions, this discussion will emphasize how one controls one's own emotions.

In this example, Secretary Clinton showed disbelief, anger, and indignation with all of the appropriate nonverbal displays to reinforce this message. She did not apologize afterward, but her aides intimated that the sharpness of her remark to the student stemmed, in part, from exhaustion and her frustration with the Congo's seemingly endless cycles of rape, genocide, and other atrocities directed toward women. (News accounts also suggested that earlier in the day she heard stories of the gang rape of women.) In effect, her aides tried to excuse her behavior.

Interestingly, a U.S. State Department representative later justified it, saying that, "It's important to understand the context here . . . an abiding theme that she has in her trip to Africa is empowering women. As the question was posed to her, it was posed in a way that said: I want to get the views of two men, but not you, the secretary of state."[32] For his part, the French-speaking student later said he had meant to say President Barack Obama.[33]

As leadership scholar Jennifer George suggests, leaders are human beings "with the full range of moods and emotions potentially available to them" even under the most controlling of circumstances.[34] Less fatigued, Clinton might have tempered her remarks; we simply do not know. However, she could control the official spin *after* the event. Given the response of the State Department and her own subsequent silence on the matter, she chose to let the record stand. By doing so, she underscored her demand for respect as a leader on her own terms, neither as somebody's wife nor as a subordinate lacking authority.

If Secretary Clinton managed an honest display of anger effectively in this situation, others would caution her against repeating such episodes. For example, when Xerox CEO Anne M. Mulcahy turned over the reins to Ursula Burns, her advice to her was to consistently hide her emotions. As Burns said, "On my face, you could tell everything in 30 seconds. You could tell exasperation. You could tell fed-up-ness. She [Mulcahy] said, 'You have to develop more of a poker face because people will watch you for everything.'"[35]

Perhaps Mulcahy knows about mirror neurons, but it is interesting that Burns did not accept all of the leadership advice she received from Mulcahy (and others) in this regard. Burns was also told to never let employees see her sweat. Her response to that was, "Oh, my God! I think that they have to see you sweat. I cannot be viewed as the solution to all problems in this company."[36]

There is evidence that Apple CEO Steve Jobs agrees with Burns. Jobs's legendary temper has been given its own name by workers at the company's Cupertino headquarters. "Being Steved" means that you have been at the business end of one of his tirades. Technology analyst Rob Enderle notes, "He uses fear more effectively than any CEO I've ever seen."[37] Yet, like any message, the moods and emotions that constitute effective leadership may well be contested. Jobs gets results, which is the gold standard for a technology analyst. The Apple employees to whom Jobs directs his anger, however, may not respond as favorably.

When it comes to managing your own emotions, the context will always determine what is appropriate and what is not in terms of the self-control you show. For this reason, heightening your sensitivity to the context is key, which is the subject of Chapter Seven. You may also recall from our discussion of Message Design Logic in Chapter One that Strategics have such context sensitivity. However, from a framing perspective, two other key ideas can help you manage your emotions: priming and reframing.

As discussed in Chapter Three, *priming for spontaneity* involves the conscious recall or rehearsal of some content before it is necessary to communicate spontaneously and automatically about it. The key here is that conscious recall leaves an unconscious imprint, so you can prime your mental models for specific language and for opportunity. But why not prime for emotion as well? Emotions can pose a special challenge because our mirror neurons will likely be sensitive to the unexpected emotional displays of others. However, thinking ahead of time of how best you can hold it together often lays a foundation for doing just that when the situation presents itself. You can do this by imagining a range of emotional responses and how you'd like to respond.

It is conceivable that Xerox CEO Ursula Burns does just that as she envisions her daily or weekly work schedules and the desired outcomes of the meetings she attends. There may be certain meetings, such as those involving the media or other outside stakeholders, in which she takes care to not tip her hand. A primed poker face is eminently doable with just a few moments of reflection in anticipation of these meetings.

Likewise, Tom, the workforce restructuring manager from one of the chapter's earlier examples, can and should prepare himself for the range of emotions that downsized employees might display: shock and relief, frustration and uncertainty, anger and resentment. He can prime himself for a more emotionally intelligent response by posing some key questions to himself before these meetings, such as, "How will I respond if employees appear mostly shocked and saddened?" "How can I best affirm their frustration?" "What should I say if they direct their vitriol to me, personally, not just to the company?" "Are there ways to preempt an angry show of hostility?" "If not, what are some possible containment strategies?" and "How do I want these meetings to end, and what's my message here?" Again, conscious recall some time prior to the meetings leaves an unconscious imprint to draw upon as they transpire. Events such as these are never totally predictable, but priming can give you a sense that you have prepared yourself for the unexpected.

The second framing concept that allows you to exert some control over your own emotions is the concept of *reframing*, which is simply the do-over. Note that in Secretary Clinton's example, there were three reframings. Her staff first tried to excuse her angry response. The State Department then justified it, and Clinton herself let her subsequent silence reaffirm her message about the legitimacy of her office. Few situations in organizational life are not amenable to reframing if you are inclined to create such opportunities for yourself.

Does Apple CEO Steve Jobs apologize to those subject to "being Steved"? Maybe not, but you can apologize for an emotional tirade if you think it is in order. You can clarify your feelings if you feel they have been misunderstood. You can reinforce a strong emotional message with a follow-up. You can explain a decision with the insight that comes from reflection and review of having made it. These situations are reframing opportunities that benefit from the wisdom of hindsight, and they should not be underestimated because all the framing principles still apply.

In summary, when it comes to emotional regulation, priming for spontaneity allows you to exert some control over your emotions in advance of their display. Reframing allows you to recast your view of "the situation here and now" in emotional terms more to your liking.

FRAMING TOOL 5.1

Critical Incident Framing

Recall the critical incident that you identified in earlier chapters, or use another one involving your leadership that you would like to analyze. Remember the focus should be on your communications as a leader with your employees, customers, or other stakeholders. Also, select an incident in which you were unhappy with the outcome.

_____

_____

_____

_____

_____

Did emotional contagion play a role in any way? Was it positive or negative? Describe the framing involved.

_____

_____

_____

_____

_____

How would you describe the level of emotional intelligence you brought to the management of this situation? What did your framing look like?

_____

_____

_____

_____

_____

What could you do differently the next time around?

_____

_____

_____

_____

(You can download this form from www.josseybass.com/go/gailfairhurst.)

A Backward Glance at Chapter Five

Leading others is often challenging and fraught with emotion. Our level of emotional intelligence is likely to be the best predictor of our framing communications in this regard. More specifically,

- Emotionally intelligent leaders see a framing opportunity when emotions run strong. They prioritize listening and, where possible, dialogue with employees or other stakeholders.

- Emotionally intelligent leaders treat toxic emotions as an opportunity to productively manage them through framing. They also treat their own emotions as data, joining reason and emotion to facilitate an effective response.

- Emotionally intelligent leaders also understand emotional contagion, the process by which moods and emotions are communicated to others. Framing is not achieved by verbal means alone, especially in emotionally charged messages.

- Humans have a tendency to mimic the expressions and emotions of others, although they may be unaware of these effects. Emotionally intelligent leaders sensitize themselves to these dynamics because high-energy framing is instrumental to emotional contagion, and the framing of authentically positive emotions increases positive emotional contagion.

- Emotional regulation is a part of emotional intelligence, and two framing concepts play a role in this regard. Priming for spontaneity can assist in controlling one's emotions in advance of a situation if one envisions a wide range of responses likely to occur. Also, framing after the fact, or reframing, allows leaders to correct the emotionally charged messages they wish to modify.

A FINAL THOUGHT

Framing requires emotional intelligence, the ability to join reason and emotion.

6

The Ethics of Framing

ETHICS IS THE STUDY of morality, or how we harm or assist others based on what we do and say.[1] Because our ethical choices so readily display themselves in our framing and actions, these choices are an open window into our leadership. Among other things, this window reveals how we morally position ourselves and others in "the situation here and now" as well as the ethical ideals for which we strive.

According to ethicists James Anderson and Elaine Englehardt, the study of our ethical choices "starts in our obligation toward one another and ends in the careful analysis of our action."[2] Such a statement concisely captures the ground that this chapter covers: our obligation to do no harm and careful analysis of our framing in this regard. It begins with a discussion of ethical codes and why they are so necessary.

Ethical Codes and Why We Need Them

Talk of ethics is quite fashionable these days as wave after wave of ethical lapses dominate the news: Ponzi schemes by the former head of NASDAQ; moral outrage over bank bailouts and executive bonuses, banks that, in turn, halted lending to many small business and individual home owners; pay-to-play politics raised to new levels by a sitting governor of Illinois who tried to sell Barack Obama's senate seat to the highest bidder; sexual peccadilloes involving governors, senators, and presidential candidates; and the enduring legacy of cultures of greed at Enron, WorldCom, and Tyco—to name just a few of the many intent on maximizing their own return to the neglect of other stakeholders.[3]

In an attempt to stave off these kinds of lapses, several organizations and professions adopt *ethical codes*, which are guides to everyday professional behavior often found in mission statements or corporate philosophies. It is unfortunate that they seem to have become mere niceties in this day and age, perfunctory exercises at best, instead of a major resource for framing communications.

How exactly do ethical codes work as a framing resource? Consider an example from my world. As an organizational communication educator and researcher, I belong to several communication professional organizations, including the National Communication Association (NCA)—the largest national organization dedicated to communication. It is made up of researchers, educators, and professionals working to understand and improve all forms of human communication. Through publications, resources, conferences, conventions, and services, NCA contributes to the greater good of education and society. Its ethical code, shown in Exhibit 6.1, admirably testifies to its organizational ideals.[4]

Exhibit 6.1.   NCA Credo for Ethical Communication

Questions of right and wrong arise whenever people communicate. Ethical communication is fundamental to responsible thinking, decision making, and the development of relationships and communities within and across contexts, cultures, channels, and media. Moreover, ethical communication enhances human worth and dignity by fostering truthfulness, fairness, responsibility, personal integrity, and respect for self and others. We believe that unethical communication threatens the quality of all communication and consequently the well-being of individuals and the society in which we live. Therefore we, the members of the National Communication Association, endorse and are committed to practicing the following principles of ethical communication:

We advocate truthfulness, accuracy, honesty, and reason as essential to the integrity of communication.

We endorse freedom of expression, diversity of perspective, and tolerance of dissent to achieve the informed and responsible decision making fundamental to a civil society.

We strive to understand and respect other communicators before evaluating and responding to their messages.

We promote access to communication resources and opportunities as necessary to fulfill human potential and contribute to the well-being of families, communities, and society.

We promote communication climates of caring and mutual understanding that respect the unique needs and characteristics of individual communicators.

We condemn communication that degrades individuals and humanity through distortion, intimidation, coercion, and violence, and through the expression of intolerance and hatred.

We are committed to the courageous expression of personal convictions in pursuit of fairness and justice.

We advocate sharing information, opinions, and feelings when facing significant choices while also respecting privacy and confidentiality.

We accept responsibility for the short- and long-term consequences for our own communication and expect the same of others.

Source: www.natcom.org/index.asp?bid=514; access date: May 23, 2010. Emphasis added.

What is important to understand about ethical codes is that they do more than embody a set of ideals, values, and commitments that help people decide on a course of action. They also supply the language for them—and that helps people who subscribe to them justify a course of action and frame a morally responsible identity for themselves when they communicate. In Chapter Two's terms, an ethical code is a cultural Discourse with its own linguistic tool bag.

For example, I teach leadership communications courses to undergraduate and graduate students, and as I have done in this book, I often critique the political and corporate leaders of the day. Regarding politics, I am careful *not* to identify my political affiliation as a Democrat, or Republican, the two major political parties that dominate U.S. politics. I always tell my students at the start of the term that it's not for me to determine who they should vote for; that is their own very personal decision. I believe it to be an unfair use of the platform that I have as a teacher and, if pressed, I would argue something akin to the sentences marked in bold in Exhibit 6.1 related to "diversity of perspective," "promoting climates of . . . understanding," and "accepting responsibility for the consequences. . . ."

However, a student might say, "But, Dr. Fairhurst, other professors have no problem telling us who they are voting for. You criticized [former U.S. president] George W. Bush just now. I'll bet you are a Democrat." To which I would respond,

> Respectfully, I disagree with my colleagues' choice to do this. I do criticize Bush, but I also criticize plenty of Democrats. I believe I can separate out people's communication behavior for analysis without moving to judgment about their worth as candidates. Such a policy of identifying one's political affiliation usually alienates large numbers of students who feel differently and equally passionate about their chosen candidate. I don't want these students dismissing my analysis because of a presumed party affiliation. I like to think of myself as an equal-opportunity critic of all leadership communications.

Note what I have done in this little exchange. My teaching stance has been questioned by a student who wants me to be more forthcoming about my politics. Because my beliefs are in line with the NCA ethical code, I am ready to draw from it, extensively if I have to, to support my (always contestable) stance as the correct one and, by implication, that I am a good teacher. To wit, a good teacher promotes diverse thinking, creates cultures of understanding, and accepts that words and actions have consequences. (Do you recognize my mental model here?) This is how a sound ethical code serves as a guide to good judgment, and it is identity-shaping.

However, from a leadership perspective, ethical codes do two more things. First, they help people cope with the contradictions and ambiguities of chaotic work environments.[5] Codes are also purposely general so that individuals can match up the specifics of just about any situation to them. Second, ethical codes shape organizational identities, not just individual identities. Indeed, most really ethical leaders diligently promote their conception of what it means *for their organizations* to behave ethically. They then try to grow the organizations accordingly.[6]

An interesting case of this on a governmental level occurred on February 13, 2008, when Prime Minister Kevin Rudd of Australia made a motion in Parliament to apologize to the "Stolen Generation" of Aborigines (see Exhibit 6.2). The Stolen Generation are the children of Briten Aboriginal and Torres Strait Islander descent who were forcibly removed from their parents' care by order of the Australian national and state governments roughly between 1869 and 1969. The reasons for the systematic removal are contested. They include the more benevolent reason of protecting the children from alleged abuse, but also the more malevolent reason of a society seeking white racial purity. Notably, the *Aborigines Protection Amending Act* of 1915 did not require authorities to establish that the children were neglected or mistreated. Nevertheless, the apology marks Rudd's attempt to shape a national identity that explicitly condemns racial practices of this nature, acknowledges the grievous harm such practices caused, and pledges to be more inclusive from here on out.

Exhibit 6.2. Motion of Apology to Australia's Aboriginal Peoples

Today we honour the indigenous peoples of this land, the oldest continuing cultures in human history.

We reflect on their past mistreatment.

We reflect in particular on the mistreatment of those who were Stolen Generations—this blemished chapter in our nation's history.

The time has now come for the nation to turn a new page in Australia's history by righting the wrongs of the past and so moving forward with confidence to the future.

We apologise for the laws and policies of successive parliaments and government that have inflicted profound grief, suffering and loss on these our fellow Australians.

We apologise especially for the removal of Aboriginal and Torres Strait Islander children from their families, their communities, and their country.

(Continued)

Exhibit 6.2. (Continued)

For the pain, suffering, and hurt of these Stolen Generations, their descendants and for their families left behind, we say sorry.

To the mothers and fathers, the brothers and the sisters, for the breaking up of families and communities, we say sorry.

And for the indignity and degradation thus inflicted on a proud people and a proud culture, we say sorry.

We the parliament of Australia respectfully request that this apology be received in the spirit in which it is offered as part of the healing of the nation.

For the future we take heart; resolving that this new page in the history of our great continent can now be written.

We today take this first step by acknowledging the past and laying claim to a future that embraces all Australians.

A future where this parliament resolves that the injustices of the past must never, never happen again.

A future where we harness the determination of all Australians, indigenous and non-indigenous, to close the gap that lies between us in life expectancy, educational achievement and economic opportunity.

A future where we embrace the possibility of new solutions to enduring problems where old approaches have failed.

A future based on mutual respect, mutual resolve and mutual responsibility.

A future where all Australians, whatever their origins, are truly equal partners, with equal opportunities and with an equal stake in shaping the next chapter in the history of this great country, Australia.

Source: www1.aiatsis.gov.au/exhibitions/apology/apology.html.

What was the ethical code from which Kevin Rudd and his government drew? We could certainly point to anti-discrimination laws in Australia. However, those existed even before Rudd was voted into office, and preceding prime ministers eschewed any such apology. Another way to answer that question is through the concept of *ethos*, which is often seen as the distinctive spirit or defining values of a culture or historical era.

An ethos lacks the formality as an ethical code, but it is no less compelling. In the West, for example, social justice, equality, and human rights are hot-button issues. Western societies have gone to war over such issues, passed laws, rewritten budgets, and seen politicians promise to redress imbalances if elected. So even with anti-discrimination laws available, Rudd and his government can draw from a social justice ethos, arguing as they did that "the time has now come" for this apology.

Other situations are likely to find a different kind of ethos operating: a sustainability ethos for all things environmental, a due process ethos pertaining to the world of legalities, or a communicative and empowerment ethos for democratic topics. Like a formal code of ethics, an ethos is a cultural Discourse that we can draw from when we are framing our message. Because the chief difference between an ethical code and an ethos is the degree of formalization and specificity associated with the former, an ethos allows the framer to speak of morality without being terribly specific.

Before moving on, answer the following questions on ethical codes and ethos:

1. Does your company have an ethical code?

   ☐ Yes

   ☐ No (Proceed to question 4)

   ☐ I don't honestly know (Proceed to question 4)

2. Can you capture it in just a few words?

   ☐ Yes, pretty easily

   ☐ No, I'd have to look it up

3. How much does it guide your actions as a leader or manager?

   ☐ A tremendous amount

   ☐ Somewhat

   ☐ Not very much

4. Is there an ethos or two that guides your actions?

   ☐ Yes, they are

   _____

   ☐ Not that I am aware of

Creating Mindfulness

An unarticulated assumption in the preceding section is that most leaders *internalize* an ethical code or ethos in which they commit themselves to act with a certain amount of integrity to do no harm. All of us know of individuals who espouse high standards or a strong set of values only to have their behavior suggest quite the opposite. The temptation is too strong here to resist using politicians as examples—when they get caught, the drama plays out in such a big way given the twenty-four-hour news cycle of cable television.

We have only to look at 2008 U.S. presidential candidate John Edwards, whose campaign themes were poverty and economic justice. When word leaked out that he was receiving $400 haircuts and flying his California hairdresser to his campaign stops, such behavior stood in sharp contrast to the lean budgets of poor working-class Americans. Nevertheless, his cancer-stricken wife, Elizabeth, defended him, although that too must have been difficult when his affair with another woman was revealed. He said that the affair had occurred when his wife's cancer was in remission (a statement that later was proven false) as if there was an "appropriate time" to stray as a candidate who strategically paraded his family values.[7]

Harvard psychologist Howard Gardner argues that individuals have to discipline themselves to practice their ethical principles consistently, which requires that they develop an "ethical cast of mind," or *ethical mind* for short.[8] For leaders this would mean asking oneself, "What kind of leader do I want to be?" "If all leaders in my profession adopted my code of ethics, what would the world be like?"[9] As is evident from such questioning, the aim is to become more conscious or mindful of desired values and standards. However, if our jobs create interminable pressure for immediate decision making, and we act first and think afterward, as Chapter Three suggests, the mindfulness required for ethical framing may be in short supply. As Goethe said, "conscience is the virtue of observers and not of agents of action."[10]

How do we create this mindfulness? Gardner proposes "rigorous self-honesty" in admitting mistakes and taking periodic time-outs to broadly reflect on how the organization is progressing using the principled terms that we intend. Gardner calls these times for reflection "positive periodic inoculations" in which life's experiences cause us to reexamine not only our chosen paths but the example that we are setting for others.[11] In the language of Chapter Three, such inoculations help us prime for a more spontaneous use of our value systems. Periodically holding events up to the light of day provided by our values functions to prime them in such a way that these functions are uppermost in our mind when we act.

Gardner also suggests stepping back from the scene of action and becoming an impartial spectator—one whose goal it is to fight for and protect that for which our organizations or institutions stand.[12] Taking an impartial stance means that there is something larger afoot than just our individual interests, something that organizational whistleblowers often demonstrate.

For example, *Time* magazine's 2002 "Person of the Year" was actually three women who blew the whistle on their respective organizations for questionable ethics: Sherron Watkins of Enron, Cynthia Cooper of WorldCom, and Colleen Rowley of the FBI.[13] Enron vice president Sherron Watkins wrote to chairman Kenneth Lay (and key Andersen Accounting partners) in the summer of 2001, warning them that the company's accounting methods amounted to a Ponzi scheme. Cynthia Cooper blew the whistle to World-Com's board over the company's cover-up of $3.8 billion in losses through its sleight-of-hand accounting methods. And FBI staff attorney Colleen Rowley wrote to FBI Director Robert Mueller detailing the Bureau's cold shoulder given to her Minneapolis field office regarding its pre-9/11 request to investigate Zacarias Moussaoui. The latter is now serving time as a 9/11 co-conspirator.

All these women took huge personal risks because they believed that there were certain governing principles at stake. Many might overlook the lack of ethics to safeguard their jobs, but as Gardner suggests, "A whistleblower steps back from those concerns and considers the nature of work and the community in a larger way."[14] Not everyone must become a whistleblower certainly, but we can learn from them.

For whistleblowers, the "stepping back" process is highly deliberative and often filled with moments of angst or even anguish. Such angst stems not from a lack of values but from a value system at work, recalibrating itself for the tension-filled situation at hand. The situation may have no objectively right or wrong answer, only paths with different kinds of consequences.

Thus what Gardner alludes to in his quote is an inherent tension between our individual interests and our obligations to the community, a tension that marks the human condition. According to Anderson and Englehardt, "The principle that we are born into obligation is deliberately contrary to the notion that we are essentially free and autonomous and accept obligation as a rational act. At some point in our prehistory, we surrendered the fullness of freedom and autonomy for the disciplines and benefits of communication."[15]

Unfortunately, few really understand and appreciate such a notion. What we experience instead is tension between cooperation and competition in our inner conversations with ourselves: "Should I blow the whistle knowing I might lose my job, or should I keep my mouth shut and hope for better times ahead?" "If I lose my job, how will I survive?" "If my company's problems are not addressed, how will I live with myself knowing its potential impact on others?"

Certainly, there can be other tensions marking our inner conversations, such as how much change versus stability is healthy for an organization; how much to be open versus closed with another; whether one should have a short versus a long term focus on bottom-line concerns, and so on. Most of the time, we know the tensions that we face in trying to clarify our values. If we don't, it does help to try to identify them, as they often become the springboard to more ethical framing. (For example, "I'm speaking up today because I could not live with myself knowing this information and its potential impact on my fellow employees.")

To sum it up, Gardner's ethical mind requires two things: first, periodic mindfulness that serves as a values clarification and priming exercise, and second, a substantial commitment to the community in ways that transcend individual interests. With these thoughts in mind, one can't help but think of the global economic crisis that struck in 2008.

It is interesting that at least one California psychologist, Kit Yarrow, sees it as a lack of introspection by top business and government leaders. These leaders operate in a highly competitive world where strength is valued above all, leaving little room for self-recrimination. Yarrow says, "It's entirely possible that these individuals haven't internalized that they've made mistakes and therefore, don't feel responsible. . . . Many of the folks involved have trained themselves to avoid introspection and second-guessing. It gives you a thick skin and sense of superiority that shields you from caring what people think of you."[16]

On one level, this is a surprising observation because executives and elected officials are often very smart people, seemingly naturally inclined to critical reflection. On another level, however, the lack of introspection as a coping mechanism may be reinforced by a turbulent environment that leaves little time to reflect. Either way, a lack of mindfulness produces a self-reinforcing cycle of one shoot-from-the-hip decision after another. It is a cycle that privileges the interests of individuals over those of the community as the path of least resistance.

Before moving on, answer the following questions:

On a scale of 1–5 (with 1 = to the lowest amount), how much time for critical reflection do you have?

If you answered a "1" or a "2," what are some specific things that you can do to create more time for critical reflection?

☐ Schedule a Sunday walk

☐ Schedule a regular time-out in your work schedule

☐ Ask a confidant to meet for coffee

☐ Select reading materials that prompt critical reflection

☐ _____

☐ _____

Moral Positioning

Writer and community organizer Saul Alinsky once observed, "Morality is a rhetorical rationale for expedient action and self-interest. . . . [We live in] a world not of angels but of angles, where men speak of moral principles but act on power principles; a world where we are always moral and our enemies always immoral . . . a world where 'good' is value dependent on whether we want it."[17]

Framing and ethics converge most directly in the ways in which we morally position ourselves and others. *Moral positioning* is simply who or what we claim to be as we try to justify some specific ends or means. As Alinsky suggests, to be human is to see and frame our actions as morally justified, rational, and often without self-interest—in contrast to how we see and frame those of others. Although Alinsky was a mid-twentieth-century activist and writer, he is not out of date. Today's leaders continue to naively exaggerate their own moral qualities, according to management scholar Mats Alvesson.[18]

There is little use deploring such a state of affairs. It is better to understand it. Indeed, Alinsky cues us in to the fact that morality is not objectively real, it is subjectively constructed. This means that there is no right and final arbiter of morality among human beings. We cannot know for sure what others' true ethics are because we cannot read their minds. What we have instead is what they make available to us in their communications and actions. Their communications are quite likely to be strategic as they position themselves as ethical or morally responsible. (Just think of how many people "fudge" their résumés to position themselves for the job market.)

Thus, we are not judging truth, ethics, or morality themselves; we are judging whether or not they are *believable* in these matters. In Chapter One's language, moral positioning is a crucial part of leaders' persuasive attempts to define the reality of "the situation here and now" and may be believed or contested for that very reason. Chapter Four even goes so far as to position truth and reality, objectivity, and legitimacy as "believability framing."

Consider a rich case comparison of moral positioning offered up in a 1996 CBS News documentary, *Who's Getting Rich and Why Aren't You?* hosted by Harry Smith.[19] As shockingly relevant today as it was in its first broadcast, the documentary explores the impact of globalization, outsourced labor practices, and skyrocketing CEO salaries on the American middle class. Among those interviewed were T. J. Rodgers, the hard-charging entrepreneur and CEO of Cypress Semiconductor; Al Dunlap, CEO of Sunbeam-Oster Corporation, also known as "Chainsaw Al" because of his massive downsizings; and Bruce Klatsky, the president and CEO of Phillips-Van Heusen Corporation, whose plant closure in Clayton, Alabama, devastated that one-industry town.

Smith posed similar questions to all three related to the consequences of their global business decisions on, for example, Americans who lose their jobs to those more cheaply paid overseas. Cypress Semiconductor's T. J. Rodgers responded:

No matter what you do, you can't save a job that doesn't have an economic right to exist. . . . I tried once to hold some American jobs that economically didn't have a right to exist. And I lost $20 million doing it until, basically, my Board of Directors and our investors said, "Thank you. Stop now. And do what you have to do." So, it's a classic lifeboat argument. Do you keep more people than the boat can support and sink the entire ship, or do you cast off until you can save what you can save? So we laid off 400 people." (Catch this on YouTube.[20])

Before coming to Sunbeam-Oster, Al Dunlap was CEO at Scott Paper Company, where he turned a hefty profit by downsizing some eleven thousand employees. On the subject of executive pay, he commented:

There's only a handful of superstar executives. You've got to compare them with the other superstars. You can't compare them with the worker on the floor . . . I never apologized when I was poor. I'm certainly not going to apologize when I'm successful. It won't happen in your lifetime. It's not a sin to be successful. (Catch this on YouTube.[21])

Bruce Klatsky of Van Heusen was asked whether the employees in Clayton, Alabama, deserved their fate of the plant closing. He said:

Did they deserve their fate? No, they didn't deserve their fate. I don't know what anybody promises you when you are put on this earth. Those people were terrific people. They came to work every day. They did their best for the company. The company did their best for them. It's a function of global economics."

Harry Smith: "Do you have any idea what's going to happen to those folks?

Klatsky: "Nope, I'm scared to death for them. I choose to focus on the 13,000 people that have survived, but that doesn't make me feel very good about the 1,000 people who didn't survive. And that's why I don't sleep as well as I used to. (Catch this on YouTube.[22])

The moral positioning of these three CEOs is quite interesting because they each draw from an ethos of global market capitalism (along with its perceived duties, rights, and consequences). The arguments that they pose draw from this Discourse and reproduce it at the same time. In fact, that is how Discourses endure. In repeated fashion, they are both the medium and outcome of our framing communications.[23] To understand the positions of the CEOs, let's examine what each makes explicit and what remains unsaid. My goal here is to underscore the strategic framing involved in moral positioning.

For example, T. J. Rodgers frames jobs as having or not having "an economic right to exist." Using a "rights" frame in this way, Rodgers makes it clear that economics is the *only* basis upon which the creation or maintenance of a job can be judged. Judged worthy, such jobs have rights. Judged unworthy, such jobs have none—thereby excluding any other legal, political, social, or moral bases for them.

Rodgers then tries to morally position himself by telling us a story of when he was temporarily swayed to hold American jobs with no rights. But he implicitly suggests that he was duty-bound to give them up when they proved too costly. He cited his obligations to his Board of Directors and investors when they called him to account. He then summarily paraphrases "the situation here and now" with the classic lifeboat metaphor, whose logic is to cast aside a few to save the many. Rodgers does not come out and directly say, "I'm playing the capitalist game of the global marketplace, and I am bound by those rules." Yet he morally positions himself in relation to key markers of this game. His tone and assured demeanor also come off as utterly rational.

Al Dunlap likewise speaks of rights, but these are the rights of an exclusive class, what he terms "superstar executives." His framing focuses on what he feels he is owed given the implied terms of membership in this elite club. For Dunlap, superstars *deserve* extraordinary compensation. Interviewer Harry Smith finds the amount of money (not supplied in the transcript) unfathomable, which prompts Dunlap to suggest that he not be compared against ordinary workers. Dunlap thus positions himself as morally superior because he is self-made and successful at the game of global capitalism.

His unapologetic demeanor also hints at a fairness issue when he says, "I never apologized when I was poor. I'm certainly not going to apologize when I'm successful." But his moral positioning of himself smacks of a false bravado. Such bravado typically evokes ridicule from others or a desired comeuppance, which many saw when Dunlap was fired from his job at Sunbeam-Oster. Moreover, he was forced to pay $15 million in a shareholder lawsuit when his management methods resoundingly failed.

Finally, there is Bruce Klatsky, a study in contrast from the other two CEOs. Low-key, earnest, and less alpha male, Klatsky's global economics argument differs not a whit from T. J. Rodgers's lifeboat argument. Yet Klatsky comes off as more morally grounded because of how he positions himself amid the consequences of his global business decisions. That is to say, he affirms the experience of the disaffected when he says, "They didn't deserve their fate. . . . Those people were terrific people. They came to work every day. They did their best for the company. . . . I'm scared to death for them . . . that doesn't make me feel very good about the 1,000 people who didn't survive. And that's why I don't sleep as well as I used to." Note how Klatsky spoke of "people," while T. J. Rodgers spoke of "jobs." Rodgers used rational argument. Klatsky took the time to also articulate his emotions for those who were downsized. As a result, he morally positions himself in a much more humane way—even though his game is likewise "global economics."

Could Klatsky merely have been feeding interviewer Harry Smith all the right lines for the sake of the camera? Of course, but there is no objective way to know this. As suggested, the key question must be, Is Klatsky's leadership performance believable? And immediately we must ask, *to whom*, because the answer to this question is always rooted in the eye of the beholder. The fact that I find Klatsky's performance believable does not prevent others from believing it to be staged, too "touchy-feely," or any other number of interpretations relative to the other CEOs.

What few appreciate sufficiently is the persuasion of oneself and others that one's moral interpretation and handling of "the situation here and now" is indeed an act of leadership. As Alinsky neatly phrased it, "All effective actions require the passport of morality."[24] Morality and moral positioning are thus crucial elements of the "the situation here and now," and joint action is best achieved when leaders argue persuasively and authoritatively to win the necessary buy-in. I continue this theme of persuasion in the next section's discussion of crucibles as framing devices.

On Crucibles and Teaching Moments

Warren Bennis and Robert Thomas have written about the value of crucibles for leadership.[25] A crucible is a test, a particularly difficult challenge to face, usually yielding hard-won lessons. *Such lessons are great fodder for teaching moments because leaders can articulate how they arrived at a particular moral position and so justify it in the process.* They can speak from their hearts about the ethical choices weighed and decided upon so that others may learn as well. An early observation in this chapter is that ethical leaders diligently promote their conception of what it means to behave ethically and then will grow the organization accordingly. Crucibles are one very good way in which to do this.

However, not all leaders see their crucibles as framing opportunities or teaching moments for ethical choices. The corporate and government leaders associated with the collapse of Enron certainly testify to this. Today, the word "Enron" is synonymous with corporate scandal and questionable accounting practices, thanks to executives like Kenneth Lay and Jeffrey Skilling. But another cautionary tale comes from one more player in that saga, Joseph Berardino, who was managing partner and CEO of Enron's accounting firm, Arthur Andersen. The collapse of Enron in 2002 hastened the dissolution of Arthur Andersen, one of the big five U.S. accounting firms, when it was found guilty of criminal charges associated with its auditing practices at Enron.[26]

After Enron's collapse, Mr. Berardino was asked to testify before the U.S. House of Representatives Committee on Financial Services on December 12, 2001. Management professors R. J. Craig and J. H. Amernic analyzed Berardino's written testimony in depth and noted that Berardino faced a difficult rhetorical challenge, to say the very least.[27] The number of jobs and individuals' life savings lost created a huge public outcry, a media blitz, and a lot of unwanted congressional attention.

Although Arthur Andersen was judged to be only one player in a multiplayer breakdown of the system, its role was featured because it brought to light a sore subject among some government officials: the lack of auditor independence from ongoing operations at Enron. Andersen appeared to be making even more money from the management consulting side of the business than the accounting side—rendering the latter, according to some, unable to perform its watchdog role without also implicating itself.

In addition, Andersen had recently paid a significant sum to settle at least two other accounting and auditing scandals. Thus, Berardino was likely sensitive to the ways in which his testimony might be used to impugn his firm in future litigation. As Craig and Amernic point out, the accusations against Arthur Andersen were nothing short of negligence and failure to exercise its duty of care. Clearly, this fits the bill for a crucible for CEO Joseph Berardino by any measure.

How does Berardino respond? Not well, according to Craig and Amernic. They argue that Berardino ultimately privileges the Discourse of the market, effectively minimizing other kinds of moral considerations:

> I am here today because faith in our firm and in the integrity of the capital market system has been shaken. . . . What happened at Enron is a tragedy on many levels. We are acutely aware of the impact this has had on investors. We also recognize the pain this business failure has caused for Enron's employees and others.

Note how the capital market has merely been "shaken," not rocked to its core. He leaves open the question as to who did the shaking or at least contributed to it. Finally, the ordering and emphasis given to investors minimizes the concerns of other stakeholders such as employees.[28]

Next we see the language of a crucible and a continued avoidance of the responsibility that comes with it:

> Many questions about Enron's failure need to be answered. . . . None of us here yet knows all the facts. Today's hearing is an important step in enlightening all of us. I am certain that together we will get to the facts.

Craig and Amernic note that "Enron's failure" points to an abstract entity, not a "we" or an "I."[29] Berardino portrays the search for the facts as a communal journey, not one in which he has been charged with supplying information related to his firm's culpability. In this example and elsewhere, we come to see that it is *Enron's* crucible, not necessarily Arthur Andersen's; the accounting firm's situation, while complex, is made to sound minor by comparison.

But Berardino's real coup de grace was a litany of mind-numbing accounting details that would overwhelm most audiences, including legislative. Here is just one small part of Berardino's testimony in this regard:

> The accounting rules dictate, among other things, that unrelated parties must have residual equity equal to at least 3 percent of the fair value of an SPE's assets in order for the SPE to qualify for non-consolidation. However, there is no prohibition against company employees also being involved as investors, provided that various tests were met, including the 3 percent test.

This quote shows the jargon-filled nature of accounting rhetoric that Berardino says is understandable to only an elite few. As Craig and Amernic argue, it is framing on two levels: framing *through* a glut of accounting details and framing *about* the glut of accounting details that are (formulated to be?) too difficult to easily comprehend.[30] Such a strategy by Berardino neutralizes these details along with Andersen's culpability. Indeed, if they can't adequately be understood, how can they be judged?

Are we judging Berardino too harshly? Is it fair to expect him to use such a public event as a teaching moment, knowing the potential legalities he might face? These are important questions, the answer to the first of which suggests that we are not misjudging Berardino. For example, consider the profile of Berardino in *Business Week* at the time:

> At times, Berardino, who made an estimated $3 million a year as CEO, seems to focus more on his personal losses than those of the shareholders and employees who lost investments and jobs. . . . He also blames forces outside of Andersen for the wave of accounting scandals currently afflicting the market. He points to shareholders

who invested in companies without examining their filings and to board members who were disengaged and failed to ask the right questions. . . . [The] prevailing view outside the firm [was that] Berardino "never said he took full responsibility for this," says Arthur W. Bowman, a longtime industry observer and founder of *Bowman's Accounting Report.* "That was the problem with everyone at Arthur Andersen. They are all so arrogant that none of them wants to take responsibility."[31]

Craig and Amernic's analysis is consistent with this viewpoint. As to the second question and whether Berardino should have used the crucible of his congressional testimony as a teaching moment, there will be differences of opinion. On strictly legal grounds, one might well answer in the negative. However, in the end Berardino was not able to stave off indictment by the U.S. Justice Department for obstruction of justice.

His testimony was viewed by many as continuing an established pattern of denial.[32] Thus, he stepped down from his job without the personal or professional absolution that can come with heartfelt introspection, the confession of one's failings, and a willingness to make amends. So one might argue that the crucible supplied by his congressional testimony would have been the perfect time, perhaps an even better move than resigning, from which Arthur Andersen could have risen from the ashes.

To conclude this discussion, use Framing Tool 6.1 to analyze the ethics, moral positioning, and crucible involved in a recent critical incident that you have faced as a leader.

 FRAMING TOOL 6.1

Critical Incident Framing

Recall the critical incident that you identified in preceding chapters or use another one involving your leadership that you would like to analyze. Remember the focus should be on your communications as a leader with your employees, customers, or other stakeholders. Also, select an incident in which you were unhappy with the outcome.

_____

_____

_____

_____

_____

_____

Were you proud of the way you acted or the way others acted under your direction? Explain your reasoning.

_____

_____

_____

_____

_____

_____

Did you justify your actions (with reference to an *ethical code* or *ethos* of some kind) or *morally position* yourself in some way? Describe how you did this.

_____

_____

_____

_____

_____

_____

What were the *crucibles* or teaching moments associated with this critical incident?

_____

_____

_____

_____

_____

_____

How could you frame and act more ethically the next time around?

_____

_____

_____

_____

_____

_____

(You can download this form from www.josseybass.com/go/gailfairhurst.)

A Backward Glance at Chapter Six

The purpose of this chapter has been to examine leadership framing from an ethical stance. A host of examples in this chapter underscore that how we go about the business of framing as leaders is fraught with ethical choices. More specifically,

- Ethics is the study of morality or how we might harm or aid another based on what we do and say. How we frame is a window into our ethics whenever we act in a leadership capacity.

- Ethical codes supply people with a set of Discursive resources, including a linguistic tool bag to use in efforts to explain ideals, values, or commitments.

- Ethos is the distinctive spirit or defining values of a culture or historical era. An ethos allows the framer to speak of morality without being very specific.

- Moral positioning is simply who or what we claim to be as we try to justify some specific ends or means. Morality is not objectively real but subjectively constructed.

- Others sit in moral judgment of us as we sit in moral judgment of others. What we judge is how believable leaders are in ethical matters as revealed in their moral positioning and behavior.

- Crucibles are great teaching moments because leaders can speak about the ethical choices weighed and decided upon so that others may learn.

A FINAL THOUGHT

Through framing, ethical leaders articulate what it means to act ethically.

7

The Leadership Context of Framing

PRECEDING CHAPTERS have highlighted the skill, science, art, emotion, and ethics of framing. This chapter discusses how framing factors into leadership when many aspects of the situation besides framing could be in play. In other words, it's not *only* about our framing communications when it comes to leadership.

The secret to understanding how framing, context, and leadership go together is to get really good at analyzing framing in all kinds of leadership situations in which you are the observer. As you evaluate and discover what you would say or do differently, you develop your mental models for leadership framing, heighten your sensitivity to the many aspects of context, and produce more framing options for yourself in the future.

Becoming that fly on the wall is relatively easy to do. First, you must focus on the "who, what, when, where, why" details of the framing involved. In other words, what in this specific situation is driving the framing by all parties involved? Second, you must figure out the "design problem" of the leader, or leaders as the case may be. Recall Reality Construction Rule #5 from Chapter One, which said that leadership is a design problem. Leaders must figure out what leadership is in the context of what they do and, through their framing and actions, persuade themselves and other people that they are doing it.[1]

Figuring out the design problem that we ourselves face as leaders is hard enough, but, you might ask, how are we to figure out how others have designed the job of leading? Admittedly, it is not an exact science. To begin with, you have to acknowledge that leadership is a very broad concept.[2] In many leadership texts, it is synonymous with influence, which explains why the term can be invoked in corporate America, remote African tribes, European soccer matches, or local Girl Scout troop cookie sales.[3] (Indeed, if I were asked the question, "How many different kinds of leadership are there?" I would have to reply, "How much time do you have?")

But despite that complexity, you do get better at sizing up the design problems of other leaders the more you perceive framing at work and the more you understand that each individual sets about the task of leading in specific ways. You, in effect, are judging their believability as leaders, just as others judge your believability as you perform in that role. When you think about it, judging people's leadership (and, by implication, how they have designed the job of it) is an everyday activity, whether it is in a conversation about the boss at the watercooler, a performance review of a manager who reports to you, a vote cast for a political leader, or the television show you turn off when a certain leader appears.

To improve your ability to analyze how framing factors into overall attributions of leadership, this chapter presents a series of leadership examples with different kinds of situational elements in play: crisis, conflict, change, challenges to authority, feeling outnumbered, ethics (or the lack thereof), a sense of service, and more. Any or all may be relevant to your station in life or suitable to your tastes in leadership, but the key is to appreciate the variety here and the ways in which framing effectiveness (or ineffectiveness) emerges

Figure 7.1. Framing and Leadership Context Questions

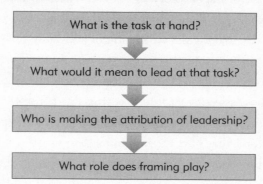

in the details of the context and the design of leadership in the moment.[4] Eliciting those details begins with getting specific, *really specific*, about leadership, by asking the questions posed in Figure 7.1.

Question 1 should get you thinking about leadership in terms of the specific task at hand. Is the leader driving the company to record-setting quarterly sales? Leading a battalion of soldiers into harm's way to secure an area? Attempting to innovate a route to the top? The task at hand is crucial in shaping what leadership actually looks like.[5] Although influence and motivation processes may be common to all, record sales growth, military supremacy, and innovation leadership are very different kinds of tasks. Why should we expect leadership to be the same in each?

Question 2 requires that you factor in those aspects of the situation that help or hinder a leader's ability to succeed. These aspects mesh with your mental models for the ideal leader to shape your specific expectations for the leadership challenge at hand. So if the question, What is my conception of an ideal leader? elicits your (always general) mental model, asking about the current situation's resources and constraints should calibrate it for the task at hand. In short, Given what is constraining and enabling about the current situation, what is effective leadership in the here-and-now? Answering these questions will also help you in Question 4, in which you must size up the role of framing relative to other aspects of the situation.

Question 3 focuses on the fact that leadership, like credibility, is in the eye of the beholder.[6] Thus it is crucial to ask, Who is actually doing the "beholding"? That is, who is assigning leadership to one or more individuals? Are you making the attribution of leadership to yourself or someone else? Is a newspaper columnist or portfolio analyst attributing leadership? Are historians gathering archival data to render their judgments? The vantage point of those assessing leadership is crucial to consider because of the information they may (or may not) be able to access, the perspective they bring, and the platform they have for expressing their views.

Question 4 encourages you to zero in on the specific role of framing in the attribution of leadership. As a result, you might focus on any or all aspects of framing by particular leaders, followers, or other stakeholders; the person or persons attributing leadership; the situational elements driving the framing, or all of these. The glossary at the end of this book can be used as a quick reminder of the framing concepts to consider in your analyses. Each framing concept is not only defined but annotated as to the chapter in which it appears, should you want to return to that discussion.

For example, when assessing the contributions of leaders and their followers, you might ask how a leader understood the *core framing tasks* and went about them. Perhaps this leader chose some interesting *master frames* around which vision-specific framing emerged. Consider whether the framing of these issues made a skillful use of *metaphorical language* or strong *argument* and whether the leader had done the *priming* necessary *for spontaneity*.

Do the same for followers or other stakeholders. Did they push back or collaborate with effective *metaphorical, simplifying,* or *believability* frames? What was the *emotional* tenor of the discussion? What were the *ethical* considerations, and did the *moral positioning* ring true? Any or all of these framing concepts might interact with aspects of the context such as the actions taken, relationship history, resource constraints, and many more.

However, your analysis of leadership dynamics need not stop there. If someone is making a leadership attribution, you might ask about that person's *mental models* for leadership or perhaps one or more *cultural Discourses* that are being used to define what leadership is. You'll recognize the cultural Discourses in play because the *tool bag* of specific language and arguments in use will have a ring of familiarity, much as we see with visionary leadership Discourse and its emphasis on vision talk and the leader-manager distinction.[7]

Context, Leadership and Framing

To recap, as you analyze the different examples of leadership in this chapter, remember to look for the following:

- What the leader's task is

- What it would mean to lead at that task when the constraints and enablements of the situation are factored in

- Who is making the attribution of leadership

- What framing elements are involved by all relevant parties

By undertaking this type of practice, you will fine-tune your ability to understand how leadership, framing, and context come together in moments of collective action both large and small.

Framing and Presidential Crises

What role does framing play in attributions of presidential leadership during a crisis? Consider what Jonathan Alter of *Newsweek* observed about George W. Bush in the days following 9/11.[8] It was Friday (September 14, 2001), actually. Bush was visiting Ground Zero for the first time. A mangled fire truck was positioned on the edge of the ruins, and Bush climbed up onto it, placing him alongside Bob Beckwith, a retired firefighter. Beckwith asked Bush if he should step down from the truck, but the president said no and draped his arm around him to signal him to stay. As the president began speaking into his bullhorn, another first responder yelled to Bush, "We can't hear you." Bush turned and replied, "I can hear *you*. The rest of the world hears you! And the people who knocked these buildings down will hear all of us soon!" (You can catch this on YouTube.[9])

Alter observed that it was a simple response to an impromptu moment, "but you could almost see the molecules of presidential leadership being rearranged." Struggling to find his voice amid the hero worship of New York Mayor Rudolph

Giuliani (Bush's motorcade had been met with cheers of "U.S.A.! U.S.A.! U.S.A.!" and "Rudy! Rudy! Rudy!"), Bush now suddenly took command—or so it appeared to Alter (and, it should be said, to many other Americans who would go on to give Bush a 90 percent approval rating shortly thereafter). As his motorcade departed, the crowd yelled "Bush! Bush! Bush!"

When Alter wrote about the event, he attributed "presidential leadership" to George W. Bush. It was an attribution that had eluded him in the early moments of the crisis when the events of 9/11 and Rudy Giuliani dominated the scene. How did framing contribute to this attribution of leadership?

Well, first you might notice Bush's framing, which was a three-part list (Chapter Four): "I can hear *you*," the president shouted through the bull-horn. "The rest of the world hears you! And the people who knocked these buildings down will hear all of us soon!" Bush was responding to someone in the crowd who was literally struggling to hear him. With a deft turn of phrase, he indicated that he as president had indeed heard them, and that the rest of the world including the perpetrators *will* hear them. It was an inspiring ad lib for a truly momentous occasion that cried out for a message of hope and resiliency among so much ruin and so many lives lost.

But one must also acknowledge the spatial and nonverbal elements here. By keeping the firefighter on stage Bush positioned himself next to an every-man, and the placement of his arm around the firefighter's shoulders was a nonverbal frame of solidarity with these first responders. In addition, Bush likely benefited from low expectations of him, especially by the media. This was a president who very nearly did not get into office, given the down-to-the-wire fight with Al Gore in the 2000 U.S. presidential election. Bush did not distinguish himself as a candidate, in part, because his use of language was common and often mangled.

So the opportunity of this moment, the expectations game for this president, his nonverbal positioning with an everyman, and deft turn of phrase "I can hear you" delivered in a three-part list, amounted to the right message for the moment. It led to Alter's judgment about molecules of presidential leadership being rearranged.

Finally, we must say something about the vantage point of Jonathan Alter as a political writer for *Newsweek*, a weekly U.S. publication that reaches millions of readers. Alter is in a key position to shape our impressions of presidential leadership because of his very public platform and presumed expertise.[10] The press socially shapes our perceptions of leadership time and again with major historical figures such as Abraham Lincoln or Mahatma Ghandi, but also modern-day ones like Nelson Mandela or Rudolph Giuliani after 9/11.[11] When influential sources decide and comment upon the leadership of one or more individuals, users of those media are likely to be influenced as well.

To summarize, the key aspects of framing and context in this presidential crisis appeared to be a potent mix of:

- The opportunity of the 9/11 moment for George W. Bush
- The lowered expectations set for candidate Bush
- His spatial positioning with an everyman
- His deft turn of phrase and three-part list that reached out to the audience
- Jonathan Alter's framing of Bush as "presidential" for an audience

Some questions to consider:

What did you like or dislike about what Bush did?

_____

_____

_____

_____

_____

Do you agree with Alter's framing of Bush at the time as presidential? Why or why not?

_____

_____

_____

_____

_____

Framing and Gendered Leadership

Anderson and Englehardt write about the moral dilemmas associated with issues of gender in leadership relationships. They relay one incident from their consultancy work that exemplifies such a dilemma:

> A female division manager related the following. "I'm the only female manager in my company. When we meet in the manager meetings, I often feel as if my colleagues just don't understand me. I would like some women colleagues at the table. Earlier today I was making a point I felt was important, when one of the other managers interrupted me and said, 'Chris, you don't really mean that. What you mean is. . . . ' He then went on to state his position. I was silenced by him. He didn't try to understand my point, and I lost the political momentum to try to express it again. I felt angry with him but was unable to do anything about it without appearing out of control."[12]

On the face of it, this example suggests a patriarchal management culture in which the male manager enacts his dominance through interrupting and translating for Chris, who relinquishes the floor.

However, it's useful to look at the framing from a number of perspectives. While Chris would probably agree that she and her fellow managers may be enacting traditional gender roles, she also suggests that her token status (as the only female manager in the company) factors into how others perceive her—regardless of her framing efforts. Organizational scientists like Rosabeth Moss Kanter would probably agree. Kanter argues that unless the ratio of majority to minority members becomes more balanced in an organization, it is indeed difficult to break down gender stereotypes.[13] Because of its impact on perception, the sex structuring of Chris's organization likely factors into the nature of her framing attempts for many observers, analysts especially.

But would the male managers in her organization see these effects? Most likely, they would not because they don't have to navigate gender stereotypes, being the (norm-setting) group in charge. They would say they are merely reacting to the substance of Chris's remarks, thus contributing to the framing communications dilemma in which tokens often find themselves.

Now take this example one step further. Using the Message Design Logic introduced in Chapter One, Chris is showing all of the signs of a Conventional. She seems to be suggesting that because she is the only female manager, she has few options but to acquiesce. She also leaves open the question as to whether she is ever able to redirect the political momentum more in her favor. I'd be inclined to test this notion with an executive coach or mentor and a push to become more Strategic. Obviously, no adviser can alter the sex structuring of Chris's organization, but advice might help her navigate conflict situations.

In particular, a coach could challenge Chris's framing of being "out of control" and ask what specific behaviors would or would not constitute being "out of control." Does a simple challenge like, "Thanks, Pete, for your clarification, but you're reducing my argument to terms I would not use," constitute being "out of control"? Alternatively, does a remark like, "Respectfully, that's not what I mean. Think of it this way—" that triggers a productive disagreement also constitute being "out of control"?

In both of these responses, Chris's Strategic strategy should be challenging but respectful (through polite language, tone of voice, facial gestures, and even a little humor, if possible). Such a demeanor keeps the focus on the task and, in this case, Chris's ability to further it, which ought to be the issue here. Chris faces real obstacles in creating the right framing, to be sure, but she need not exacerbate those obstacles herself.

To summarize, what are the key aspects of framing and context in this case of gendered leadership? It is a combination of two or more of these elements:

- Male dominance through interruption and translation of Chris, a female manager

- Sex structuring of Chris's organization and gender stereotypes (perhaps) by all involved

- Chris's Conventional communications style and apparent acquiescence through silence

Some questions to consider:

If you were Chris, what would you have said?

_____

_____

_____

_____

What should Chris have done differently?

_____

_____

_____

_____

Framing and a Changing of the Guard

Barbara Nelson is finance manager who has worked for two manufacturing companies in the last five years. She prefers to call them "Company A" and "Company B." The changing of the guard in both companies was a study in contrasts for her. When Company A changed management teams, new Manager A coming in had a reputation for being a good guy. "Great," she thought. "I can't wait to meet him." Curiously, though, only a perfunctory announcement was made of his arrival. There were no employee meetings, no rounds of interviews to see what was working and what was not, not even management-by-walking-around to introduce himself.

In the first meeting Manager A scheduled with Barb and other managers reporting directly to him, his cell phone rang constantly. Each time, he would excuse himself from the meeting and apologize. In talking with the other managers afterward, no one felt as if they had been heard or that a meaningful discussion with Manager A had taken place. It was not a good first impression.

Barb Nelson concluded, "He might have been a great individual contributor in his last job. But as a manager, he was going through the motions in this one and doing a very poor job of it."

Barb now works at Company B, which recently had its own changing of the guard with the arrival of Manager B. "It was like a breath of fresh air compared to Manager A," she said. The first thing Manager B did was to schedule meetings with groups of managers and employees, including the hourly workers, to introduce himself. At each meeting, he emphasized three things. First, he would continue to have quarterly meetings with all employees where questions could be asked and answered. Second, he would be making some unpopular decisions, but they would be biased in favor of company growth. If it looked like the company was turning down business, it was because the company could not sustain what some customers were demanding.

Third, he directed the company's managers to undertake a series of structured interviews with all employees to discern what Company B was doing right and why they liked working there. No negative questions would be asked; the emphasis would be on accentuating the positive. When the interviews were completed and results compiled, he committed to sharing the results at the next quarterly meeting.

Barb Nelson was left with a great first impression of Manager B. "He was no less results-driven than Manager A," she said. "Yet Manager B found a way to keep his eye on the ball *and* develop relationships with his people." As Barb sized up her two work experiences, the key aspects of framing with Managers A and B are particularly interesting. Many are *gestures* that others read as framed messages.

Manager A makes little effort to introduce himself, while Manager B makes every effort. Manager B uses his introduction to prepare the workforce for some unpopular decisions ahead, while Manager A is silent on this issue. Manager B signals a commitment to keep the lines of communication open, while Manager A is silent on this issue too. With the company-wide interviews, Manager B emphasizes the positive and what is working in Company B's culture, while Manager A is still silent. Finally, Manager A's attachment to his cell phone, fairly or not, prioritizes others over those who report directly to him, which leaves Barb Nelson to suggest that he was just going through the motions—"and doing a very poor job of it." Interestingly, no mitigating circumstances stood out to Barb that would explain Manager A's tepid introduction to Company A.

To summarize, what are the key aspects of framing and context in these two cases of management transition? They combine several factors:

- Manager A did not live up to his advance billing; he did not seem interested in building a relationship with employees from the start.

- Barb's mental model for Manager A served as a baseline when evaluating Manager B.

- The effort Manager B made to be

  - Relationship-oriented *and* results-driven

  - Explicit about value commitments such as open communication

  - Positive, not trying to fix what wasn't broken

  - Able to manage a collective identity, a "we" instead of an "I"

Some questions to consider:
Are you more like Manager A or Manager B?

_____

_____

_____

Are there any mitigating circumstances to justify Manager A's behavior? Is there anything else that Manager B should have done?

_____

_____

_____

_____

Framing and Servant Leadership

How does framing factor into the servant leadership? A great example is provided by Greg Mortenson, the subject and coauthor of *Three Cups of Tea*.[14] This book recounts the transformation of Mortenson from a young mountaineer in 1993 (who failed to climb to the top of K2, the world's second-highest mountain) to philanthropist and servant leader. Over the next ten years, Mortenson sought money and directed the building of schools, especially for girls, in the poorest regions of Pakistan and Afghanistan.

Although Mortenson's personal journey is itself inspiring, an early lesson from his father really stands out. Irvin "Dempsey" Mortenson and his wife, Jerene, were Lutheran missionaries to Tanzania in Africa as Greg was growing up. Dempsey's greatest achievement in this regard was raising money for and founding Tanzania's first teaching hospital, the Kilimanjaro Christian Medical Centre. At its dedication ceremony, Mortenson recalls of his father:

> He began by thanking his Tanzanian partner at the hospital, John Moshi, who Dempsey said was just as responsible for the medical center's success as he was. "I have a prediction to make," he said in Swahili, looking so at peace with himself that Greg remembers, for once, his father didn't seem awkward speaking in front of a crowd. "In ten years, the head of every department at Kilimanjaro Christian Medical Centre will be a Tanzanian. It's your country. It's your hospital," he said. "I could feel the swell of pride from the Africans," Mortenson remembers. "The expats [expatriates] wanted him to say, 'Look what we've done for you.' But he was saying, 'Look what you've done for yourselves and how much more you can do.'" "My dad got blasted by the expats for that," Mortenson says. "But you know what? It happened. The place he built is still there today, the top teaching hospital in Tanzania, and a decade after he finished, all the department heads were African. Watching him up there, I felt so proud that this big, barrel-chested man was my father. He taught me, he taught all of us, that if you believe in yourself, you can accomplish anything."[15]

One of the individuals to whom *Three Cups of Tea* is dedicated is Dempsey Mortenson, "for showing us the way, while you were here." Indeed, it would be the lessons of a father on helping the poor to help themselves that would inspire the leadership of the son. Years later, Greg Mortenson helped to build 130 schools *in partnership* with the villages he tried to serve.

This event has a number of contributing elements to it. First, of course, is the strong contrast that Greg observed between the framing of "Look at what you've done for yourselves . . . " compared to the expatriates' framing of "Look at what we've done for you." Second are two strong emotional undercurrents, Greg's observation of "the swell of pride from the Africans" and the seeming peacefulness of his father, an apparent departure from the awkwardness the latter had shown previously. Finally, Dempsey's prediction proved true over time, which only heightened Greg's admiration of him. The chemistry of these components for Greg avoids a patronizing style, however benevolent. Instead, it favors of a style of leading that is respectful, egalitarian, and servantlike—perhaps the only combination of qualities suitable to the intercultural context in which Greg would later find himself.

To summarize, what are the key aspects of framing and context in this case of servant leadership? It is a combination of these factors:

- A contrast between Dempsey's framing and the expatriates' framing over who should be credited for the Tanzanian medical center

- The emotional undercurrents supplied by the Africans' swell of pride and Dempsey's calm

- A prediction by Dempsey that eventually proved true

- Greg's admiration for Dempsey, whose value system stressed helping people help themselves

Some questions to consider:

Do you know any servant leaders? What, in particular, distinguishes each one's performance as a leader?

_____

_____

Do you find this person to be inspirational in the same way that Dempsey was to his son? Why or why not?

_____

_____

_____

_____

_____

Framing and Union Leadership

On November, 19, 2009, a *New York Times* story about union leadership opened with the case of Julia Rivera. She reported being elated when her union of hotel and restaurant workers, Unite Here, selected her to become a union organizer.[16] But her pride quickly turned to anger as she soon became a victim of a practice known as "pink sheeting." In pink sheeting, union leaders surreptitiously elicit highly personal and negative information from one's past, which they then write down on a pink form for future use.

In Rivera's case, her father had sexually abused her. Learning this, union leaders apparently pressured her to use this information as a hook to recruit new members. It was a testimonial of the order, "Thanks to the union, I overcame my problems." To make matters worse, new union organizers like Julia Rivera were forced to pink sheet other workers to increase the union's size and number of recruiters. Rivera said, "I was scared not to do what they said. . . . To me, it was sick. It was horrible."

Asked about pink sheeting practices, Unite Here's president, John W. Wilhelm, denounced them, saying, "I have zero tolerance for inappropriate intrusions into people's private and personal lives. I have not personally used these techniques, and I have taken a very strong stand against them."[17] But he also asserted that the practice was rare within Unite Here and was more likely a propaganda campaign by its rival, Service Employees International Union. Apparently, Unite Here split apart earlier in the year and part of it merged with the services employees union.

Wilhelm was convinced that Service Employees was raiding his union; however, he pledged to eradicate any pink sheeting practices. This led to new member recruitment guidelines in both 2008 and 2009. But even after these were issued, several former Unite Here organizers interviewed by the *New York Times* reported that little had changed. Apparently, the sheets were no longer pink and had been renamed "motivation sheets"—but they were still in use. Questions targeting the risks and difficulties in one's personal life remained, as did data entries of a highly personal nature involving sexual abuse, substance abuse, anxiety disorders, and the like.

These were then followed by statements by former Unite Here organizers who morally positioned themselves as against repugnant recruiting practices, not sympathizers of another union. Also, at least one Unite Here current organizer echoed John Wilhelm's sentiments about the practice of pink sheeting amounting to a union-busting propaganda campaign by the rival union.

What are we to make about framing, leadership, and context in this apparently "they said, they said" situation? Without question, this is difficult—especially because *everything* we know is filtered through the newspaper's reporting of this situation. On a strictly emotional level, the stories told may trigger mirror neurons and cause some readers to sympathize with those whose secrets have been told. Other readers may see the decision by former union organizers to speak up as an act of leadership and pay particular attention to the large number of quotes from disgruntled union organizers versus that of John Wilhelm and his sympathizer.

But for a veteran of ugly union campaigns, Wilhelm's position may resonate and appear much more credible than the "sour grapes" attributed to those who left the union. Readers might also have an opinion of the *New York Times* that could impact their attributions of leadership. Fans of conservative media might see the paper as left-leaning and likely to emphasize the plight of the unions, while others might see the paper's reporting as balanced.

To summarize, what are the key aspects of framing and context in this case of union leadership? It depends on one or more of the following:

- The plausibility and emotional resonance of the stories of former union organizers
- How developed one's mental models are for union campaigns and media outlets
- One's ethical Discourses for leadership influence and motivational tactics
- The credibility of the former union organizers, current union leadership, and media outlets like the *New York Times*

Some questions to consider:

From your perspective, who is showing leadership in this case and why?

_____

_____

_____

Can you cite other instances of contested leadership?

_____

_____

_____

_____

_____

Framing and Charismatic Leadership

At this writing, Governor Arnold Schwarzenegger faces a severe economic crisis in his state of California, which is reportedly close to bankruptcy. However, in 2007 Schwarzenegger was on the front cover of *U.S. News & World Report*'s "America's Best Leaders" issue for his handling of the California wildfires.[18] The title of the article read, "A Film Hero Up to Playing the Real Role," suggesting that the Governor had reprised his 1984 action hero role in the movie

The Terminator to deal with the fire and its problems.[19] Schwarzenegger appeared to echo its Discourse when touring one of the local assistance centers at Cuyamaca College. He was asked about those wildfire survivors who might become victims of fraud:

> The fraud situations? Well, let me tell you, I made it very clear that if anyone uses this time where people are most vulnerable to commit fraud, they will regret it for the rest of their lives. We will find these people. We will do everything that we can, and the state will do everything it can, to go and prosecute those people and put them away.[20]

In *The Terminator*, Schwarzenegger is a menacing cyborg who would not be deterred from accomplishing his mission. In the excerpt from the speech quoted here, Schwarzenegger combines similar tough-talking language from his movie roles, celebrity, his distinctive Austrian accent, and an athletic body adorned in a suit to position an identity for himself as a moral standard-bearer for California's citizens. In the *U.S. News* interview, Schwarzenegger even acknowledges the conscious use of his celebrity as a strategic resource.[21] As the chief spokesman for the state of California, the framing of the "Governator," an amusingly apt nickname accorded to him, appears as a mighty force against those who would defraud the state's most vulnerable citizens.

However, it is not only Schwarzenegger's celebrity that contributes to how he plays the charisma game. When interviewed for the *U.S. News & World Report* story, he talked about being on the front lines "with the people," both victims and first responders.[22] Such talk was reminiscent of movie roles where he could jump into action. In this case, he could attend to such small things as diapers and baby formula in addition to more standard concerns with health and well-being in a fire-ravaged area.

However, while the magazine was certainly shaping the Governor's image as one of "America's Best Leaders," Schwarzenegger and his staff cleverly assisted this effort through the official Governor's Web site, which chronicled the Governor's every move during the crisis.[23] This included photographs, video clips, and texts of his news conferences, in which he often stood at the microphone flanked by dutiful representatives of California's state agencies. There were also visits to relief centers in which he was photographed engaged in conversation, suggesting a hands-on monitoring of the relief effort.

In effect, the public relations effort of Schwarzenegger's staff produced a model image of a crisis governor. They highlighted key individual framing efforts, including his moral positioning on matters of fraud, visually evocative press conferences and visits to relief centers, and tough-talking "Terminator" language as a show of determination. Moreover, although it was never voiced in the midst of the crisis, Schwarzenegger was likely aware of the heavy criticisms that Governor Kathleen Blanco of Louisiana received for her management of the relief effort associated with Hurricane Katrina. So "jump into action" nicely captures his image-shaping efforts, if not his crisis management itself.

To summarize, what are the key aspects of framing and context in this case of charismatic leadership? It is a combination of these elements:

- "Terminator" Discourse to address the current crisis, complemented by Schwarzenegger's distinctive Austrian accent and his athletic-looking body

- Strategic use of his celebrity

- Strategic use of technology through the official Governor's Web site, which framed Schwarzenegger as a leader who jumped into action

- Inevitable comparisons to Governor Blanco's leadership during Hurricane Katrina

Some questions to consider:

Was talking in "Terminator" Discourse effective? Does being a celebrity leader have any downside to it?

_____

_____

_____

How does technology assist or interfere with the framing process for leaders?

_____

_____

_____

Framing and Resistance Leadership (Whistleblowing)

Whistleblowing is not for the faint of heart. Even though, as Chapter Six reported, three women received *Time* magazine's "Person of the Year" honors in 2002 for blowing the whistle in their respective organizations, few whistleblowers are rewarded for their resistance leadership. (The resistance they show is usually to some established authority structure or organization.)

Arguably, most whistleblowers suffer the fate of Roger Boisjoly, the Morton Thiokol engineer who blew the whistle on the dangers associated with O-rings (a type of gasket) in NASA's Space Shuttle *Challenger* disaster. In a 1985 memo, an ensuing task force, and heated discussion at or around the time of the fatal launch on January 28, 1986, Boisjoly expressed his objections to the space shuttle launch and the operation of the O-rings under conditions of dangerously cold temperatures.

Largely ignored, Boisjoly watched in horror as the *Challenger* blew up. Shortly thereafter, he was asked to testify before a presidential review committee ordered by President Reagan, which he did by sharing his pre-launch warnings along with NASA's and Morton Thiokol's rejection of them. Upon his return to work, he was shunned by management and certain of his colleagues, forcing him to leave to become a lecturer on workplace ethics.[24]

Many outside Morton Thiokol or NASA would attribute real leadership, even heroism, to Boisjoly because of the way he placed concern for human health and safety ahead of the bottom line. However, management and others inside those two organizations implicitly framed him as a traitor or snitch. Despite laws in many countries that protect whistleblowers, very few cases of whistleblowing actually end up in court, let alone Congress. Moreover, the process of workplace shunning represents the dark side of leadership that few write about because the purveyors of this game deny that they do it.

Usually orchestrated by management, shunning can produce termination, suspension, demotion, wage reduction, or harsh mistreatment by other employees, many of whom may fear for their own jobs unless they parrot the company line. As a result, the shunning game often creates an "outsider," a person who is now "not one of us." It is a particularly effective form of workplace bullying because shunning is a strategically ambiguous maneuver.

The person who is shunned is often left with only (increasingly) vague feelings of disenfranchisement as in, "Hmmm, John no longer speaks with me about this issue. I wonder . . ., " or "I expected to hear from Human Resources this week. I haven't yet, which is kind of odd." It thus becomes possible for the shunning firm to claim deniability should it be forced into a legal setting. Suffice it to say, framing whistleblowers as traitors through workplace shunning is not a display of leadership at its finest. Consider also that some seven years later, on February 1, 2003, another structural failure caused the loss of the Space Shuttle *Columbia* during re-entry after a two-week mission. A blue ribbon commission concluded that NASA had learned little from the first disaster.[25]

To summarize, what are the key aspects of framing and context in this case of resistance leadership shown by whistleblower Boisjoly? They are a combination of several factors:

- A heightened sense of urgency to discover the factors contributing to the disaster

- Boisjoly's decision to publicly speak the truth about his prelaunch warnings, knowing the culture at Morton Thiokol

- Boisjoly's framing from an ethos of safety and reliability

- The implicit framing of Boisjoly as a traitor through shunning

- Morton Thiokol's value system, which privileged the bottom line over human safety and relied upon the company's ability to force compliance through authority

Some questions to consider:

Does Boisjoly qualify as a resistance leader or a reluctant one? Is there a difference?

_____

_____

_____

Can you cite other instances of resistance leadership through whistleblowing? What were the outcomes for the leaders involved?

_____

_____

_____

_____

_____

Framing and Community Organizing

Mid-twentieth-century community organizer and leader Saul Alinsky wrote passionately about the needs of a community to move past its rationalizations for (sometimes years of) inaction.[26] As a community organizer, Alinsky was a self-described "agitator" likely to provoke defensive reactions and ambivalence about how to proceed. In Message Design Logic terms, he is a classic Strategic all the way. His leadership challenge was to spur collective action by fighting inertia, breaking down defensiveness, and inducing change.

One story he told involved a meeting with some Canadian First Nations leaders (the specific tribe was unnamed) who invited him to help them address their plight at the margins of Canadian society. Similar to American Indians, these Canadians were segregated and subject to a host of discriminatory practices. Apparently, they did not take kindly to Alinsky's "get organized" message. Alinsky writes,

> The dialogue went something like this (I should preface this by noting that it was quite obvious what was happening since I could see from the way the Indians were looking at each other they were thinking: "So we invite this white organizer from south of the border to come up here and he tells us to get organized and to do these things. What must be going through his mind is: 'What's wrong with you Indians that you have been sitting around here for a couple of hundred years now and you haven't organized to do these things?'" And so it began):
>
> Indians: Well, we can't organize.
>
>   Me: Why not?

Indians: Because that's a white man's way of doing things.

Me: (I decided to let that one pass though it was obviously untrue, since mankind from time immemorial has always organized, regardless of what race or color they were, whenever they wanted to bring about change.) I don't understand.

Indians: Well, you see, if we organize, that means getting out and fighting the way you are telling us to do and that would mean that we would be corrupted by the white man's culture and lose our own values.

Me: What are these values that you would lose?

Indians: Well, there are all kinds of values.

Me: Like what?

Indians: Well, there's creative fishing…when you whites go out and fish, you just go out and fish, don't you?

Me: Yeah, I guess so.

Indians: Well, you see, when we go out and fish, we fish creatively.

Me: Yeah. That's the third time you've come around with that. What is this creative fishing?

Indians: Well, to begin with, when we go out fishing, we get away from everything. We get way out in the woods.

Me: Well, we whites don't exactly go fishing in Times Square, you know.

Indians: Yes, but it's different with us. When we go out, we're out on the water, and you can hear the lap of the waves on the bottom of the canoe, and the birds in the trees and the leaves rustling, and—you know what I mean?

Me: No, I don't know what you mean. Furthermore, I think that's just a pile of shit. Do you believe it yourself?

This brought a shocked silence. It should be noted that I was not being profane purely for the sake of being profane, I was doing this purposefully. If I had responded in a tactful way, saying, "Well, I don't quite understand what you mean," we would have been off for a ride around the rhetorical ranch for the next thirty days. Here profanity became literally an up-against-the-wall bulldozer."[27]

Alinsky noted that the conversation continued with "creative welfare" and a number of other "creative" rationalizations for inaction over the years—that he would challenge. Interestingly, the National Film Board of Canada, which was doing a documentary on Alinsky's work, had filmed parts of this episode. At a screening for Canadian development workers, with both Alinsky and several of the Indians present, Alinsky observed:

> The white Canadian community development workers kept look-ing at the floor, very embarrassed, during the unreeling of the scene, and giving sidelong looks at the Indians. After it was over one of the Indians stood up and said, "When Mr. Alinsky told us we were full of shit, that was the first time a white man has talked to us as equals—you [referring to the development workers] would never say that to us. You would always say "'Well, I can see your point of view but I'm a little confused,' stuff like that. In other words you treat us as children."[28]

Framing through a strategic use of obscenity is not something I have addressed in this book. However, Alinsky makes the case for its effectiveness, as he calls it, an "up-against-the-wall bulldozer" designed to break through to the real issues. Again, there's clearly a Strategic communications style surfacing here.

What is especially interesting is the collective sensemaking of the Indian community in which the political correctness of the Canadian development workers was framed as demeaning, akin to treating the Indians as children. This must have come as quite a surprise to the development staff who probably felt their communications were doing just the opposite. Unlike Mr. Alinsky, they had studiously avoided offending the people they were working with—only to be told that that is exactly what they had been doing. It would appear that the First Nations leaders delivered their own "up-against-the-wall bulldozer" by introducing a parent-child frame seriously in need of repair.

To summarize, what are the key aspects of framing and context in this case of community organizing? It is a potent mix:

- Alinsky's ethical code helps people to help themselves
- His Strategic communications style, agitating through challenges to "creative" inertia and moving past defensiveness

- His strategic use of obscenity and brutally frank talk

- Evidence of the Indians' sensemaking through contrasting the egalitarian framing by Alinsky compared to the "treatment as children" framing by the Canadian development workers

Some questions to consider:

What do you think of the frankness of Alinsky's talk? Do you use obscenity for emphasis and stress in your framing?

_____

_____

_____

Why is sensemaking an important concept to use in the analysis of leadership here?

_____

_____

_____

_____

_____

Now It Is Your Turn

Now that you have read the examples of different kinds of leadership presented in this chapter, it should be clear that framing is not the only thing that matters with respect to leadership. But it is centrally important, and your task as a responsible leader is to increase your awareness of the role played by your own framing communications relative to other contextual elements. You can do this by continuing to treat leadership as a design problem. As suggested, the best way to do all this is to get specific, really specific, about your tasks as a leader and how framing communications factor into these tasks.

Can you recall a critical framing incident as a leader or manager in which you *failed to meet* your expectations for yourself? Can you recall another critical framing incident in which you *exceeded* your expectations for yourself?

For each critical framing incident, answer the questions in Framing Tools 7.1 and 7.2 and note the picture that emerges.

FRAMING TOOL 7.1

Failed Leadership

Describe a critical incident in which you failed to meet expectations for yourself as a leader.

_____

_____

_____

_____

_____

What aspects of the situation were in play in terms of resources or constraints?

_____

_____

_____

_____

_____

How did these situational factors impair or otherwise impact your ability to lead?

_____

_____

_____

_____

_____

In what ways did your framing and actions in this incident *not* meet your expectations?

_____

_____

_____

_____

_____

What do you hope to do differently the next time around?

_____

_____

_____

_____

(You can download this form from www.josseybass.com/go/gailfairhurst.)

FRAMING TOOL 7.2

Successful Leadership

Describe a critical incident in which you met expectations for yourself as a leader.

_____

_____

_____

_____

What aspects of the situation were in play in terms of resources or constraints?

_____

_____

_____

_____

How did these situational factors assist or otherwise impact your ability to lead?

_____

_____

_____

_____

_____

In what ways did your framing and actions in this incident meet your expectations?

_____

_____

_____

_____

_____

What do you hope to do the same or differently the next time around?

_____

_____

_____

_____

_____

(You can download this form from www.josseybass.com/go/gailfairhurst.)

A Backward Glance at Chapter Seven

This chapter is designed to help you understand how framing mixes with other aspects of the context when leadership is the judged outcome. More specifically,

- The secret to unlocking the answers to the question of how framing, context, and leadership all go together is twofold. First, you must focus on the "who, what, when, where, why" details of the situation at hand to discern the framing at work. Second, you must figure out the design problem of the leader or leaders involved.

- Reality Construction Rule #5 from Chapter One stipulates that leadership is a design problem. Leaders must figure out what leadership is in the context of what they do and, through their framing and actions, persuade themselves and other people that they are doing it.

- Your analysis of leadership as a design problem should begin by answering four key questions:

  - What is the task at hand? Any designation of leadership should be grounded in the task.

  - What would it mean to lead at that task? Any attribution of leadership requires that the specific constraints and enablements of the context be meshed with one's mental models for leadership (which are always general). This will produce an image of what it would mean to lead at a *specific* task.

  - Who is making the attribution of leadership? The vantage point of those assessing leadership is always impacted by the information they may or may not have, the perspective that they bring, and the platform they have for expressing their views.

  - What is the role of framing in this leadership situation? Once the first three questions are answered, the relatively more or less important role of framing communications can be determined. The glossary at the end of the book can also be used to analyze specific framing components and their impact on leadership effectiveness.

A FINAL THOUGHT

Three of the most important aspects of leadership framing are context, context, and context.

8

The Applications of Framing

THE POWER OF FRAMING can apply directly to your everyday communications—in two distinct ways. First, imagine that you and I are having a conversation at your local coffee shop, and you ask my advice as an executive coach about a framing dilemma you face. In this first part of the chapter, you will find a number of common framing dilemmas and my advice as to how to apply the power of framing to achieve your objectives. Using the Message Design Logic terminology of Chapter One, I will be attempting to move you from a Conventional response to a more Strategic one in most cases.

Second, for projects that are somewhat wider in scope, such as those involving organizational change, I provide a strategic framing template that is also downloadable. This tool should help you think through all of the aspects of framing when you are approaching a new subject and need to apply its power for maximum effect.

Conversations

Now, imagine that conversation we are having over coffee . . .

The Job Interview

Framing Dilemma: You are interviewing for a manager's job and the first thing the interviewer says is "Tell me about yourself." This is a deceptively simple opening; you can blow the interview without a good response.

Framing Advice: This is a fairly predictable interview tactic, so prime yourself for a "spontaneous" response ahead of time. (Chapter Three) Also:

- Say something that is both ordinary and extraordinary about yourself. The former makes you easy to relate to, while the latter communicates your uniqueness.

- Try to impart at least a little of your leadership philosophy in answering the question; this establishes that you see yourself as a leader.

- Use humor, if possible, to establish rapport.

- Use a three-part list to organize your ideas. This increases the chances that the interviewer will remember your answer. (Chapter Four)

- After you've finished answering, stop talking, pause, and pleasantly look back at the interviewer while controlling whatever signs of nervousness that you may be experiencing.

The Elevator Pitch

Framing Dilemma: You are planning to attend a trade association meeting and want to do a lot of networking there. However, you always find it difficult to introduce yourself given the technical nature of your job. You are seeking advice as to how best to do this.

Framing Advice: This is another predictable framing opportunity for which priming is key. Remember also Rhonda Abrams's advice from Chapter

Three.[1] She said to keep it short, avoid jargon, and be memorable, which are all good things to do. You might also:

- Determine how the people you'll be meeting relate to what you do, and tailor your language accordingly.

- Introduce some humor or use an easily understood analogy explaining what you do. For example, "I'm the quarterback in the group who depends mightily on a strong offensive line of account reps. . . ." (Chapter Four)

- Keep it simple by keeping it general, as in, "I manage people in the communications industry," or "I manage people on the accounting side of my company." (Chapter Four)

- Alternatively, relate what you do to your questioner's job description. (Chapter Two)

- Remember to smile, maintain eye contact, offer up a strong handshake, and have a business card ready.

Seeing Systems

Framing Dilemma: You work for a small manufacturing company that produces a new but hugely successful commodity product overseas. Over the last ninety days, demand has spiked significantly, causing stock-outs. The sales force is out selling this product, but they get frustrated when they lose orders because the company doesn't maintain high enough inventory levels to meet the ever-increasing demand.

When a stock-out occurs, the time needed to fill the order ranges from 30 to 120 days. Because customers can't wait that long, they take their business elsewhere.

The real problem, as you see it, is that Sales staff are compensated based on dollars sold in their respective territories. They complain to Marketing that it is not maintaining proper stocking levels. Marketing has to ensure that it accurately forecasts inventory levels for Purchasing to order and maintain in inventory. Purchasing has been told to scale back inventories to a one-month safety stock level, but this level isn't enough to support the increasing demand of this product.

The Purchasing team is measured based on the number of inventory turns annually and isn't making a distinction between fast- and slow-moving products, so it scales back indiscriminately on ordering across all products. You believe that these issues are related to the use of different metrics, metrics based on people acting from within their own divisional "silos."

Framing Advice: This is a classic case of what Peter Senge wrote about regarding the inability of organizations to "see systems" or patterns of interdependencies, which debunks the notion that organizational actors are free agents.[2] As a result, all of the communications in the world will not fix this problem unless the system can be changed. So:

- Target the right audience and do whatever you need to do to get the right players at the table. Schedule a meeting with only those divisional leaders who have the authority to make and negotiate standard operating procedures and policy.

- Define the problem using master frames and metaphors associated with who the team is. (Your division or the entire organization?) Avoid thinking in silos; instead embrace systems thinking. Be ready to surface mental models for "silo thinking" for those involved. (Chapter Two, Chapter Four)

- Bolster your arguments with contrasting examples of different metrics and their unintended consequences. (Chapter Four)

- Encourage leaders to set new objectives with system constraints in mind (for example, Sales must forewarn new customers of the ninety-day lead time; Purchasing should know that when Marketing provides a number, it should point out the ninety-day wait; consider a contingency emergency request of product of, say, five hundred units that will always be on hand for all customers, and so on.)

- Monitor and follow up regarding the workability of the new system.

Identity Matters

Framing Dilemma: You are one of those leaders whose identity always seems to be reduced to a demographic category (generally because you are a rarity), however well intentioned. For example, you are one of "too few" female managers, African American leaders, and so on.

Framing Advice. If you don't wish to make an issue of your difference, take a page from the playbook Barack Obama seems to have used when running for office.[3] Frame yourself as a leader "who happens to be" female or "who happens to be" black, or whatever. As such:

- Don't speak of your demographic identity unless others bring it up.

- Refrain from using familiar cultural Discourses associated with demographic issues. (Chapter Two)

If you do wish to make your demographic category an issue, frame yourself in those terms:

- Frequently categorize yourself in terms of your demographic identity in everyday conversation. (Chapter Four)

- Draw from affirmative action cultural Discourses or others associated with equal or civil rights. (Chapter Two)

E-Mail Communications

Framing Dilemma: You have just been told by one of your staff that your style of communicating over e-mail is inappropriate. She described your face-to-face communications as direct and your joking style as a bit "in your face." In e-mail, she said, your heavy use of capital letters comes off as yelling. Also, people do not know when you are joking in e-mail—or strategically using humor to criticize. Others were afraid to come forward; she was "elected" to tell you.

Framing Advice: Your challenge here is to first listen, *really* listen to this feedback. Then:

- Ask for specific examples, how widespread the perception is, or other clarifying questions that you might have.

- Consider your mental model for this source. How credible is she? (Chapter Two)

- Consider this feedback; does it ring true given your mental model for yourself? (Chapter Two)

  - If so, pledge to reflexively monitor your e-mail communications in the future regarding capital letters' usage and humor.

  - If not, consider the consequences of living with the fear-based mental model that others appear to have of you. (Chapter Two)

Problem Setting

Framing Dilemma: You are working in a complex, uncertain environment. Change is happening so quickly you hardly have time to keep up. However, one of the most important things that you do as a leader is to set or define problems for the teams that report to you. Your framing dilemma is to "read the tea leaves" and then communicate what you know to your people so they can solve the problem.

Framing Advice: Your job as the leader is *not* to solve problems yourself, it is to frame them and ask the right questions. So it is important to:

- Make your objectives and goals clear from the start.
- Define the problem if it is "tame" enough. (Chapter One Notes)
- Alternatively, if it is a "wicked problem," pose the hard questions. (Chapter One)
- Communicate the conditions of the environment as you see them, including resources and constraints.
- Consciously surface mental models as necessary. (Chapter Two)
- Encourage pushback and experimentation, and allow opportunities to fail. (Chapter Three)
- Help people envision a range of possible futures if called upon.
- Consider charging them with a "soft mission," one that empowers them to adapt to the circumstances as dictated.
- Stress accountability associated with the outcomes.
- Stress communication and the need for continuous updating with you.

Ethical Codes

Framing Dilemma: You are an HR manager, and one of your employees, Jane, just confessed to you that she has known about a possible case of sexual harassment that she did not previously disclose to you. As it turns out, Jane is friends with a young woman in another department, who disclosed to her that her recently divorced boss was making sexually inappropriate comments to her. But, as a friend, she asked Jane to keep it quiet.

Two months later, however, at the office holiday party, Jane began to question her decision to keep silent. When the friend drank way too much alcohol, her boss didn't call her a cab; instead, he booked her a hotel room and paid for it himself. It was not known what may have happened between this young woman and her boss, if anything, but Jane now felt compelled to tell you what she knew. Upon hearing this news, you are upset with Jane because she should have known better as a staff member in HR. As it turns out, Jane's friend also has a pending sexual harassment lawsuit against her old boss in another company.

Framing Advice: Your job is to channel your emotion into making Jane understand the potential ramifications of her silence:

- In the strongest possible terms, express disapproval of Jane's actions, citing the company's ethical code along with the ethos of an HR unit. (Chapter Six)

- Stress and spin the possible unintended consequences of her silence, for example, lawsuits against the company (Jane's friend can claim that "an HR representative" knew of her concerns); lawsuits against Jane personally were she to be a supervisor, and so on. (Chapter Four)

- Give Jane the actual wording she should have used to morally position herself when telling her friend that, as a staff member in HR, she was ethically bound to report any perceived sexual harassment. (Chapter Six)

- Consider introducing a master frame to Jane that also functions as a catchphrase (and thus more easily remembered) for *any* situation in HR, for example, "If you know it, you own it." (That is, if you know of a rule violation—in this case, perceived sexually harassment—you must report it to your supervisor, because your knowing silence will be taken as permission for it to continue.) (Chapters Two and Four)

- Repeat the master frame, using a wide variety of examples to explain it. (Chapter Four)

Managing Your Boss

Framing Dilemma: Your manager thinks she is a democratic leader, but more often than not, she will make statements like, "You have my permission to . . . " or "I have 51 percent of the vote around here." Moreover, she has a way of micromanaging you once assignments are made. You've decided to talk to her about this because you feel you deserve more autonomy.

Framing Advice: A performance review is often a good context in which to raise this concern. If this is not possible, schedule a time when your boss is unhurried and has time to talk and reflect. Then:

- State your goal of seeking more autonomy and provide a feeling statement related to it. ("When you supervise every part of a task like that, it makes me feel that you don't trust my judgment.") (Chapter Four)

- Perception check with her. Does she share your frame that she regards it as necessary to see and control every step of a job?

- Be prepared to give specific examples; tell a story or two. (Chapter Four)

- Demonstrate how it is in her best interest to leave you alone. Use strong arguments and suggest a trial period. (Chapter Four)

- Agree on a schedule for touching base, if necessary.

- During your next performance review, make any progress (or lack thereof) on this issue a topic for discussion.

Working Interculturally

Framing Dilemma: Your management team is growing, adding members whose countries of origin are not your own. You are concerned that although they have been with the company for a while, they have some culture-based practices that are proving difficult to penetrate. For example, one of your "X country" team leaders is stressing the hierarchical relationship with his people above all else—including meeting performance criteria. You have scheduled a one-to-one meeting with him to learn more about the reports you've been getting.

Framing Advice: In this meeting you are trying to productively manage the tension between cultural sensitivity and productivity. Understand and label that tension in the meeting. Also:

- This is a good time to surface cross-cultural differences in mental models around the role of authority. Such models usually surface when targeting specific practices and answering questions like, "Why do you think that way?" (Chapter Two)

- Use examples, tell stories, and build as much redundancy into this conversation as possible to reinforce the message. (Chapter Four)

- Monitor and follow up.

Show Your Emotional IQ (1)

Framing Dilemma: Your company has just announced that it plans to downsize a large number of workers. Several of your employees have requested a meeting with you to address questions that they have. Reports from your staff suggest that several of them are freaking out. You have agreed to meet with them, but are concerned that a meeting like this could get out of hand.

Framing Advice: Before meeting with your employees, make sure you have the most up-to-date information about the downsizing and the resources to be made available to them, and that you have clarified sentiments you want to express. Then, at the meeting:

- Listen, *really* listen to your employees' stories of potential hardship.

- Be as honest as possible. If there is uncertainty about any of the information (even the details) you are offering, say so, pledge to get more information, and communicate about it as soon as you are able. (Chapter Six)

- Acknowledge and affirm employees' emotions, making sure that the concern you show is genuine. Don't be afraid to label their emotions (surprise, uncertainty, anger, and so on), identify with them, or suggest helpful ways in which they might be managed. (Chapter Five)

- Don't be afraid of morality-talk. Remember Tom, the toxin handler in Chapter Five?[4] He said, "Somebody had to look at them and talk to them openly and honestly and say this is not your fault. It's not something you did; it's not something you said." (Chapter Five, Chapter Six)

- Position (or frame) yourself as a conduit to get employees the resources that they need.

- Pay attention to your nonverbal and symbolic framing by refraining from arrogant or insensitive displays of wealth and power. (Remember the CEOs from the American automobile industry who flew on private jets to testify before Congress asking for a government bailout. Ouch!) (Chapter One, Chapter Five)

Show Your Emotional IQ (2)

Framing Dilemma: One of your most reliable employees is going through a painful separation and divorce. You have genuine empathy for the situation, but this person's emotional state is beginning to seriously affect job performance. You have requested a meeting to talk over the road ahead.

Framing Advice: Show the genuine concern that you feel for this person, but balance it with a concern for the task. For example:

- Offer up one or more feeling statements as in "I've been through a divorce myself [or seen several divorces close-up, or whatever is true], and I know that there will be some difficult days ahead. I empathize with you." (Chapter Five)

- Listen carefully to what this person has to say.

- Broach the subject of performance by asking if the employee has felt any effect on the job.

  - If the answer is yes, ask about ways in which this might be managed better, remaining sensitive to the employee's needs.

  - If the answer is no, communicate your view of recent performance issues with one or more specific examples. Try to secure the employee's understanding, if not agreement. (Chapter One)

- Suggest joint problem solving to manage this difficult time period.

- Suggest some useful resources (for example, counseling, reading, exercise, and so on) and wish the employee well. (Chapter Five)

Gender Politics

Framing Dilemma: You are one of the few female managers in a male-dominated division. The men with whom you work often comment upon your appearance, the effect of which further singles you out as a token female.

Framing Advice: Remarks like this can play out in many different ways. It is important to get as accurate a reading as to the speaker's intentions as possible and respond accordingly. In general,

- Use humor, even sarcasm, to diminish the focus on appearances. You might smile and say something like, "And the same goes for you, Bill. I see you've managed to wear matching socks today."

- Work on smooth segues back to the task, "Thanks, this is my lucky suit. I have a feeling my team's sales will be beating yours by a mile this month."

- Compliment back, but exemplify how you wish to be complimented. Note that this is a "hinting" strategy, which not everyone will pick up on.

- If this occurs in the context of other sexually harassing comments, plainly and firmly communicate the unwanted nature of the attention: "This is nothing short of sexual harassment. It is unwanted and will be reported unless you stop making such comments."

Making the Case for Change

Framing Dilemma: Your teams have gotten awfully good at making deadlines with only seconds to spare. You want to change this kind of last-minute effort in favor of a more thoughtful process.

Framing Advice: Take a page out of the playbook of high-reliability organizations (Chapter Three):

- Surface and name the mental model involved in last-minute thinking. (Chapter Two)

- Argue that success, even last-minute success, breeds complacency and resting on your laurels. (Chapter Four)

- Instead, frame last-minute success as "near-failure." (Chapter Three)

- Encourage team learning by asking, "What could we do better the next time around?" Develop concrete action plans.

- Encourage follow-through on these plans and monitor results.

Enhance Your Speaking Style

Framing Dilemma: You have been told that you come off as too meek to be a manager. You are deferential and soft-spoken, essentially speaking in a monotone. You have excellent ideas, but they are not appreciated in meetings because they appear to lack conviction.

Framing Advice: Channel your inner alpha:

- Practice taping your voice and exaggerating your voice variation. Read children's books into the recorder. This kind of material will help develop in you a sensitivity to natural inflection points so that you frame with emphasis and stress with your work content. (Chapter Five)

- Please don't end your sentences with rising inflections, okay? You are nonverbally framing yourself as uncertain or insecure when you consistently do so. (Chapter One, Chapter Five)

- Throw your body into your delivery. Gesture for emphasis and stress. Move into the audience if you are in a public speaking venue. Expect it to feel awkward the first time or two. (Chapter Five)

- Build redundancy into your arguments to reinforce your key points, as in, "My point is, essentially, this . . . " (Chapter Four)

Tone Down Your Speaking Style (1)

Framing Dilemma: You played football in college and you still look the part. You have been told that you have an intimidating presence. Not only are you physically imposing, your voice is a bit loud. Truth be told, you also have been known to bark orders at people during hectic periods to get the job done. You have been asked to speak to three or four hundred sales reps from your division for an upcoming meeting. You really want to engage the audience, but you fear that your reputation might precede you and your physicality might be off-putting. You are struggling with how to get them past the intimidation factor.

Framing Advice. There are several ways to counter-frame others' perception of you as intimidating:

- Before your talk starts, "work the room" as politicians do by greeting those you know—and introducing yourself to those you do not know. Shake hands, maintain direct eye contact, and smile— all of which can minimize the distance between you and your audience.

- Use self-deprecating humor. Laugh at yourself (perhaps joke about one too many blows to the head in football games); it eases tension and makes you appear more human.

- Stress your approachability. Solicit questions or input from the audience. Listen, *really* listen to what they are saying and answer them as best you can.

- Move into the audience and away from the podium as much as possible. Maintain eye contact, and smile if the content allows it.

- Don't put your entire talk on PowerPoint. Use slides only as tags for your main points to keep the focus on you.

- Don't stonewall in answering questions. Be as honest as possible. If you don't know the answer, say so and offer to try to get one.

Tone Down Your Speaking Style (2)

Framing Dilemma. You are a female leader working in the financial services industry where working with alpha males is the norm. You have been told that you come off as too aggressive—and what they don't actually say, but mean, is "for a woman."

Framing Advice: This is a tough one because gender expectations are factoring in here—men can be aggressive, but women can't? That's not fair! But female leaders generally don't win the fairness argument on this (just as male leaders who come off as too soft by being inclusive and participatory also don't win the fairness argument). You have a few options:

- Consciously consider your mental models for aggressiveness versus assertiveness. Knowing the difference between the two, you can more easily curb your aggressiveness if you so choose. Work on priming for and displaying assertiveness instead. Also, be ready to account for yourself and your actions in ways that show others the differences between the two. (Chapter Two, Chapter Three)

- Don't change your style. Let your results speak for themselves; however, try to gauge to what extent *not changing* impacts your promotability—and whether you can live with these consequences.

- Don't change your style, and ask for an executive coach who can help you to *situationally* adapt your style better.

Turning Down a Job

Framing Dilemma: You work for a multinational firm and have had your share of international assignments. Your boss has another opportunity for you, which you want to decline. Your partner does not want to move again. When you suggest to your boss that he consider other candidates, your boss indicates that their family situations (read, the presence of children) make it difficult.

Framing Advice: Politely, but firmly, say "thank you, but no thank you" however many times you are asked. You might also:

- Remind your boss of your international assignments to date. List them on paper if necessary.

- Make your arguments explicit; fairness dictates equal treatment regardless of whether one has children or not. (Chapter Four)

- If applicable, suggest an alternative arrangement that might satisfy both the aims of the assignment and your work location preferences.

Framing for Campaigns

Some of your communications tasks give you time to reflect and plan in advance. These tasks are usually broader in scope and may take on a campaign-like quality because they involve organizational change. For example:

- You have a kernel of an idea that could develop into a profitable vision for your firm. You are seeking input and buy-in from others with whom you work as you formulate this idea into an organizational vision.

- You have a strategic plan that you must communicate effectively. Your people must adopt the plan, although each team has a choice as to how they do so.

- As a senior leader in a marketing division, you have to set the terms for the creation of new marketing campaigns for your major accounts.

- The press is reporting financial misdeeds on the part of your organization. You must account for and defend your organization's handling of the budget to multiple constituencies, which is calling for a coordinated public relations effort.

FRAMING TOOL 8.1

Framing Involving Big Projects or Campaigns

A. What is the opportunity or problem you need to address?

_____

_____

_____

_____

B. What is your basic message, idea, or case for change? Write it on the lines below.

_____

_____

_____

_____

C. What are your core framing tasks associated with this project? List and describe them on the lines below. (Chapter Two)

1._____

_____

_____

2._____

_____

_____

3._____

_____

_____

4._____

_____

_____

5._____

_____

_____

6._____

_____

_____

D. Who would the key stakeholders be and why? (Chapter Two)

_____

_____

_____

_____

_____

_____

E. What framing challenges do you face? (Chapters One, Two, and Three)

1. What do you know about the mental models of all involved? How different are they? How well developed are they? Do stakeholders need time or information (or both) to further develop their mental models?

_____

_____

_____

_____

_____

2. Are the various stakeholder groups "speaking different languages," that is, using different cultural Discourses? In formulating your basic message to them, are there terms or arguments that should be avoided because of the Discourses with which they align?

_____

_____

_____

_____

_____

3. What constraints do you face and what resources are needed to overcome them? Do you have a plan for acquiring these resources?

_____

_____

_____

_____

_____

4. Do you need agreement from everyone, or is alignment (behavioral compliance only) sufficient?

_____

_____

_____

_____

_____

F. What are your framing aesthetics? What is the emotional landscape like? (Chapter Four, Chapter Five)

1. Can you breathe more life into the wording of your basic message through metaphors or other language tools? Don't be afraid to experiment with narrative or different word choices. Write them on the lines below.

_____

_____

_____

_____

_____

2. Are you providing a new angle or fresh take to stimulate new thinking by your stakeholders? Can you communicate the value-added through a central master frame?

_____

_____

_____

_____

_____

3. Do you need to simplify the message you are trying to get out? Or build redundancy into the message?

_____

_____

_____

_____

_____

4. How might you position gains or losses, or both?

_____

_____

_____

_____

_____

5. Are you believable? What are you saying and doing that will make people trust you?

_____

_____

_____

_____

_____

6. What role do emotions play in your basic message? Do you expect emotional contagion to be operating? Are you consciously trying to regulate emotions in a certain way? If so, how do you plan to do this?

_____

_____

_____

_____

_____

7. Does your message have any potential inconsistencies that will confuse your stakeholders? What might they be?

_____

_____

_____

_____

_____

8. If appropriate, can you inject some humor into your message? How might you do this (for example, with a funny story or anecdote)?

_____

_____

_____

_____

_____

9. Finally, estimate how many aspects of your message strategy you have under control, then list them. What else is likely to give you a sense of presence as a communicator, such as your nonverbal communication, physical appearance, use of technology, stage and setting, and so on?

_____

_____

_____

_____

_____

G. What are your framing ethics? (Chapter Six)

1. What ethos or aspects of your ethical code are relevant to the campaign you are planning?

_____

_____

_____

_____

_____

2. Will you frame or morally position yourself in a particular way? Explain.

_____

_____

_____

_____

_____

3. If all leaders adopted your code of ethics or a certain ethos for this effort, what would this organization look like? Would this be something of which to be proud?

_____

_____

_____

_____

_____

H. Framing tactics checklist for campaigns:

☐ Will you prime for spontaneity? Rehearse before you speak? If not, you may put out an incomplete or inconsistent message. (Chapter Three)

☐ Is there a chance that your strategic plan may come off as another "program of the week"? If so, be ready to challenge this framing.

☐ Have you already planned to give your people the opportunity to weigh in with their concerns? If not, provide this framing opportunity.

☐ Are you willing to risk evolution of the vision and changes to the strategic plan based on what your people say? If not, be prepared to live without their buy-in.

☐ Will you frame (read, translate) the vision and strategic plan in terms of their role responsibilities? Can you demonstrate your enthusiasm for the vision and strategic plan?

☐ Can you link the vision with other strategic initiatives in your organization so your people understand the big picture?

☐ Do you plan to frequently communicate about the vision and strategic plan? Is it worked into the everyday fabric of the organization?

I. In conducting this "campaign," are you acting in a leadership capacity? Explain. (Chapter Seven)

_____

_____

_____

_____

_____

J. Other framing issues to consider:

_____

_____

_____

_____

_____

(You can download this form from www.josseybass.com/go/gailfairhurst. Feel free to adapt it to suit your needs.)

This book's preface began with David Foster Wallace's story about the two young fish who are greeted by an older one; when the latter asks about the water, the two younger fish swim on as one says to the other, "What the hell is water?" In the spirit of Wallace's keen observations about the realities of life, the hope is that this book's closing marks a continuation of your journey to understand the power of your framing communications as a leader.

Ultimately, this involves a renewed commitment to connect with others in morally responsible ways. It means abandoning the view that communication is a simple transmission or something you just do automatically. It asks instead that you see framing as the means by which you create and manage meaning with others to create reality in the process. Finally, it asks that you see meaning creation as the milieu in which all communications operate—for *this* is the water.

A FINAL THOUGHT
Can you teach others to know about the water?

GLOSSARY OF FRAMING TERMS

Agreement (Chapter Two)

Agreement is one measure of framing effectiveness when others buy into our framing attempts.

Alignment (Chapter Two)

Alignment is one measure of framing effectiveness when the basis for coordinated action is understanding and willingness to comply, rather than agreement.

Believability frames (Chapter Four)

Believability frames are the language we use to establish our credibility, and that what we are saying is truthful, objective, and legitimate.

Case-based reasoning (Chapter Three)

Case-based reasoning involves deriving a course of action by comparison of the situation here and now with examples instead of working from a set of rules. *Mental models* function like a library of cases, especially when used by experts.

Complex metaphors (Chapter Four)	Complex metaphors involve an intricate organization of a series of comparisons, not literally applicable. Such metaphors are often the basis of stories or other narrative forms.
Conventionals (Chapter One)	According to Message Design Logic, Conventionals are people who have some sensitivity to framing because they generally follow the rules for communicating with others. They do what is appropriate to the situation and readily follow social norms. They tend to be reactive, not proactive, with respect to the context.
Core framing tasks (Chapter Two)	Core framing tasks are the dominant patterns of effective leadership communications in one's job. Leaders and managers should try to:

- Develop a collective sense of goals, objectives, and strategies.

- Instill knowledge of the organization's environment and its work.

- Generate enthusiasm, confidence, optimism, cooperation, and trust.

- Encourage flexibility in decision making and change.

- Construct and maintain a meaningful organizational identity.

Crucible (Chapter Six)	A crucible is a test, a particularly difficult challenge that usually leads to hard-won lessons.
Cultural Discourse (Chapter Two)	Cultural Discourse is an era-based system of thought with its own linguistic *tool bag* of terms, metaphors, themes, and familiar arguments that *culture* members draw upon in the moment of communicating.
Culture (Chapter Two)	Culture is the collective experience of an era—its defining events, people, objects, and concepts, which give rise to ways of seeing and talking about the world.

Emotional contagion (Chapter Five)	Emotional contagion occurs when the emotions and energy levels of an individual or a group influence others, consciously or unconsciously, to adopt a matching mood (see Barsade, 2002).
Emotional intelligence (Chapter Five)	Emotional intelligence involves the ability to join emotion and reason effectively. Psychologists Mayer and Salovey describe it as "the ability to perceive emotions, to access and generate emotions so as to assist thought, to understand emotions and emotional knowledge, and to reflectively regulate emotions so as to promote emotional and intellectual growth" (1997, p. 5).
Emotional regulation (Chapter Five)	Emotional regulation involves the management of one's own emotions. It is one of the features of emotional intelligence.
Ethical codes (Chapter Six)	Ethical codes are guides to everyday professional conduct. They are also a *cultural Discourse* and *tool bag* that enables people to decide on a course of action, justify it, and frame a preferred identity at the same time.
Ethical mind (Chapter Six)	Ethical mind requires that individuals discipline themselves to practice their ethical principles consistently.
Ethos (Chapter Six)	Ethos is the distinctive spirit or defining values of a *culture* or historical era.
Expressives (Chapter One)	According to Message Design Logic, Expressives are people who are apt to be least sensitive to the framing concept. Their primary goal is simply to express themselves; they lack an edit function. However, they are often viewed as more honest than *Strategics*, who can be perceived as manipulative.
Frames (Chapter One)	Frames are the mental pictures that are the basis for framing communications.

Framing (Chapter One)	Framing involves the ability to shape the meaning of a subject, to define its character and significance through the meanings we include and exclude, as well as those we emphasize when communicating.
Gain and Loss Frames (Chapter Four)	A gain frame spins or emphasizes the potential rewards of choosing one particular course of action, while a loss frame spins the disadvantages and the potential losses.
Hebb's Law (Chapter Three)	Hebb's Law states, "Neurons that fire together, wire together"—meaning that the more often you think of things in connection with each other, the more likely you are to recall them together in the future. It is the basis for *priming for spontaneity* (see Doidge, 2007).
High-reliability organizations (Chapter Three)	High-reliability organizations are concerned with preventing failure and maximizing reliability rather than promoting success and maximizing efficiency. Examples include aircraft carriers, police and fire organizations, and NASA.
Language forms (Chapter Four)	The concept of "language forms" employs a number of specialized terms:

Metaphorical language portrays a subject's resemblance to something else that is not literally applicable.

Story frames a subject through narrative.

Contrast describes what a subject is not.

Spin places a subject in a positive or negative light.

Jargon and *catchphrases* frame a subject in familiar terms.

Analogy frames a subject's parallels to another subject.

Argument frames a subject in reasoned, rational terms.

Feeling statements frame a subject in terms of felt emotions.

Categories frame a subject in terms of its membership (or not) in a class or group.

Three-part lists organize a subject in easily remembered "threes."

Repetition dramatizes a subject through parallel form.

Leaders (Chapters One and Two)

Leaders are people who tend to be the architects of change. They establish direction through a vision for the organization, develop strategies to achieve change, align people toward the mission and vision of the organization, and motivate and inspire to overcome obstacles and resource imbalances. (Compare *managers.*) For *wicked problems*, leaders ask key questions and facilitate a collaborative process by which individuals work together to arrive at solutions.

Leadership as design problem (Chapters One and Seven)

The design problem for leaders is to figure out what leadership is in the context of what they do and, through their framing and actions, persuade themselves and others that they are doing it (see Kelly, 2008).

Managers (Chapters One and Two)

Managers are the people in charge of everyday problem solving. Their goal is to lend stability to the organization through planning, budgeting, and staffing activities. (Compare *leaders.*)

Massed practice (Chapter Three)

Massed practice involves learning through immersion in a *culture.*

Master frames (Chapters Two and Four)

Master frames are more encompassing than ordinary *frames*, umbrella-like in their power to mobilize the collective efforts of a group or community.

Mental models (Chapter Two)

Mental models are deeply held images of how the world works. They organize our thoughts and assist us in understanding and remembering. They also lead us to make predictions about what will happen next (see Senge, 1990).

Message Design Logic (Chapter One)

Message Design Logic is Barbara J. O'Keefe's term for the three kinds of communicator styles she posits in her research program: *Expressive, Conventional,* and *Rhetorical.* (I use the term *Strategic* in place of *Rhetorical* in this book.) In her view, these styles determine how we produce messages and interpret those of others, especially as situations gain in complexity.

Miracle questions (Chapter Three)

Miracle questions lead us to envision a hoped-for future and use fantasy to develop *mental models* in the absence of experience.

Moral positioning (Chapter Six)

Moral positioning is who or what we claim to be as we try to justify some specific end or means.

Preoccupation with failure (Chapter Three)

Preoccupation with failure is the mark of an effective *high-reliability organization.* It involves remaining in a mindful state to guard against system failures.

Priming for spontaneity (Chapter Three)

Priming for spontaneity involves conscious recall of some content (*mental model,* opportunity, or language) that leaves an unconscious imprint for later automatic and spontaneous expression.

Rules-based reasoning (Chapter Three)

Rules-based reasoning involves deriving a course of action from a set of rules; less complex than *case-based reasoning.*

Sensemaking (Chapter One)

Sensemaking is the ability to understand a situation well enough to act or "go on" in it.

Simple metaphors (Chapter Four)

Simple metaphors liken one subject to another through a direct comparison that makes sense, even though it is not literally applicable.

Simplifying frames (Chapter Four)

Simplifying frames reduce the chaos and complexity of the moment into more understandable terms.

Strategics (Chapter One)

According to Message Design Logic, Strategics are people with a heightened sensitivity to language, which makes them rather precise when choosing the terms they use. While they understand the context-shaping features of language, they may be prone to charges of manipulation.

**Tame problems
(Chapter One)**

Tame problems are manageable—they can require work to solve, but the general outline of the solution is usually clear from the start. This is in contrast to *wicked problems*.

"The situation here and now" (Chapter One)

"The situation here and now" is a phrase used to capture what aspects of the context leaders and others need to define through their framing.

Tool bag (Chapter Two)

The tool bag sums up the linguistic resources that a *cultural Discourse* supplies. These include terminology and metaphors for ideas and concepts, themes for stories, categories for understanding, and habitual forms of argument.

**Wicked problems
(Chapter One)**

Wicked problems are overwhelmingly complex, intractable, and not subject to easy or expected solutions. Unlike *tame problems*, they are constantly morphing into new problems, the solutions to which require leaders to foster the necessary collaborations among relevant individuals.

NOTES

Preface

1. See Wallace (2008).

2. Shannon and Weaver (1949) are the source of the "Sender → Message → Receiver" model. For a useful discussion, see Axley (1984).

3. See Gross (2009).

4. Harry Truman was the thirty-third President of the United States.

5. In writing about Foucault's view of power, Dreyfus and Rabinow (1983) quote a personal communication from him: "People know what they do; they frequently know why they do what they do; but what they don't know is what they do does" (p. 187).

6. See Luntz (2007); Scheufele and Tewksbury (2007).

7. See Wittgenstein (1953).

8. "Coalition of the willing" was the language used by George W. Bush to refer to the allies that joined the United States in the invasion of Iraq during his presidency.

9. See Gross (2009).

Chapter One

1. For the uninitiated, baseball is a ball game played between two teams, nine players to a team. The goal is for a player to hit a pitched ball and run a series of four bases in a diamond-shaped field without being caught and tagged as "out." Each team tries to score as many runs as possible. More specifically, a "pitcher" throws the ball to a "batter." A "ball" occurs when a pitched ball is not swung at by the batter and does not pass through the strike zone (an area over home plate between the batter's shoulders and knees). A "strike" occurs when the batter swings at a pitched ball and misses it; when a pitch passes through the strike zone but the batter does not swing; and when a struck ball behaves in one of several ways referred to as "foul tips." See the entry for "baseball" (n.d.) at Dictionary.com Unabridged. Retrieved January 10, 2010, from http://dictionary.reference.com/browse/baseball.

2. Simons (1976) and Weick (1979) are among a number of authors who report this story.

3. See Papanikolas (2007) for more details.

4. My own definition of framing has been influenced most heavily by Bateson (1972), Goffman (1974), Entman (1993), and Weick (1979). For example, spurred by a trip to the Fleishacker Zoo in San Francisco, Gregory Bateson (1972) observed monkeys engaging in combat-like behavior that was clearly not combat, but play. Rooted in the mathematical theory of logical types, Bateson's view of framing derived from the meta-communicative level at which some messages contextualize others. Erving Goffman (1974) argued that human beings are in a near-constant struggle over how to make sense of the world around them.

He used the word *frame* to mean a definition of the situation, that is, a summary answer to the question, "Just what is going on here?" It is this concept that I draw from in defining "the situation here and now." Goffman's frame analysis reveals the very structuring of this experience through a number of concepts, including *primary frameworks*, which are culture-based interpretive schemes (more or less well developed) that impact how humans view the world, but also constitute rules for social action. In the area of mass media, Robert Entman's (1993) definition is frequently cited as an example of micro-level framing: "To frame is to select some aspects of a perceived reality and make them more salient in a communicating text, in such a way as to promote a particular problem definition, causal interpretation, moral evaluation, and/or treatment recommendation" (p. 52). By contrast, more macro-level frames emphasize what Goffman suggests are primary frameworks, or what this book terms "mental models." Finally, Karl Weick (1979) notes, "Organizations, despite their apparent preoccupation with facts, numbers, objectivity, concreteness, and accountability, are in fact saturated with subjectivity, abstraction, guesses, making do, invention, and arbitrariness . . . just like the rest of us" (p. 5). For this reason, organizational leaders too often think that they react to the environment when instead they shape or create it through the way in which they interpret—that is, frame—equivocal inputs.

5. You can see many of Robert Murray's interactions with the press for yourself on YouTube. Locate clips by searching www.youtube.com/ under "Robert Murray Mine."

6. See Papanikolas (2007) for more details. These quotes were taken from Murray's news conference of August 7, 2007, and illustrate the unflinching optimism Murray showed in the early days of the collapse.

7. Lippmann (1922) first used the expression "the picture inside our heads" to refer to the fact that people act based upon perceptions, not "objective reality" (p. 3).

8. Deborah Tannen (1979) reviews the pre-1979 literature on frames, scripts, and schemata in the fields of linguistics, artificial intelligence, cognitive psychology, social psychology, sociology, and anthropology. Tannen makes the case that all of these concepts involve underlying expectations, where the cumulative effect of one's experiences of the world becomes organized in such a way as to observe redundancies, form prototypes, and predict what is likely to occur in new, albeit similar, situations.

9. See Riesbeck and Schank (1989) on case-based reasoning, which suggests complex mental models form from a library of cases, making it more likely that experts reason from cases rather than simple rules.

10. Sensemaking can assume a variety of forms: a rational means-end calculation in the mind's eye, a gut feel for one choice over another, or a communication process in which people arrive at a consensus about which interpretation of "the situation here and now" is the right one.

11. See Wittgenstein (1953, no. 508) and, for an extended discussion, Shotter (2007).

12. From Weick's (1986) discussion of eloquence (p. 583).

13. See Langfitt (2007).

14. See Berkes (2007).

15. See Goldman (2007).

16. See Langfitt (2007).

17. Both Fairhurst (2007) and Kirtzman (2001) make this point.

18. For example, see Kotter (1990), Kanter (1983), Senge (1990), and Hickman (1990).

19. While many have written about "wicked problems" across social science disciplines, Rittel and Webber (1973) originated the expression in planning.

20. Grint (2005) recommends that managers deal with tame problems. Those with a command-and-control style should handle crises, while leaders are best suited for wicked problems.

21. The labeling and argument for leadership as a "design problem" is drawn from Kelly and colleagues (2006).

22. Kanter (1983) first posed this question in *The Change Masters*.

23. This is otherwise known as the "Hitler Problem," which Bass and Riggio (2006) discuss: Was Hitler a transformational leader or not, given the immorality of his actions? It raises the question of whether *leadership* should be regarded as tantamount to positive contributions to society only.

24. See Grint's (2000) discussion of the persuasive aspects of leadership performances.

25. See Haass (2009), p. 216. Haass worked in the administrations of both George H.W. Bush, the forty-first president of the United States, and George W. Bush, the forty-third president.

26. However, there was one stipulation; the donor was adamant about remaining anonymous. For this reason, the Chancellor could only speculate as to why she received this honor.

27. Interestingly, the Chancellor and two colleagues have researched and written about high-trust organizations (Shockley-Zalabak, Morreale, & Hackman, 2010).

28. See Chancellor Shockley-Zalabak's podcast, "College Is Possible," at www.uccs.edu/~chancellor/site/media/index.shtml; Access date: May 14, 2010.

29. See Sinclair (2005) for an extended discussion of the use of the body in leadership.

30. As Randall Stutman of CRA, Inc. would often remark, "the way you do anything is the way you do everything."

31. O'Keefe's work on message design logic is extensive (O'Keefe, 1988, 1991, 1992, 1997; O'Keefe & Lambert, 1989, 1995; O'Keefe, Lambert, & Lambert, 1993).

32. The theory of message design logic predicts that in some situations individuals will behave similarly and other situations, usually high in complexity, they will show different styles (O'Keefe, 1997).

33. The scale items are derived chiefly from explanations provided by O'Keefe (1988, 1997) and Willihnganz, Hart, and Willard (2002), who apply her work to organizations. Although the format and thematic content of the scale parallels early scale development by O'Keefe and her students, the specific items of the inventory are not drawn from this work.

34. The *Strategic* label is not specific to O'Keefe, who uses the term *Rhetorical* instead. *Strategic* is thought to be more user-friendly to a business audience, a precedent set by Randall Stutman of CRA, Inc.

35. Joe Biden referred to Barack Obama as "clean."

36. Given Gore's vice presidential experience and an economy in reasonable shape, many pundits believed that the race was "his to lose" over then-governor George W. Bush.

37. See Thamel's (2009) report in the *New York Times*, from which all of the quotes are drawn.

38. See Gerlach (2006).

39. Also, on May 25, 2006, President George W. Bush was quoted as saying, "I learned some lessons about expressing myself maybe in a little more sophisticated manner" (Gerlach, 2006).

40. O'Keefe (1997) argues that the acquisition of a design logic is a long process, extending well into adulthood. It is also a progression from Expression to Conventional to Rhetorical (her term for the style I refer to as *Strategic*), thus people who have developed the latter are able to assume the other design logics as necessary, while just the opposite is true for Expressives.

41. See the NHS Institute Innovation and Improvement Report on Carly Fiorina (2006).

42. For further information on Fiorina's tenure at Hewlett-Packard, see www.businesswings.co.uk/articles/Carly-Fiorina; access date: May 17, 2010.

43. See Fiorina (2006), p. 206.

44. On the subject of Mark Hurd's early tenure at Hewlett-Packard, see http://money.cnn.com/magazines/fortune/fortune_archive/2005/08/08/8267666/index.htm; access date: May 17, 2010.

45. The *60 Minutes* segment ran October 5, 2006.

46. When the December 2005 tsunami hit several Asian and African nations, President George W. Bush asked his father and his immediate predecessor, George H. W. Bush and Bill Clinton, to lead a massive private relief effort to help victims.

47. See Parker (2006).

Chapter Two

1. Nor are Catholics known for their charitable giving (Greeley & McManus, 1987). A correlation perhaps?

2. See the January 16, 2006, article on Martin Luther King in the *Cincinnati Enquirer* (Johnston, 2006).

3. See Spitzberg (2003) for an extended discussion of communication skill assessment.

4. Martin Luther King Day is the third Monday of January every year in the United States.

5. See Foucault (1972, 1973, 1995) or Dreyfus and Rabinow (1983). I am following Alvesson and Kärreman (2000) in the definition and application of the term *Discourse*.

6. The "tool bag" metaphor is based on Potter and Wetherell's (Potter, 1996, 1997; Potter & Wetherell, 1987; Wetherell, 1998) recasting of Foucault's Discourse as an interpretative repertoire. However, it is not my intention to reduce Foucault's view of Discourse to *just* a repertoire or linguistic tool bag. His writings on power and knowledge especially are wide-reaching in their effects. Interested readers are urged to delve deeper into his work in this regard.

7. See Luntz (2007).

8. See Bennis and Thomas (2002).

9. Ibid., p. 10. Foucault would likely agree with Bennis and Thomas's basic idea that geeks and geezers were shaped by powerful histori-cal forces. Their side-by-side comparison of eras parallels Foucault's (1972, 1980) archeology. Foucault's writings (1983, 1990, 1995) on genealogy, or the ways in which Discourse reveals itself in the prac-tices of a given era, are also quite relevant to the ways in which Ben-nis and Thomas define the tools and practices of geeks and geezers.

10. See also du Gay, Salaman, and Rees (1996) and Tracy and Trethe-way (2005).

11. Jason Delambre's company is Interdependent Energies, LLC (www.InterdependentEnergies.com).

12. Those who have been influenced by Foucault's work suggest that people are not subject to just one Discourse but many, depending upon work-life circumstances. Here there is a large body of work to consider (Ashcraft & Mumby, 2004; Daudi, 1986; Grant et al., 2004; Holmer-Nadesan, 1996; Laclau & Mouffe, 1985).

13. Indeed, Foucault says there is no agency outside of Discourse; human beings can only move from one discursive network to another.

14. As mentioned, Foucault's archeological method (1972, 1995) was rooted in the comparison of socio-historical eras.

15. These tool bags signify potentials or possibilities until realized in the act of framing. However, by considering such potentials we can get a sense of where our words come from when we speak, words that coalesce into the frames we construct and the conversations we begin.

16. See work by Senge and colleagues (Ancona et al., 2007; Senge, 1997; Senge et al., 1999; Senge et al., 1994), which shapes this book's discussion of mental models.

17. This is not to suggest that the city leaders' mental models necessar-ily lacked this distinction—only that they chose not to make it.

18. See Bryant (2009a).

19. See Bryant (2009b).

20. See Helgesen (1990).

21. See Senge (1990).

22. See Bryant (2009c).

23. A version of Framing Tool 2.2 appeared in Fairhurst and Sarr (1996).

24. The concept of mental models is akin to the psychological construct of *schema*, discussion of which can be found in Fiske and Taylor (1984).

25. For a discussion of sensemaking as the ability to go on in a situation, see Wittgenstein (1953).

26. For further discussion of the development of mental models, see Senge (1990) but also Fiske and Taylor (1984) in the context of schema.

27. See Senge (1990) for further discussion on the need to surface mental models.

28. The expression "core framing tasks" is taken directly from sociologists Robert Benford and David Snow's work on framing in social movements (Benford & Snow, 2000; Snow & Benford, 1992).

29. Although others have written about the leader-manager distinction (Hickman, 1990; Zaleznik, 1977), Kotter's (1990) work is perhaps best known.

30. Benford and Snow (2000) also adopt specific terms for core framing tasks in social movements associated with problem setting and solving: *diagnostic framing* (problem identification and attributions), *prognostic framing* (articulating proposed solutions and plans of attack), and *motivational framing* (a "call to arms" or rationale for acting in concert for the good of the department); p. 615.

31. While George's (2000) work provides the general framework for Framing Tool 2.4, specific components are also based in Conger and Kanungo (1998), Fairhurst (1993a, 1993b), Locke (1991), and Yukl (1998). Moreover, this framework is not intended to essentialize leadership by suggesting these are the only core framing tasks of leader-managers. Rather, it is a starting place to stimulate thinking about the dominant communication patterns of one's job.

32. See Kotter (1990, 1995).

33. When speaking of master frames, media framing expert Stephen Reese (2003) observes, "All frames are not equal in their ability to cause information to cohere, making sense out of the world" (p. 13). The term "master frame" is drawn from Benford and Snow (2000; Snow & Benford, 1992) and others who write about framing processes in social movements and the media (Gamson, 1992; Pan & Kosicki, 2003; Reese, Gandy, & Grant, 2003).

34. See "About Xavier: Michael J. Graham, S.J., President," 2010; available online: www.xavier.edu/about/Fr-Graham.cfm; access date: May 18, 2010.

35. "UC|21 Academic Plan," 2006; available online: www.uc.edu/uc21/; access date: May 18, 2010.

36. This view of alignment is a simplified version of Snow et al. (1986), who refer to it as "the linkage of individual and SMO [social movement organizations] interpretive orientations, such that some set of individual interests, values, and beliefs and SMO activities, goals, and ideology are congruent and complementary" (p. 464).

37. See Donnellon, Grey, and Bougon's (1986) discussion of equifinal meaning.

38. For a discussion of a "difference that connects," see Barge and Fairhurst (2008).

39. Graham's remarks were quoted in Good Shepherd Catholic Church's *Flock Report* (Huber, 1994).

Chapter Three

1. See Dreyfus and Rabinow (1983) for a discussion of Foucault and this quote.

2. See Mead (1956), p. 136.

3. See Weick (1979, 1995).

4. See Weick (2001), p. 92. Italics are in the original.

5. See Kellerman (1992) for an extensive discussion of this topic.

6. See Harley (2008) for a discussion of implicit memory.

7. For further discussion of the tip-of-the-tongue experiments, see Harley (2008).

8. See Reese, Gandy, and Grant (2003).

9. See the research of Gelbard-Sagiv et al. (2008).

10. Historically, conventional thinking was that every brain function had one and only one hardwired location. If that brain function was somehow lost, it was not considered recoverable. See Doidge (2007), p. 17.

11. See Doidge (2007).

12. As Doidge (2007) suggests, this challenges Descartes' classic mind-body dualism.

13. Hebb's law is cited in Doidge (2007), as is Schatz's restatement, "neurons that fire together wire together" (p. 63).

14. Alsop's remarks can be found in Kantrowitz (2005), p. 60.

15. The Tanglewood Music Center is dedicated to advanced musical study and is affiliated with the Boston Symphony and Boston Pops Orchestra.

16. See Doidge (2007), p. 202.

17. See Bryant (2009d).

18. See Jones (2009).

19. From *The New York Times* obituary of Crystal Lee Sutton (Hevesi, 2009), including an interview with Ms. Sutton at Alamance Community College, which she attended in the 1980s, p. B15.

20. See Alinsky (1971).

21. See Hevesi (2009), p. B15.

22. The traditions are a critical part of the Alcoholics Anonymous program along with the twelve steps. See www.al-anon.alateen.org; Access date: May 19, 2010.

23. On *Saturday Night Live*, Jane Curtain played Shana Alexander, while Dan Ackroyd played James Kilpatrick.

24. James Kilpatrick is a Washington-based syndicated columnist. For his article on Alexander, see Kilpatrick (2005).

25. See Abrams (2007), p. J3.

26. See Ludeman and Erlandson (2004, 2006).

27. As quoted in Parker (2008).

28. See Brooks (2008).

29. Much of the literature around case-based reasoning casts it as a powerful method for computer reasoning as well as a key tool in human reasoning (Cheetham & Goebel, 2007; Kolodner, 1993).

30. See Glaser and Chi (1988).

31. See Riesbeck and Schank (1989).

32. See Riesbeck and Schank (1989), p. 10. This example was also presented in *The Art of Framing* (Fairhurst & Sarr, 1996).

33. The work of Edward Taub is reviewed in Doidge (2007).

34. See Doidge (2007).

35. See Doidge (2007), p. 156.

36. See Weick, Sutcliffe, and Obstfeld (1999).

37. See Weick and Roberts (1993).

38. See Weick and Sutcliffe (2001).

39. My research on this topic was conducted with François Cooren (Cooren & Fairhurst, 2004; Fairhurst, 2007; Fairhurst & Cooren, 2004).

40. See Weick and Sutcliffe (2001).

41. See Shotter and Cunliffe (2003), pp. 24–25.

42. See de Shazer (1988, 1991).

43. See Berg and de Shazer (1993).

44. See Durrant and Kowalski (1993).

45. A technique that therapists use in tandem with miracle questions is *exception framing*, where therapists help clients find exceptions to seemingly intractable problems. For example, if a client says, "I'll

never be able to get my boss to notice me," the therapist might ask, "Was there ever a time when your boss did notice you?" Surprisingly, most clients can usually name an exception. The skilled therapist then uses that foot in the door to slowly unfreeze apparent realities that look so hard and fast (de Shazer, 1988, 1991).

46. See Duck (1993), p. 11.

47. See Kendall's work as cited in Doidge (2007), p. 218.

Chapter Four

1. See it on YouTube: www.youtube.com/watch?v=PbUtL_0vAJk; access date: May 20, 2010.

2. This is otherwise known as *anaphora* in rhetorical studies.

3. See Grint (2000), p. 297.

4. At the same time, one should also not overexaggerate the importance of Martin Luther King Jr. Clearly, he benefited from the many events and participants that led up to the delivery of the "I have a dream" speech (Grint, 2000).

5. See Weick (1986), p. 585.

6. See Garber (2008), p. XIII.

7. See S. Martin (2007), p. 1.

8. See Laborde (1988), p. 85

9. See Verrengia (2005).

10. See Laborde (1988)

11. See Dass (2008), p. 68

12. For an extended discussion of metaphors and sensemaking, see Lakoff and Johnson (1980).

13. See Laborde (1988).

14. It is because of these innovations that *Black Enterprise* featured her in the magazine as 2009 Corporate Executive of the Year (Alleyne, 2009).

15. Ibid., p. 92.

16. Edwin Young's title is zone multicultural director for his firm.

17. The nonstandard use of "aks" instead of "ask" (which, incidentally, I observed only once in two conversations) derives from African American Vernacular English (so-called Black English).

18. See Snow and Benford (1992).

19. From the NoVo Web site at www.novofoundation.org/; access date: May 20, 2010.

20. See Bailey (2009), p. 79.

21. See Meacham (2008).

22. See Weisberg (2008).

23. The American Recovery and Reinvestment Act of 2009 is an economic stimulus package enacted by the U.S. Congress in February 2009 based on proposals made by President Barack Obama. See Heath and Heath (2009), p. 59.

24. See A. Martin (2009).

25. Prospect theory has a long history (Kahneman & Tversky, 1979; Kahneman & Tversky, 1984; Tversky & Kahneman, 1981).

26. However, reviews of the literature suggest that there is often complex psychology and interactional processes at work here (Bazerman, 1984; Brummans et al., 2008; Dewulf et al., 2009; George et al., 2006; Kennedy & Fiss, 2009; Putnam & Holmer, 1992).

27. See Lewis (in press), but also Dewulf et al. (2009).

28. See Bryant (2009e).

29. See Bryant (2009f).

30. Much of the material in this section was first introduced in Fairhurst and Sarr (1996).

31. See Deetz (1985).

32. Colbert's "truthiness" was Merriam-Webster's 2006 Word of the Year. See www.merriam-webster.com/info/06words.htm; access date: May 20, 2010.

33. "The sky is falling" is from the children's story of Chicken Little, who has to be taught courage and to see that the sky is not about to fall.

34. See Deetz (1985).

35. D. Martin (2009) draws this statement by Cronkite from a 1973 interview with the *Christian Science Monitor*.

36. See Deetz (1985).

37. See Ramer (2007).

38. See Gerlach (2006).

39. See Weick (1986), p. 581.

Chapter Five

1. For example, see Schillinger (2006).

2. I would have to include myself in that category. Emotions were always a part of my research program on the language aspects of leadership, but rarely a central part.

3. Several books and articles on emotional intelligence make these points (Caruso, Mayer, & Salovey, 2002; Fisher & Ashkanasy, 2000; George, 2000; Goleman, 1995; Goleman, Boyatzis, & McKee, 2002).

4. See Damasio (1994), p. 53.

5. See Mayer and Salovey (1997), p. 5.

6. This case is drawn from Fairhurst, Cooren, and Cahill (2002).

7. Ibid.

8. See Isaacs (1999), p. 83.

9. See Frost (2003), p. 3.

10. See Fairhurst et al. (2002) for more details.

11. Barsade (2002) bases this on the support found for the *circumplex model of emotion*, which he describes in detail.

12. This definition draws from Schoenewolf (1990). See also Barsade (2002) for a discussion of the impact of high energy on mood

contagion. Following Barsade, I use the term *emotion* as a broad, affective label that includes mood. However, moods are sometimes distinguished from emotions. The former are persistent, low-intensity feeling states that carry across situations (Reber, 1985), while the latter are higher-intensity but more fleeting feeling states (Tellegen, 1985).

13. See Barsade (2002) for a review of the research on attentional processes.

14. Mimicry has been discussed by a number of authors (Dinberg, 1982; Hatfield, Cacioppo, & Rapson, 1992, 1994; Iacoboni, 2008).

15. See Barsade (2002) for a review of this research.

16. See Haviland and Lelwica (1987) and Wild, Erb, and Bartels (2001).

17. See Iacoboni (2008), p. 111.

18. Ibid., p. 4

19. However, empathy is likely a multifaceted construct with emotional or mood contagion as just one component (Barsade, 2002).

20. See Mehrabian (1972).

21. See Barsade (2002) for further discussion.

22. See Kelly and Barsade (2001).

23. Pearson made *Fortune* magazine's "Toughest Bosses" issue (Dorsey, 2001).

24. See Dorsey (2001, p. 78).

25. Sadly, it wasn't until Pearson moved to Tricon Global Restaurants Inc. (KFC, Pizza Hut, and Taco Bell) that he modified his style. Pearson attributed his change in style to David Novak, Tricon's chairman and CEO, who taught him that he could ask tough questions without always having to prove that he was the smartest guy in the room (Dorsey, 2001).

26. See Barsade (2002).

27. Ibid.

28. Ibid.

29. See work by George (1991, 2000; George & Brief, 1992).

30. See Karacs (2009). This report includes a video excerpt from the encounter.

31. See Barsade, Brief, and Spataro (2003), p. 22.

32. See http://blogs.wsj.com/washwire/2009/08/11/state-department-clarifies-clinton-remark-to-student/; access date: May 22, 2010.

33. See www.huffingtonpost.com/2009/08/11us-official-struggles-to-_n_257069.html; access date: May 22, 2010.

34. See George (2000), p. 1032.

35. See Bryant (2010), p. 9.

36. Ibid., p. 9.

37. See Pilkington (2009).

Chapter Six

1. See Anderson and Englehardt (2001), p. 9.

2. Ibid., p. 9.

3. Most of the incidents in this paragraph should leap to mind—or others equivalent to the ones I was thinking of. A couple of details may be useful, though: Bernie Madoff (the Ponzi artist) was a non-executive chairman of the NASDAQ stock market, and Rob Blago-jevich was the governor of Illinois charged with seeing a lucrative opportunity in the privilege of naming a senator.

4. See also Eisenberg, Goodall, and Tretheway (2007) for an interesting discussion of this code of ethics.

5. For an excellent discussion on this point, see Wheatley (1992).

6. See, for example, Kornberger and Brown (2007) and Schein (1985).

7. See Seelye and Phillip (2008) for a summary of the ABC news interview with John Edwards on family values and his contrary behavior.

8. See Gardner (2007).

9. Ibid.; see p. 52 for Gardner's phrasing of the questions.

10. As cited in Alinsky (1971), p. 25.

11. See Gardner (2007), p. 55.

12. Ibid., p. 52.

13. See Lacayo and Ripley (2002).

14. See Gardner (2007), p. 52.

15. See Anderson and Englehardt (2001), p. 24.

16. See Jones (2008).

17. See Alinsky (1971), pp. 13–14.

18. See Alvesson (in press).

19. See CBS News, 1996.

20. This interview with T. J. Rodgers can be seen on YouTube: www
    .youtube.com/watch?v=lfJcpO-pCdc; access date: May 23, 2010.

21. The interview with Al Dunlap can be seen on YouTube: www
    .youtube.com/watch?v=Bw9ieef7DTc;; access date: May 23, 2010.

22. The interview with Bruce Klatsky can be seen on YouTube: www
    .youtube.com/watch?v=qbUHSqiUPFw;; access date: May 23, 2010.

23. See Giddens (1979, 1984).

24. See Alinsky (1971), p. 44.

25. See Bennis and Thomas (2002).

26. Although the verdict was subsequently overturned by the U.S. Supreme
    Court, Arthur Andersen has not returned as a viable business.

27. See Craig and Amernic (2004).

28. Ibid., pp. 827–829.

29. Ibid., p. 829.

30. See Craig and Amernic (2004), p. 832. See also Moore (1994).

31. See Byrne (2002).

32. Ibid.

Chapter Seven

1. The labeling and argument for leadership as a "design problem" is drawn from Kelly and colleagues (2006).

2. The definitions of leadership are so broad that several scholars have concluded that searching for *the* definition of leadership is futile (Alvesson & Sveningsson, 2003; Barker, 1997; Rost, 1991).

3. See Collinson (2006) for an interesting discussion of the equation of leadership and influence.

4. This view is consistent with Kelly (2008), who treats leadership as a set of language games, following Wittgenstein (1953).

5. This point has been made by Robinson (2001), Gronn (2000), and Fairhurst (2007).

6. Attributional views of leadership are well established (Calder, 1977; Meindl, 1995; Meindl, Ehrlich, & Dukerich, 1985).

7. Recall that in Chapter Two, visionary Discourse was discussed in terms of the work of John Kotter, Warren Bennis, and Peter Senge. It emphasizes that a key distinction between leaders and managers is that the former creatively define a vision, while the latter implement it.

8. See Alter (2001).

9. You can see George W. Bush's Ground Zero moment on You-tube: http://www.youtube.com/watch?v=MiSwqaQ4VbA or search "George Bush 9/11 Bullhorn Speech." Access date: May 24, 2010.

10. Following Grint (2000), the hyping of a leader's performance is called "social shaping."

11. *New York Times* columnist Bob Herbert observed of Giuliani, "He moves about the stricken city like a god. . . . People wanted to be in his presence" (Kirtzman, 2001), p. 305.

12. From Anderson and Englehardt (2001), p. 119.

13. Kanter (1977) found that token women are going to feel greater performance pressure, social isolation, and role entrapment than

will women who have some peers in their organizations. Tokens are created when women comprise 15 percent or less of the managerial population.

14. See Mortenson's discussion of his father in Mortenson and Relin (2007).

15. Ibid., p. 38.

16. See Greenhouse (2009), p. B1.

17. Ibid., p. B5.

18. For a more in-depth analysis of this case, see Fairhurst and Cooren (2008).

19. See Kelly (2007).

20. "Gov. Schwarzenegger Tours the Local Assistance Center at Cuyamaca College," Office of the Governor Web site, October 28, 2007; http://gov.ca.gov/speech/7956/; access date: May 24, 2010.

21. See Kelly (2007), p. 51.

22. Ibid., pp. 50–51.

23. Office of the Governor Web site, http://gov.ca.gov/, includes a variety of reports like the one cited in Note 20.

24. See "Roger Boisjoly and the Challenger Disaster." Online Ethics Center for Engineering and Research, n.d. Retrieved May 28, 2005, from www.onlineethics.org/cms/7123.aspx. Also Roger Boisjoly, "Ethical Decisions—Morton Thiokol and the Space Shuttle *Challenger* Disaster: Telecon Meeting." Online Ethics Center for Engineering and Research, n.d. Retrieved May 28, 2005, from www.onlineethics .org/cms/profpractice/ppessays/thiokolshuttle.aspx.

25. See Dunn (2003) on the point that NASA may be doomed to more tragedies because of its culture.

26. See Alinsky (1971).

27. Ibid., pp. 109–112.

28. Ibid., p. 112.

Chapter Eight

1. See Abrams (2007), p. J3.

2. See Senge (1990).

3. See S. Cohen (2008) for a discussion of Obama's racial identity politics.

4. See Frost (2003) on leaders who are toxin handlers.

REFERENCES

Abrams, R. (2007, August 19). It might be time to start honing "elevator pitch" for your business. *Cincinnati Enquirer*, p. J3.

Alinsky, S. D. (1971). *Rules for radicals: A pragmatic primer for realistic radicals.* New York: Vintage.

Alleyne, S. (2009, September). Refashioning the familiar: Candace Matthews updates the Amway brand and sales force while fine-tuning the global message. *Black Enterprise*, pp. 86–94.

Alter, J. Seeing history for yourself. (2001, December 31). *Newsweek*. Available online: www.newsweek.com/2001/12/30/seeing-history-for-yourself .html. Access date: June 12, 2010.

Alvesson, M., & Kärreman, D. (2000). Varieties of discourse: On the study of organizations through discourse analysis. *Human Relations, 53*, 1125–1149.

Alvesson, M., & Sveningsson, S. (2003). The great disappearing act: Difficulties in doing "leadership." *Leadership Quarterly, 14*, 359–381.

Alvesson, M. (in press). The leader as saint—leadership through moral peak performance. In M. Alvesson & A. Spicer (Eds.), *Metaphors we lead by*. London: Routledge.

Ancona, D., Malone, T. W., Orlikowski, W. J., & Senge, P. (2007, February). In praise of the incomplete leader. *Harvard Business Review*, pp. 92–100.

Anderson, J. A., & Englehardt, E. E. (2001). *The organizational self and ethical conduct: Sunlit virtue and shadowed resistance*. Fort Worth, TX: Harcourt.

Ashcraft, K. L., & Mumby, D. K. (2004). *Reworking gender: A feminist communicology of organizations*. Thousand Oaks, CA: Sage.

Axley, S. R. (1984). Managerial and organizational communication in terms of the conduit metaphor. *Academy of Management Review, 9*, 428–437.

Bailey, J. (2009, September). Daddy Givebucks. *Fast Company*, pp. 74–79.

Barge, J. K., & Fairhurst, G. T. (2008). Living leadership: A systemic, constructionist approach. *Leadership, 4*, 227–251.

Barker, R. A. (1997). How can we train leaders if we do not know what leadership is? *Human Relations, 50*, 343–362.

Barsade, S. G. (2002). The ripple effect: Emotional contagion and its influence on group behavior. *Administrative Science Quarterly, 47*, 644–675.

Barsade, S. G., Brief, A. P., & Spataro, S. E. (2003). The affective revolution in organizational behavior: The emergence of a paradigm. In J. Greenberg (Ed.), *Organizational behavior: The state of the science* (pp. 3–52). Mahwah, NJ: Erlbaum.

Bass, B. M., & Riggio, R. E. (2006). *Transformational leadership* (2nd ed.). Mahwah, NJ: Erlbaum.

Bateson, G. (1972). *Steps to an ecology of the mind*. New York: Ballantine.

Bazerman, M. H. (1984). The relevance of Kahneman and Tversky's concept of framing to organizational behavior. *Journal of Management, 10*, 333–343.

Benford, R. D., & Snow, D. A. (2000). Framing processes and social movements: An overview and assessment. *American Sociological Review, 26*, 611–639.

Bennis, W. G., & Thomas, R. J. (2002). *Geeks and geezers: How era, values, and defining moments shape leaders.* Boston: Harvard Business Press.

Berg, I. K., & de Shazer, S. (1993). Making numbers talk: Language in therapy. In S. Friedman (Ed.), *The new language of change.* New York: Guilford Press.

Berkes, H. (2007, August 23). Murray says Crandall Canyon Mine to be closed. *NPR Transcripts.* Available online: www.npr.org/templates/story/story.php?storyId=13866983. Access date: May 14, 2010.

Brooks, D. (2008, December 8). On foreign policy, Obama will adopt insights developed in Bush years. *Cincinnati Enquirer,* p. B9. Reprinted from a *New York Times* editorial of December 7, 2008.

Brummans, B. H., Putnam, L. L., Gray, B., Hanke, R., Lewicki, R. J., & Wiethoff, C. (2008). Making sense of intractable multiparty conflict: A study of framing in four environmental disputes. *Communication Monographs, 75,* 25–51.

Bryant, A. (2009a, August 2). In a near-death event, a corporate rite of passage: John T. Chambers. *New York Times,* p. 2.

Bryant, A. (2009b, July 26). No doubts: Women are better managers: Carol Smith. *New York Times,* p. 2.

Bryant, A. (2009c, October 25). He prizes questions more than answers: Tim Brown. *New York Times,* p. 2.

Bryant, A. (2009d, July 5). Charisma? To her, it's overrated: Wendy Kopp. *New York Times,* p. 2.

Bryant, A. (2009e, June 28). Stumping for votes, every day: Daniel P. Amos. *New York Times,* p. 2.

Bryant, A. (2009f, June 14). On his team, would you be a solvent, or the glue? Will Wright. *New York Times,* p. 2.

Bryant, A. (2010, February 21). We're family, so we can disagree: Xerox's new chief tries to redefine its culture. *New York Times,* p. 1.

Byrne, J. A. (2002, August 12). Joe Berardino's fall from grace. *Business Week.* Available online: www.businessweek.com/magazine/content/02_32/b3795001.htm, Access date: June 12, 2010.

Calder, B. J. (1977). An attribution theory of leadership. In B. M. Staw & G. R. Salancik (Eds.), *New directions in organizational behavior* (pp. 179–202). Chicago: St. Clair Press.

Caruso, D. R., Mayer, J. D., & Salovey, P. (2002). Emotional intelligence and emotional leadership. In R. E. Riggio, S. E. Murphy & F. J. Pirozzolo (Eds.), *Multiple intelligences and leadership* (pp. 55–74). Mahwah, NJ: Erlbaum.

CBS News. (1996, August 8). *Who's getting rich and why aren't you?* Documentary; production company: CBS News; executive producer: Linda Mason; senior producer: Stephen Blauber; presenter and reporter: Harry Smith.

Cheetham, W., & Goebel, K. (2007). Appliance call center: A successful mixed-initiative case study. *Artificial Intelligence Magazine, 28*, 89–100.

Cohen, S. (2008, January 6). Does Obama win mean US voters are color-blind? *Cincinnati Enquirer*, p. A6.

Collinson, D. L. (2006). Rethinking followership: A post-structuralist analysis of follower identities. *Leadership Quarterly, 17*, 179–189.

Conger, J. A., & Kanungo, R. N. (1998). *Charismatic leadership in organizations*. Thousand Oaks, CA: Sage.

Controversial leaders: Carleton S. Fiorina. (2006, March). *NHS: Institute for Innovation and Improvement*, no. 9. Available online: www.executive.modern. nhs.uk/inview/inviewarticle.aspx?id=64. Access date: May 14, 2010.

Cooren, F., & Fairhurst, G. (2004). Speech timing and spacing: The phenomenon of organizational closure. *Organization, 11*, 797–828.

Craig, R. J., & Amernic, J. H. (2004). Enron discourse: The rhetoric of a resilient capitalism. *Critical Perspective on Accounting, 15*, 813–851.

Damasio, A. R. (1994). *Descartes' error*. New York: Putnam.

Dass, T. K. (2008). Human resource processes and the role of the human resources function during mergers and acquisitions in the electricity industry. Unpublished dissertation, University of Cincinnati.

Daudi, G. (1986). *Power in the organization*. Cornwall, UK: T.J. Press.

Deetz, S. A. (1985). Critical-cultural research: New sensibilities and old realities. *Journal of Management, 11*, 121–136.

de Shazer, S. (1988). *Clues: Investing solutions in brief therapy.* New York: Norton.

de Shazer, S. (1991). *Putting difference to work.* New York: Norton.

Dewulf, A., Gray, B., Putnam, L., Lewicki, R., Aarts, N., Bouwen, R., & van Woerkum, C. (2009). Disentangling approaches to framing in conflict and negotiation research: A meta-paradigmatic perspective. *Human Relations, 62,* 155–194.

Dinberg, U. (1982). Facial reactions to facial expressions. *Psychophysiology, 26,* 643–647.

Doidge, N. (2007). *The brain that changes itself.* New York: Penguin.

Donnellon, A., Grey, B., & Bougon, M. G. (1986). Communication, meaning, and organized action. *Administrative Science Quarterly, 31,* 43–55.

Dorsey, D. (2001, August). Andy Pearson finds love. *Fast Company,* p. 78.

Dreyfus, H. L., & Rabinow, P. (1983). *Michel Foucault.* Chicago: University of Chicago Press.

du Gay, P., Salaman, G., & Rees, B. (1996). The conduct of management and the management of conduct: Contemporary managerial discourse and the constitution of the "competent manager." *Journal of Management Studies, 33,* 263–282.

Duck, J. D. (1993, November/December). Managing change: The art of balancing. *Harvard Business Review,* pp. 109–118.

Dunn, M. (2003, August 2). Columbia investigator fears NASA won't change. *Cincinnati Enquirer,* 2003. Available online: www.space.com/mission-launches/sts107_osheroff_030801.html. Access date: June 12, 2010.

Durrant, M., & Kowalski, K. M. (1993). Enhancing views of competence. In S. Friedman (Ed.), *The new language of change.* New York: Norton.

Eisenberg, E., Goodall, H. L., Jr., & Tretheway, A. (2007). *Organizational communication: Balancing creativity and constraint* (6th ed.). New York: St. Martin's Press.

Entman, R. (1993). Framing: Toward a clarification of a fractured paradigm. *Journal of Communication, 43,* 51–58.

Fairhurst, G. T. (1993a). The leader-member exchange patterns of women leaders in industry: A discourse analysis. *Communication Monographs, 60*, 321–351.

Fairhurst, G. T. (1993b). Echoes of the vision: When the rest of the organization talks Total Quality. *Management Communication Quarterly, 6*, 331–371.

Fairhurst, G. T. (2007). *Discursive leadership: In conversation with leadership psychology*. Thousand Oaks, CA: Sage.

Fairhurst, G. T., & Cooren, F. (2004). Organizational language in use: Interaction analysis, conversation analysis, and speech act schematics. In D. Grant, C. Hardy, C. Oswick, N. Phillips, & L. Putnam (Eds.), *The Sage handbook of organizational discourse* (pp. 131–152). London: Sage.

Fairhurst, G. T., & Cooren, F. (2009). Leadership and the hybrid production of presence(s). *Leadership, 4*, 1–22.

Fairhurst, G., Cooren, F., & Cahill, D. (2002). Discursiveness, contradiction and unintended consequences in successive downsizings. *Management Communication Quarterly, 15*, 501–540.

Fairhurst, G. T., & Sarr, R. A. (1996). *The art of framing: Managing the language of leadership*. San Francisco: Jossey-Bass.

Fiorina, C. (2006). *Tough choices: A memoir*. New York: Penguin.

Fisher, C. D., & Ashkanasy, N. M. (2000). The emerging role of emotions in work life: An introduction. *Journal of Organizational Behavior, 21*, 123–129.

Fiske, S. T., & Taylor, S. E. (1984). *Social cognition*. New York: Random House.

Foucault, M. (1972). *The archeology of knowledge and the discourse on language*. London, UK: Tavistock.

Foucault, M. (1973). *The order of things*. New York: Vintage Books.

Foucault, M. (1980). *Power/knowledge: Selected interviews and other writings 1972–1977*. New York: Pantheon.

Foucault, M. (1983). The subject and power. In H. L. Dreyfus & P. Rabinow (Eds.), *Michel Foucault: Beyond structuralism and hermeneutics* (pp. 208–226). Chicago: Chicago University Press.

Foucault, M. (1990). *The history of sexuality* (Vol. 1). New York: Vintage Books.

Foucault, M. (1995). *Discipline and punish.* New York: Vintage Books.

Frost, P. J. (2003). *Toxic emotions at work.* Boston: Harvard Business Press.

Gamson, W. A. (1992). The social psychology of collective action. In A. D. Morris & C. M. Mueller (Eds.), *Frontiers in social movement theory* (pp. 53–76). New Haven, CT: Yale University Press.

Garber, M. (2008). *Patronizing the arts.* Princeton, NJ: Princeton University Press.

Gardner, H. (2007, March). The ethical mind: A conversation with psychologist Howard Gardner. *Harvard Business Review,* pp. 51–56.

Gelbard-Sagiv, H., Mukamel, R., Harel, M., Malach, R., & Fried, I. (2008, October 3). Internally generated reactivation of single neurons in human hippocampus during free recall. *Science, 322,* 96–101.

George, J. M. (1991). State or trait: Effects of positive mood on prosocial behavior. *Journal of Applied Psychology, 25,* 778–794.

George, J. M. (2000). Emotions and leadership: The role of emotional intelligence. *Human Relations, 53,* 1027–1055.

George, J. M., & Brief, A. P. (1992). Feeling good—doing good. A conceptual analysis of the mood at work—organizational spontaneity relationship. *Psychology Bulletin, 112,* 310–329.

George, E., Chattopadhyay, P., Sitkin, S. B., & Barden, J. (2006). Cognitive underpinnings of institutional persistence and change: A framing perspective. *Academy of Management Review, 31,* 347–365.

Gerlach, D. (2006, June 19). Fighting words. *Newsweek,* p. 38.

Giddens, A. (1979). *Central problems in social theory.* Berkeley: University of California Press.

Giddens, A. (1984). *The constitution of society.* Berkeley: University of California Press.

Glaser, R., & Chi, M.T.H. (1988). Overview. In M.T.H. Chi, R. Glaser, & M. J. Farr (Eds.), *The nature of expertise* (pp. xv–xxviii). Mahwah, NJ: Erlbaum.

Goffman, E. (1974). *Frame analysis.* Philadelphia: University of Pennsylvania Press.

Goldman, R. (2007, August 8). Mine owner faces old foes after collapse. *ABC News.* Available online: http://abcnews.go.com/print?id=3456428. Access date: May 14, 2010.

Goleman, D. (1995). *Emotional intelligence.* New York: Bantam.

Goleman, D., Boyatzis, R., & McKee, A. (2002). *Primal leadership: Realizing the power of emotional intelligence.* Boston: Harvard Business Press.

Grant, D., Hardy, C., Oswick, C., & Putnam, L. (2004). *The Sage handbook of organizational discourse.* London: Sage.

Greeley, A., & McManus, W. (1987). *Catholic contributions: Sociology and policy.* Chicago: Thomas More Press.

Greenhouse, S. (2009, November 19). Some organizers protest their union's tactics. *New York Times,* pp. B1, B5

Grint, K. (2000). *The arts of leadership.* Oxford, UK: Oxford University Press.

Grint, K. (2005). Problems, problems, problems: The social construction of "leadership." *Human Relations, 58,* 1467–1494.

Gronn, P. (2000). Distributed properties: A new architecture for leadership. *Educational Management and Administration, 28,* 317–338.

Gross, D. (2009, April 6). The peril of financial linguistics. *Newsweek,* p. 34.

Haass, R. N. (2009). *War of necessity, war of choice: A memoir of two Iraq wars.* New York: Simon & Schuster.

Harley, T. A. (2008). *The psychology of language: From data to theory* (3rd ed.). New York: Psychology Press.

Hatfield, E., Cacioppo, J., & Rapson, R. L. (1992). Primitive emotional contagion. In M. S. Clark (Ed.), *Review of personality and social psychology: Emotion and social behavior* (pp. 14, 151–177). Thousand Oaks, CA: Sage.

Hatfield, E., Cacioppo, J., & Rapson, R. L. (1994). *Emotional contagion.* New York: Cambridge University Press.

Haviland, J. M., & Lelwica, M. (1987). The induced affect response: 10-week-old infants' responses to three emotion expressions. *Developmental Psychology, 23,* 97–104.

Heath, D., & Heath, C. (2009, September). The gripping statistic. *Fast Company*, pp. 59–60.

Helgesen, S. (1990). *The female advantage: Women's ways of leadership*. New York: Doubleday Currency.

Hevesi, D. (2009, September 15). Crystal Lee Sutton, 68: The real-life "Norma Rae." *New York Times*, p. B15.

Hickman, C. R. (1990). *Mind of a manager, soul of a leader*. Hoboken, NJ: Wiley.

Holmer-Nadesan, M. (1996). Organizational identity and space of action. *Organization Studies, 17*, 49–81.

Huber, R. (1994, March/April). Everything you've always wanted to know about . . . Father Michael Graham, S.J. *The Flock Report*, Cincinnati, Ohio, Good Shepherd Church: 6–7, 14.

Iacoboni, M. (2008). *The new science of how we connect with others: Mirroring people*. New York: Farrar, Straus & Giroux.

Isaacs, W. (1999). *Dialogue and the art of thinking together*. New York: Doubleday Currency.

Johnston, J. (2006, January 16). Martin Luther King Jr.: An enduring inspiration. *Cincinnati Enquirer*, pp. D1, D3.

Jones, D. (2008, October 20). Why "sorry" isn't in many CEOs' vocabularies anymore. *USA Today*. Available online: www.usatoday.com/money/companies/management/2008-10-20-ceo-apologies_N.htm. Access date: June 12, 2010.

Jones, M. (2009, December 27). Crystal Lee Sutton: The organizer; A mill girl rebels. *New York Times Magazine*, pp. 35–36.

Kahneman, D., & Tversky, A. (1979). Prospect theory: An analysis of decision under risk. *Econometrica, 47*, 263–292.

Kahneman, D., & Tversky, A. (1984). Choice, values, and frames. *American Psychologist, 39*, 341–350.

Kanter, R. M. (1977). *Men and women of the corporation*. New York: Basic Books.

Kanter, R. M. (1983). *The change masters*. New York: Simon & Schuster.

Kantrowitz, B. (2005, October 24). When women lead. *Newsweek*, pp. 46–76.

Karacs, I. (2009, August 12). Hillary: "I'm Secretary of State, Not Bill." TimesOnline. Available online: www.timesonline.co.uk/tol/news/world/us_and_americas/article6790980.ece. Access date: May 22, 2010.

Kellerman, K. (1992). Communication: Inherently strategic and primarily automatic. *Communication Monographs, 59*, 288–300.

Kelly, B. (2007, November 19). America's best leaders: A film hero up to playing the real role. *U.S. News & World Report*, pp. 50–51.

Kelly, S. (2008). Leadership: A categorical mistake? *Human Relations, 61*, 763–782.

Kelly, J. R., & Barsade, S. G. (2001). Mood and emotions in small groups and work teams. *Organizational Behavior and Human Decision Processes, 86*, 99–130.

Kelly, S., White, M. I., Martin, D., & Rouncefield, M. (2006). Leadership refrains: Patterns of leadership. *Leadership, 2*, 181–201.

Kennedy, M. T., & Fiss, P. C. (2009). Institutionalization, framing, and diffusion: The logic of TQM adoption and implementation decisions among U.S. hospitals. *Academy of Management Journal, 52*, 897–918.

Kilpatrick, J. (2005, July 3). Farewell to a lovely writer, debating partner. *Cincinnati Enquirer*, p. E4.

Kirtzman, A. (2001). *Rudy Giuliani: Emperor of the city*. New York: Perennial.

Kolodner, J. (1993). *Case-based reasoning*. San Mateo, CA: Morgan Kaufmann.

Kornberger, M., & Brown, A. D. (2007). "Ethics" as a discursive resource for identity work. *Human Relations, 60*, 497–518.

Kotter, J. P. (1990). *A force for change: How leadership differs from management*. New York: Free Press.

Kotter, J. P. (1995, March-April). Leading change: Why transformation efforts fail. *Harvard Business Review*, pp. 59–67.

Laborde, G. Z. (1988). *Fine tune your brain: When everything's going right and what to do when it isn't . . . .* Palo Alto, CA: Syntony.

Lacayo, R., & Ripley, A. (2002, December 30). "Persons of the Year 2002: The Whistleblowers." *Time.* Available online: www.time.com/time/magazine/article/0,9171,1003998,00.html. Access date: June 22, 2010.

Laclau, E., & Mouffe, C. (1985). *Hegemony and socialist strategy.* London: Verso.

Lakoff, G., & Johnson, M. (1980). *Metaphors we live by.* Chicago: University of Chicago Press.

Langfitt, F. (2007, August 16). Cause of Utah mine collapse disputed. *NPR Transcripts.* 16:00–17.00 PM. 12838379. Available online: www.npr.org/templates/story/story.php?storyId=12838379 Access date: June 12, 2010.

Lewis, L. K. (in press). Organizational change: Creating change through strategic communication. New York: Wiley-Blackwell.

Lippmann, W. (1922). *Public opinion.* New York: Macmillan.

Locke, E. A. (1991). *The essence of leadership.* New York: Lexington Books.

Ludeman, K., & Erlandson, E. (2004, May). Coaching the alpha male. *Harvard Business Review*, pp. 58–67.

Ludeman, K., & Erlandson, E. (2006). *Alpha male syndrome.* Boston: Harvard Business Press.

Luntz, F. (2007). *Words that work: It's not what you say, it's what people hear.* New York: Hyperion.

Martin, A. (2009, January 22). How green is my orange? PepsiCo tracks carbon footprints to the breakfast table. *New York Times*, pp. B1, B8.

Martin, D. (2009, July 18). Walter Cronkite, 92, dies; Trusted voice of TV news. *New York Times*, pp. 1, A15.

Martin, S. (2007). *Born standing up: A comic's life.* New York: Scribner.

Mayer, J. D., & Salovey, P. (1997). What is emotional intelligence: Implications for educators. In P. Salovey & D. Sluyter (Eds.), *Emotional development, emotional literacy, emotional intelligence* (pp. 3–31). New York: Basic Books.

Meacham, J. (2008, June 23). God, politics and the making of a joyful warrior. *Newsweek*, pp. 31–33.

Mead, G. H. (1956). *Social psychology* (A. Strauss, Ed.). Chicago: University of Chicago Press.

Mehrabian, A. (1972). *Nonverbal communication.* Chicago: Aldine-Atherton.

Meindl, J. R. (1995). The romance of leadership as a follower-centric theory: A social constructionist approach. *Leadership Quarterly, 6,* 329–341.

Meindl, J. R., Ehrlich, S. B., & Dukerich, J. M. (1985). The romance of leadership. *Administrative Science Quarterly, 30,* 78–102.

Moore, D. C. (1994). Feminist accounting theory as a critique of what's "natural" in economics. In P. Mirowski (Eds.), *Natural images in economic thought* (pp. 583–610). Cambridge, UK: Cambridge University Press.

Mortenson, G., & Relin, D. O. (2007). *Three cups of tea: One man's mission to promote peace . . . one school at a time.* New York: Penguin.

O'Keefe, B. J. (1988). The logic of message design: Individual differences in reasoning about communication. *Communication Monographs, 55,* 80–103.

O'Keefe, B. J. (1991). Message design logic and the management of multiple goals. In K. Tracy (Eds.), *Understanding face-to-face interaction: Issues linking goals and discourse* (pp. 131–150). Mahwah, NJ: Erlbaum.

O'Keefe, B. J. (1992). Developing and testing rational models of message design. *Human Communication Research, 18,* 637–649.

O'Keefe, B. J. (1997). Variation, adaptation, and functional explanation in the study of message design. In G. Philipsen (Ed.), *Developing Communication Theories* (pp. 85–118). Albany: State University of New York Press.

O'Keefe, B. J., & Lambert, B. (1989). *Effects of message design logic on the communication of intention.* San Francisco: Speech Communication Association.

O'Keefe, B. J., & Lambert, B. (1995). Managing the flow of ideas: A local management approach to message design. In B. R. Burleson (Ed.), *Communication Yearbook 18* (pp. 54–82). Thousand Oaks, CA: Sage.

O'Keefe, B. J., Lambert, B. L., & Lambert, C. A. (1993). *Effects of message design logic on perceived communication effectiveness in supervisory relationships.* Washington, DC: International Communication Association.

Pan, Z., & Kosicki, G. M. (2003). Framing as a strategic action in public deliberation. In S. D. Reese, O. H. Gandy, & A. E. Grant (Eds.), *Framing public life: Perspectives on media and our understanding of the social world* (pp. 35–61). Mahwah, NJ: Erlbaum.

Papanikolas, T. (2007, August 7). Who is Bob Murray? ksl.com. Available online: www.ksl.com/index.php?nid=481&sid=1601688. Access date: May 14, 2010.

Parker, K. (2006, February 4). This Clinton badly needs a clue. *Cincinnati Enquirer*, p. B11.

Parker, K. (2008, November 15). How long do you have to pay for saying something dumb? *Cincinnati Enquirer*, p. D5.

Pilkington, E. (2009, June 23). What's driving Steve Jobs? *Guardian*. Available online: www.guardian.co.uk/technology/2009/jun/23/steve-jobs-liver-transplant. Access date: June 12, 2010.

Potter, J. (1996). *Representing reality: Discourse, rhetoric and social construction.* London: Sage.

Potter, J. (1997). Discourse analysis as a way of analyzing naturally occurring talk. In D. Silverman (Ed.), *Qualitative research: Theory, method and practice* (pp. 144–160). London: Sage.

Potter, J., & Wetherell, M. (1987). *Discourse and social psychology.* London: Sage.

Putnam, L. L., & Holmer, M. (1992). Framing, reframing, and issue development. In L. L. Putnam & M. E. Roloff (Eds.), *Communication and negotiation* (pp. 128–155). Newbury Park, CA: Sage.

Ramer, H. (2007, November 11). How to drive voters from stump to polls. *Cincinnati Enquirer*, p. A10.

Reber, A. S. (1985). *Dictionary of psychology.* New York: Penguin.

Reese, S. D. (2003). Prologue—framing public life: A bridging model for media research. In S. D. Reese, O. H. Gandy, & A. E. Grant (Eds.), *Framing public life: Perspectives on media and our understanding of the social world* (pp. 7–31). Mahwah, NJ: Erlbaum.

Reese, S. D., Gandy, O. H., & Grant, A. E., Eds. (2003). *Framing public life.* Mahwah, NJ: Erlbaum.

Riesbeck, C. K., & Schank, R. C. (1989). *Inside case-based reasoning.* Mahwah, NJ: Erlbaum.

Rittel, H., & Webber, M. (1973). Dilemmas in a general theory of planning. In *Policy Sciences* (Vol. 4, pp. 155–169). Amsterdam: Elsevier.

Robinson, V.M.J. (2001). Embedding leadership in task performance. In K. Wong & C. W. Evers (Eds.), *Leadership for quality schooling* (pp. 90–102). London: Routledge/Falmer.

Rost, J. C. (1991). *Leadership for the twenty-first century.* New York: Praeger.

Schein, E. (1985). *Organizational culture and leadership.* San Francisco: Jossey-Bass.

Scheufele, D. A., & Tewksbury, D. (2007). Framing, agenda setting, and priming: The evolution of three media effects models. *Journal of Communication, 57,* 9–20.

Schillinger, L. (2006, September 20). "Foreign Office: The French and Germans have remade the BBC series. Why?" *Slate Magazine.* Available online: www.slate.com/id/2150015/. Access date: May 21, 2010.

Schoenewolf, G. (1990). Emotional contagion: Behavioral induction in individuals and groups. *Modern Psychology, 15,* 49–61.

Seelye, K. Q., & Phillip, K. (2008, August 8). Edwards admits to extramarital affair. *New York Times.* Available online: http://thecaucus.blogs .nytimes.com/2008/08/08/abc-news-edwards-admits-to-extramarital-affair/?hp. Access date: June 12, 2010.

Senge, P. (1990). *The fifth discipline.* New York: Doubleday.

Senge, P. (1997). Through the eye of the needle. In R. Gibson (Ed.), *Rethinking the future* (pp. 123–145). London: Brealey.

Senge, P., Kleiner, A., Roberts, C., Ross, R. B., & Smith, B. J. (1994). *The fifth discipline fieldbook.* New York: Doubleday Currency.

Senge, P., Kleiner, A., Roberts, C., Ross, R., Roth, G., & Smith, B. (1999). *The dance of change: The challenges of sustaining momentum in learning organizations.* New York: Doubleday Currency.

Shannon, C., & Weaver, W. (1949). *The mathematical theory of communication.* Urbana: University of Illinois Press.

Shockley-Zalabak, P., Morreale, S., & Hackman, M. (2010). *Building the high-trust organization: Strategies for supporting five key dimensions of trust.* San Francisco: Jossey-Bass.

Shotter, J. (2007). *"Getting it": "Withness"-thinking and the dialogical . . . in practice.* London: Unpublished manuscript.

Shotter, J., & Cunliffe, A. L. (2003). Managers as practical authors: Everyday conversations for action. In D. Holman & R. Thorpe (Eds.), *Management and language* (pp. 1–37). London: Sage.

Simons, H. (1976). *Persuasion: Understanding, practice, and analysis.* Reading, MA: Addison-Wesley.

Sinclair, A. (2005). Body possibilities in leadership. *Leadership, 1,* 387–406.

Snow, D. A., & Benford, R. D. (1992). Master frames and cycles of protest. In A. D. Morris & C. M. Mueller (Eds.), *Frontiers in social movement theory* (pp.133–155.) New Haven, CT: Yale University Press.

Snow, D. A., Rochford E. B., Jr., Worden, S. K., & Benford, R. D. (1986). Frame alignment processes, micromobilization, and movement participation. *American Sociological Review, 51,* 464–481.

Spitzberg, B. H. (2003). Methods of interpersonal skill assessment. In J. O. Greene & B. R. Burleson (Eds.), *Handbook of communication and social interaction skills* (pp. 93–134). Mahwah, NJ: Erlbaum.

Tannen, D. (1979). What's in a frame? Surface evidence for underlying expectations. In R. O. Freedle (Ed.), *New directions in discourse processing* (pp. 137–181). Norwood, NJ: Ablex

Tellegen, A. (1985). Structure of mood and personality and their relevance to assessing anxiety, with an emphasis on self-report. In A. H. Tuma & J. D. Maser (Eds.), *Anxiety and the anxiety disorders* (pp. 681–706). Mahwah, NJ: Erlbaum.

Thamel, P. (2009, December 27). A last man off the bench rides a blog and an attitude to stardom. *New York Times,* p. 9.

Tracy, S. J., & Tretheway, A. (2005). Fracturing the real-self<—>fake-self dichotomy: Moving toward "crystallized" organizational discourses and identities. *Communication Theory, 15*, 168–195.

Tversky, A., & Kahneman, D. (1981). The framing of decisions and the psychology of choice. *Science, 211*, 453–458.

Verrengia, J. B. (2005, April 17). Einstein's influence, legacy still expanding. *Cincinnati Enquirer*, p. A22.

Wallace, D. F. (2008, September 19). David Foster Wallace on life and work. *Wall Street Journal*, p. W14.

Weick, K. (1979). *The social psychology of organizing* (2nd ed.). Reading, MA: Addison-Wesley.

Weick, K. (1986). The management of eloquence. In D. R. Hampton, C. E. Summer & R. A. Webber (Eds.), *Organizational behavior and the practice of management* (pp. 581–586). Glenview, IL: Scott, Foresman.

Weick, K. (1995). *Sensemaking in organizations.* Thousand Oaks, CA: Sage.

Weick, K. (2001). Leadership as the legitimation of doubt. In W. Bennis, G. Spreitzer, & T. Cummings (Eds.), *The future of leadership: Today's top leadership thinkers speak to tomorrow's leaders* (pp. 91–102). San Francisco: Jossey-Bass.

Weick, K., & Roberts, K. H. (1993). Collective mind in organizations: Heedful interrelating on flight decks. *Administrative Science Quarterly, 38*, 357–381.

Weick, K., & Sutcliffe, K. M. (2001). *Managing the unexpected: Assuring high performance in an age of complexity.* San Francisco: Jossey-Bass.

Weick, K., Sutcliffe, K. M., & Obstfeld, D. (1999). Organizing for high reliability: Processes of collective mindfulness. In (B. M. Staw & L. L. Cummings, Eds.), *Research in organizational behavior* (pp. 21, 81–123). Stamford, CT: JAI Press.

Weisberg, J. (2008, September 29). Message: Get a message. *Newsweek*, p. 30.

Wetherell, M. (1998). Positioning and interpretative repertoires: Conversation analysis and post-structuralism in dialogue. *Discourse & Society, 9*, 387–412.

Wheatley, M. J. (1992). *Leadership and the new science: Learning about organizations from an orderly universe.* San Francisco: Berrett-Koehler.

Wild, B., Erb, M., & Bartels, M. (2001). Are emotions contagious? Evoked emotions while viewing emotionally expressive faces: Quality, quantity, time course and gender differences. *Psychiatry Research, 102*, 109–124.

Willihnganz, S., Hart, J. L., & Willard, C. A. (2002). The logic of message design in organizational argument. In D. Holman & R. Thorpe (Eds.), *Management and language: The manager as a practical author* (pp. 104–120). London: Sage.

Wittgenstein, L. (1953). *Philosophical investigations.* Oxford, UK: Blackwell.

Yukl, G. (1998). *Leadership in organizations* (4th ed.). Upper Saddle River, NJ: Prentice Hall.

Zaleznik, A. (1977, May/June). Managers and leaders: Are they different? *Harvard Business Review, 55*, 67–78.

THE AUTHOR

GAIL T. FAIRHURST is a professor of communication at the University of Cincinnati. Her Ph.D. is from the University of Oregon. Her research and writing interests are in organizational communication and the linguistics of leadership. Across a variety of projects, she is currently exploring leaders' sensemaking in creativity-based organizations undergoing major organizational change, interim leadership, the collaborative mind-set of leaders unaccustomed to sharing control, and the role of a more discursive, social, and cultural view of leadership than found in leadership psychology.

She has published more than sixty articles in communication and management journals, including *Communication Monographs, Human Communication Research, Management Communication Quarterly, Academy of Management Journal, Academy of Management Review*, and *Organization Science*, as well as several book chapters, most recently in the *Sage Handbook of Leadership*, the *Sage Handbook of Organizational Discourse*, and the

Handbook of Business Discourse. She is the author of two other books, including *Discursive Leadership: In Conversation with Leadership Psychology* (Sage, 2007) and *The Art of Framing: Managing the Language of Leadership* (Jossey-Bass, 1996), both award-winning. She has also received "Article of the Year" awards from both the International Communication Association and the National Communication Association. She is a Fellow of the International Communication Association, a Fulbright Scholar, and an associate editor for the journal *Human Relations.*

In addition to her university research and teaching, she has been a process consultant, trainer, and executive coach. She has worked with Procter & Gamble, Kroger, Merrill Lynch, McDonald's, Boeing, State Farm Insurance, General Electric, the U.S. Air Force and Department of Energy, Fluor Daniel, and Children's Hospital of Cincinnati, among others. She was also head of the Department of Communication at the University of Cincinnati for five years and has held visiting appointments at Procter & Gamble, Copenhagen Business School (Denmark), and Lund University (Sweden). She can be reached at fairhug@ucmail.uc.edu.

INDEX

Page references followed by *fig* indicate an illustrated figure; followed by *t* indicate a table; followed by *e* indicate an exhibit.